NEWS AS DISCOURSE

COMMUNICATION

A series of volumes edited by
Dolf Zillmann and Jennings Bryant

NEWS AS DISCOURSE

TEUN A. VAN DIJK

University of Amsterdam

 LAWRENCE ERLBAUM ASSOCIATES, PUBLISHERS

1988   Hillsdale, New Jersey   Hove and London

P N
4783
.D543
1988

Lawrence Erlbaum Associates, Inc., Publishers
365 Broadway
Hillsdale, New Jersey 07642

Library of Congress Cataloging in Publication Data

Dijk, Teun Adrianus van, 1943–
  News as discourse / by Teun A. van Dijk.
    p. cm.
    Bibliography: p.   *# 16465092*
    Includes index.
    ISBN 0-8058-0828-0
    1. Newspapers.   2. Discourse analysis.   I. Title.
  PN4783.D543 1987
  070'.0141—dc19

4-12-90
Ac

Printed in the United States of America
10 9 8 7 6 5 4 3 2

CONTENTS

PREFACE

This book presents a new, interdisciplinary theory of news in the press. Against the background of developments in discourse analysis, it is argued that news should be studied primarily as a form of public discourse. Whereas in much mass communication research, the economic, social, or cultural dimensions of news and news media are addressed, the present study emphasizes the importance of an explicit structural analysis of news reports. Such an analysis should provide a qualitative alternative to traditional methods of content analysis. Also, attention is paid to processes of news production by journalists and news comprehension by readers, in terms of the social cognitions of news participants. In this way news structures can also be explicitly linked to social practices and ideologies of newsmaking and, indirectly, to the institutional and macrosociological contexts of the news media.

After a survey, in Chapter 1, of recent studies of news in different disciplines, both in the United States and Europe, Chapter 2 discusses the respective levels and dimensions of the structures of news reports in the press. Besides the usual linguistic, grammatical analysis of news language, an account is given of the important notions of topic and news schema, which represent the overall content and the conventional form of news reports. Finally, stylistic and rhetorical structures of news are analyzed. It is shown that these various structures of the news are systematically related to the cognitive and social conditions of news production, as well as to the processes of understanding by the readers. At several levels, the ideological dimensions of news structures are being analyzed.

Chapters 3 and 4 feature the more empirical, cognitive, and social psychological approach to news production and reception. They report results of field studies on everyday news production as source text processing by journalists and on recall of news stories by readers. Their theoretical basis derives from current advances in text processing within cognitive psychology and Artificial Intelligence. At the same time, however, the processes of production and understanding news have an important social dimension, so that they should be accounted for in terms of social cognitions of newsmakers and readers. This also allows the integration of our account into a sociological analysis of news and news media.

This book should be of interest for students and researchers in the fields of mass communication, discourse analysis, linguistics, and cognitive and social psychology. To facilitate comprehension for readers from different disciplines, these chapters also feature an introduction to the respective theoretical notions used in the analysis of news structures and processes.

Originally, this book was planned as part of a larger study, which also included applications and case studies on reporting in the world's press (the coverage of the assassination of Bechir Gemayel of Lebanon in September 1982) as well as studies on the portrayal of ethnic minority groups and squatters in the news. Since such a book would have become too voluminous, it was decided to publish the case studies as a separate book, *News Analysis*, which may be read as a companion volume to the present study, and which is also published in this series. Both books summarize the result of work on news I have been engaged in since the end of the 1970s.

The field studies reported in this book were carried out with the assistance by the following students of the University of Amsterdam: Sjoukje de Bie, Juliette de Bruin, Hellen Claver, Jane Alice Coerts, Gemma Derksen, Barbara Diddens, Jeroen Fabius, Guus Gillard d'Arcy, Michel Gijselhart, Karin Greep, José Hermans, Dienke Hondius, Kitty Jansman, Nico de Klerk, Liesbeth Klumper, Rie Kromhout, Stan Liebrand, Anja Lok, Marianne Louwes, Ingeborg van Oosterom, Hans Pols, Anke Riem, Patrice Riemens, and Tijl Rood. I would like to thank them all for their contributions and their enthusiasm. I am also indebted to Piet de Geus for his assistance with the usual computer chores related to present-day scholarly work. Finally, I would like to thank Jennings Bryant for his fast and positive advice to publish this book in this series.

Teun A. van Dijk

1

THE STUDY OF NEWS

INTRODUCTION: GOALS AND PROBLEMS

A Discourse Approach to Media Analysis

The aim of this book is to propose a new theoretical framework for the study of news in the press. The main feature of our approach is to analyze news primarily as a type of text or discourse. The first major consideration in such an analysis is the structures of news discourse, such as the various levels or dimensions of description and the units or categories used to explicitly characterize such levels or dimensions. This analysis should answer the important question about the structural specifics of news discourse as compared to other types of discourse. For instance, in English we may use the term "news story," and this suggests that news might be a special kind of narrative. Yet, we also know that it differs from the kind of stories we tell in everyday conversations or in children's books or in novels. Hence, we must specify why and how news stories are different. Similarly, news in the press is a specific kind of mass media discourse, which suggests possible family resemblances with news on radio and TV or with other discourse types in the newspaper, such as editorials or advertisements. Such a qualitative approach to the news is typical for the various branches of the new discipline

1

of discourse analysis, including text linguistics, narrative analysis, stylistics or rhetoric. In the next chapter we address this textual dimension of the news.

Yet, this is only part of the story. Discourse analysis is an interdisciplinary discipline. It is also interested in the analysis of the various contexts of discourse, that is, in the cognitive processes of production and reception and in the sociocultural dimensions of language use and communication. Therefore, the second major question to be answered deals with the processes involved in the production, the understanding and the uses of news in the context of mass-mediated communication. In particular, we are interested in the complex relationships between news text and context: How do cognitive and social constraints determine the structures of news and how are the understanding and the uses of news influenced by its textual structures? Obviously, our approach to news is especially relevant for mass communication research if we are able to specify such relationships. If not, our analysis would at most contribute to a new, and more explicit content analysis of media messages. Although this would certainly be a legitimate aim, we would be unable to place such an analysis within a more interesting explanatory and theoretical framework. We also want to know why news has its particular structure and what role such structures play in mass communication.

A single book cannot possibly answer all of these questions. Our aims must be more restricted. A single monograph could be dedicated to, for instance, the style of news discourse or to the uses of news by the readers. Therefore, we focus on topics that have been neglected in earlier research, that is on news structures and their cognitive processing, both in production and in understanding. For instance, we propose a partial theory of so-called news schemata, that is, of the conventional forms and categories of news articles in the press. From a cognitive point of view, we deal with the memory processes involved in the understanding, representation, and retrieval of news events by the journalist in news gathering and writing and by the reader in processes of reconstructing news events in knowledge and belief updating. This allows us to make explicit the well-known role of news values and ideologies in the production and understanding of news. Since such values and ideologies are also inherently social, we thus hope to build a bridge between the psychological and the sociological studies of news. Indeed, the psychological dimension of our study is not merely cognitive. Rather, it should be called 'sociocognitive'. In this respect, it is also an application and further extension of current developments in the new field of social cognition. At the same time, it provides a more explicit basis for actual work on news production in microsociology, e.g., from an ethnomethodological point of view, which also deals with processes of understanding and representing news events.

This approach seems to imply a critique of other approaches to media analysis in general and of other research about the news in particular. Yet, this critique requires some qualification. We do find that few approaches pay sufficient attention to the study of news as discourse in its own right. This is particularly true of the macrosociological approaches to news. We also believe that the cognitive dimension of news production and understanding has been neglected. Nevertheless, several studies have been conducted in the past decade that are very relevant for our own analysis, and we have integrated their results into our own theoretical framework.

Much like discourse analysis, the study of mass communication is an interdisciplinary enterprise. Yet, despite influences from several disciplines, especially those of the social sciences, mass communication research has developed as an autonomous and self-contained discipline. Such a development has both advantages and disadvantages. The major advantage, obviously, is that the many phenomena of mass communication will receive specific and expert attention, without being subsumated simply as particular instances of more general phenomena, such as communication, information, discourse, understanding, professional routines, or institutional control. The disadvantage, however, is that such an autonomous discipline does not keep abreast with highly relevant developments in other disciplines and might soon lag behind the development of its own theoretical framework. With an eye on the important insights into the media and news obtained in mass communication research, therefore, we hope that our study will stimulate the interdisciplinary cross-fertilization that may result from our special attention to the structures of news discourse and the processes of social cognition in news production and understanding.

News in the Press

Before we begin the theoretical analysis, we must first explain the concept of news and define our empirical database. However, no a priori definition will suffice; rather the definition must come from the whole theory. We can only try to make explicit our everyday intuitions about news, and then specify approximately what empirical object we want to analyze and theorize about.

The notion of news is ambiguous. First, we have the general notion of news, meaning 'new information', as we find in such everyday sentences as "I have bad news for you" or "What is the latest news from your son?" Clearly, the notion of news we are dealing with is both different but also has meaning components in common with this more general notion. Our notion of news, then, is part of a second class of meanings, which involve the media and mass communication. It is used in such expressions as "Have you read the news about the rising interest rate"? or in "Did you watch the news last night"? Even this class of media news notions contains interesting ambiguity. From the two examples just given, we see that news may be understood as new information or as a news article but also as a TV program in which news is presented, as demonstrated in the phrase "The Ten O'Clock news." In other words, the notion of media news in everyday usage implies the following concepts:

1. New information about events, things or persons.
2. A (TV or radio) program type in which news items are presented.
3. A news item or news report, i.e., a text or discourse on radio, on TV or in the newspaper, in which new information is given about recent events.

This study will focus on news as presented in 3. That is, we deal with a type of text or discourse as it is expressed, used, or made public in news media or public information carriers such as TV, radio, and the newspaper. Nevertheless, some ambiguity remains. That is, news in that case may refer to a news item or news article in the physical sense—news one can see, read, or clip from the paper. It may also refer to the content or meaning of such an article or item, as when we speak about the latest news about Lebanon. In this case, we do not mean the concrete article or item, of course, but the latest media news information. This distinction is even clearer when we use negation: After all, news may also not appear in the paper or on TV. In other words, there is a notion of media news involving the whole discourse, including its physical shape, and a notion of media news which is close to the first meaning mentioned previously and which has a more semantic nature: new information as given by the media and as expressed in news reports. We will analyze the first of these two notions, and for clarity, we will often use the term "news discourse" to avoid ambiguity.

After this brief exercise in conceptual analysis of the everyday notion of news, a specific restriction must be made. We are concerned mostly with news in the press, that is with news discourse or news articles published in daily newspspers. We neglect news items on TV or radio, although we take research results about such news into account. Apart from personal interest, there are several reasons for this choice. First, many studies in the last decade have concentrated on TV news since it usually has a vast public and, therefore, may have a more central role in public information processing. It should be noted, however, that newspaper news also has a crucial role in mass communication, not only in our own western societies but also in societies where TV is still a rare commodity, and few discourse studies have been conducted explicity of newspaper news. Second, in the course of several case studies, we have obtained specific insights into the structures of news in the press based on a vast collection of newspapers from many countries in the world (van Dijk, 1984b).

Finally, we should also clarify the notion of newspaper news. Although our intuitions seem to be rather clear on that point (we recognize a news article when we see one), the notion is not entirely without problems. In most cases, we can distinguish between a news article and an advertisement, and in many countries the word ADVERTISEMENT must be printed above an ad in the paper. But what about the weather report, the lists of radio and TV programs, the comics, the book reviews, or arts and performances sections? Some of these also give new information and therefore are part of the general characterization of news in the press. Yet, we exclude these discourse types from our analyses and focus on news articles in the narrow sense, that is, news discourse about past political, social, or cultural events. This excludes at least all text types that have a programmatic nature (they are about future events), although it does not yet rule out reviews of performances or editorials. The latter could be excluded by differentiating between informative and evaluative discourse, but that distinction is notoriously problematic. Genuine news articles may feature opinions, despite the ideological belief of many journalists that news only gives the facts and not opinion. This is even more obvious in background articles, which are a specific type of news article. Finally, we also exclude listings of the stock exchange, international currency change rates, lists with movements of ships, and similar types of practical information about actual states of affairs. From this brief attempt to differentiate between news articles in the strict sense and other types of informative or evaluative texts in the paper, it may already be seen that it is not so easy to make our intuitive notions explicit in clear-cut theoretical categories. A real definition of a news discourse in the paper requires an extensive and explicit theoretical description of structures (both formal and semantic), uses, and functions. This is one of the major aims of this book.

EARLIER STUDIES OF NEWS: A BRIEF REVIEW

From Anecdotical to Sociological Accounts

Many studies of news have an anecdotical nature. They are often written by ex-journalists, who tell about their experiences and who provide either friendly advice or harsh criticism of the media and their news. Such studies make fine reading, and their journalistic approach gives us insights into the everyday life and routines of newsmakers that may be useful as data for more systematic and explicit analyses in the everyday sociology of news production. Typical for such studies is the case approach. That is, the authors deal with an issue by illustrating it on well-known cases of reporting: a presidential election campaign; the race riots of the sixties; Watergate; or

other important social and political problems, issues, and events. From
these examples it may be inferred that this approach is popular in the
United States (Wicker, 1978). Here, the rather special role of TV anchorpersons has also stimulated quite a few studies (Powers, 1978). Although
this work focuses mostly on domestic events, we also find studies that deal
with international reporting—though again from a U.S. point of view
(Rosenblum, 1981). Thus, in a narrative style, Rosenblum describes how
foreign correspondents work, how they gather news, what kind of problems
they have (typically censorship in Third World countries), and how much of
the news can be characterized as coups and earthquakes. The political
philosophy of such work is usually liberal. The press is urged to perform a
critical role. Rosenblum ends his book with a statement typical for many of
these books about news and reporting (Rosenblum, 1981):

> A democracy cannot function without an informed electorate, and this applies no
> less to foreign affairs than to domestic matters. Foreign policy cannot be left
> unchecked to a Washington elite, to specialists or to interested lobby groups.
> World crises, if foreseen in time, sometimes can be avoided. But without reliable
> reporting from abroad, citizens are vulnerable and weak. If many Americans do
> not realize this, only reporters and editors—Knickerbocker's madmen—can
> drive it home to them. (p. 223)

Not all pretheoretical studies are merely anecdotical. In fact, some of
them are well-documented and based on extensive research. The MIT
News Study Group videotaped and analyzed more than 600 hours of TV
news (Diamond, 1978). Yet, their interest remains within the framework of
how the press covered political candidates for the respective presidential
elections in the United States, the role of anchorpersons, or how the audience is seduced by entertainment on TV. Again, this study emphasizes the
role of "responsible journalism", and the need for critical "press watchers"
(p. 240). Similarly, in his studies of the press and TV news, Epstein (1973,
1975) shows how the press handled such primary national topics in the
United States as the Pentagon Papers, The Vietnam War, the Black Pan-
thers, and Watergate and how TV news is gathered, selected, and presented. The former study (Epstein, 1973), based on fieldwork with the TV
network NBC, attempts to show how news depends not only on the facts but
also on the structure of the organization of news production. This dependence is discussed in rather informal terms and not by systematic content
analysis. Like several other studies written at the end of the 1970s (e.g.,
Gans, 1979), such an approach provides valuable insights into the journalistic routines, values, and constraints in news production. Here, we witness a transition to a more systematic and theoretically explicit form of news
study, which is still lacking in the anecdotical approach or the documentary
studies of the news (Barrett, 1978; Abel, 1981). Many of these studies are

interested in how the news is biased and distorts events (Altheide, 1974; Cirino, 1971). Data are usually interview fragments and tables of figures rather than close analysis of news output. Indeed, one hardly ever finds extensive fragments of news text in most of these studies. Conceptually, the analysis of news production focuses of problems of organization, journalistic routines and values, and corporate or political control (Bagdikian, 1971, 1983). These examples represent some of the better known studies of the news on TV and in the press. Yet, as social analysis they remain rather superficial and macrolevel, and as news analysis they are impressionistic. They often tell stories instead of analyzing them. We may call them observer accounts of the news.

From Macrosociology to Microsociology

The organization of news production has several dimensions and levels of description. Some of the studies previously mentioned pay extensive attention to the overall organization of news media institutions, for example, in terms of their public or corporate control structure, their management, the hierarchy of editors and other journalists involved, and the daily routines of newsgathering. Thus, in an influential study, Gans (1979) provides many details about how news is produced both at the networks and with such magazines as *Newsweek* or *Time*. Extensive field work gives us a view of the newsroom, the beats, the professional routines, the news values, and the range of topics that may be covered by the news media. Here we are closer to what news production is actually about, and a relationship is established between the social constraints and actual values and topics that underlie the news. Nevertheless, although Gans' study may be called an exemplary result of sociological fieldwork, observation, and analysis, it remains at the intermediate level of description. We still have no idea exactly how an editorial meeting takes place—who says what and when. The same is true for newsgathering activities during the beat or for the contacts between reporters and their sources. We still ignore how the journalist interprets these news environments and how such interpretations shape his or her reproduction of news events and news discourse. We need a still closer look, a microanalysis of news production processes.

Such a microanalysis can be found in Tuchman (1978a). Her book, perhaps the most interesting and innovating sociological study of news production, takes an ethnomethodological approach. While it has in common with the previously mentioned studies an interest for the daily routines of reporters and editors, such routines are described as everyday accomplishments of reconstructing reality as news and, at the same time, as enactments of the institutional processes in which newsmaking takes place. News is not characterized as a picture of reality, which may be correct or biased, but as a frame through which the social world is routinely constructed. Thus, reporters operate within a net, which is a strategic organizational device to draw upon news sources as effectively as possible. They are placed with bureaucratic institutions, which guarantee a steady flow of reliable news. At the same time, newsworthiness of events may be negotiated between members of media institutions and the organizations they cover. This also allows the newsmakers to manage the unexpectable and to produce a fixed amount of news, independent of what really happens and within the constraints of deadlines or budget limitations. Classifications of news events allow reporters to assign newsworthiness to such events, while at the same time leaving them the freedom to negotiate upon variation. Coming closer to the eventual product of such newsmaking practices, Tuchman finally pays attention to the "web of facticity" that is spun by newsmakers to create an illusion of credibility, but which ultimately legitimizes the status quo. She shows this by an analysis of film shots and stories, which systematically make different representations of disasters, riots, demonstrations, on the one hand, and of legitimated leaders on the other hand. The women's movement is used as an important illustration of how newsmaking reconstructs social events. Although the emphasis of her book is on the social and ideological dimensions of news construction, this and other examples of analysis show how a close microanalysis also requires systematic descriptions of news as a product of newsmaking practices, even when only a few steps are made toward such a description.

A somewhat similar approach may be found in Fishman (1980). He is also interested in the close sociological analysis of newsmaking and studies how journalists go through several phases where they "detect occurrences, interpret them as meaningful events, investigate their factual nature, and assemble them into stories" (p. 16). He discusses the organizational constraints, the work in the newsroom, the beat, and the methods of verification. Through field work he is able to witness these respective methods of participants in the interpretation and construction of news events, and he shows how many of these events are already predefined by public authorities such as the police. Their documents and information are taken by the reporter on his or her beat to be the definition of the news situation. Fishman concludes that the methods of making news and the dependence on external sources and documents leads to a uniform, ideological picture of the world. This ideology is largely defined in terms of the constraints on the practicalities of newsmaking. Although there are also differences with Tuchman's study, notably on the theoretical level, we find a similar approach to the definition of news ideology in Fishman's study. That is, ideology is not assumed to be rooted in the socioeconomic and cognitive conditions of newsmakers.

From Sociological and Ideological
Analysis to Systematic Content Analysis

All the studies discussed so far are the work of Americans. Despite their differences we have grouped them together. Although there is a large distance between the anecdotical approaches that contain nice stories about anchorpersons or personal experiences of journalists, on the one hand, and the much more theoretical approaches from a microsociological point of view, we also find similarities. First, the issues studied are mostly rooted in American political and social life. Second, the sociopolitical stance of these studies is usually liberal and mildly critical of the status quo. Many studies focus on errors or bias in the newsmedia, and make proposals for improvement, usually formulated from the point of view of human and civil rights, and journalistic responsibility.

When we move to the other side of the ocean, we find that many British studies of the last decade have some of these critical points in common but are rather different on other points. First, practically no British work on news has a purely microsociological (ethnomethodological) perspective. In fact, most work is formulated within a tradition of political sociology (or social political science). Second, much of this work has a Marxist orientation and is closely related to work in France or Italy, such as the work of French structuralists like Barthes, Foucault, Derrida, Pêcheux, or Althusser. This orientation pays more attention to the ideological analysis of the media and of news, especially from a historical and socioeconomic perspective. Third, and related to the previous points, is the interest for the class-defined nature of news, news production, and the media. This means that the topics chosen for closer analysis much more often deal with class struggle. And finally, there is more attention for systematic content or discourse analysis, partly also under the influence of French structuralism. In these respects, this work is an important contribution to the study of news and a necessary supplement to the more empirically and microsociologically-oriented studies previously discussed. On the whole, then, British work is more macrosociologically inspired, but due to its interest in ideological analysis, there are more concrete examples of actual news discourse descriptions. Finally, because more linguists in Britain are interested in news analysis, some beginning interaction can be found between them and researchers in mass communication.

It is impossible to even briefly review all British work on news. Therefore, we mention only some characteristic highlights from different directions of research in Britain. Indeed, it is necessary to stress that such differences exist, despite the general characterization given in the previous paragraph. Not all British media sociologists are Marxists, and not all are influenced by French structuralism; even within important centers, such as Leicester, Birmingham, Glasgow and London, people and work may be very different.

It is difficult to pinpoint exactly the beginnings of these new developments in British media research, although, as usual, the end of the 1960s or the beginning of the 1970s provides a rather obvious break. The political background of this break runs parallel to the one in the United States and Western Europe and can also be found in linguistics and discourse analysis. One influential, political study by the Leicester group (Halloran, Elliott, & Murdock, 1970) examined the media coverage of a large demonstration in London against the presence of the United States in Vietnam. By close observation of the activities of TV crews and newspaper reporters, and through an analysis of content, they found, among other things, how the media redefined an otherwise peaceful demonstration as essentially violent, due to their special attention to one minor incident. Similarly, an other event of the sixties, namely the actions of the Mods and the Rockers, led to a very influential study by Cohen (1980), which also paid extensive attention to the role of the news media. His major thesis, reflected in the title of his book, was that the general moral panic, as it was mainly formulated in the (popular, tabloid) press, defined these various groups of youngsters as "folk devils". He showed that the media, along with the authorities (the control structure), work with a model of deviancy amplification. That is, the media account of an initial problem—through various stages of misperception, sensitization, dramatization and escalation—contributes to increased deviance and hence to the confirmation of stereotypes. The orientation of this study is mainly sociological, based on field work and social data, and does not systematically describe media texts. Yet, the categories introduced by Cohen do allow translation into discourse analytical concepts.

This special interest in the media preoccupation with deviance can be found back in several subsequent studies. Cohen & Young (1981) edited a volume in which many general studies about newsmaking were reprinted, of which several specifically dealt with deviance, outgroups, or social problems. Demonstrations, crime waves, drug use, mental illness, violence, and racism are some of these issues. Along with American researchers such as Tuchman, Fishman, and Molotch & Lester (1974), we find in the revised 1981 edition of this volume nearly all those who have set the stage for British media research in the 1970s, such as Chibnall, Hall, Murdock, Cohen, Young, Morley, Husband, and others. The do-it-yourself media sociology proposed by the editors at the end of their book aptly summarizes the kind of questions that underlie much of this work, despite the substantial methodological and theoretical differences between the various authors or schools involved: which are the patterns of selection, which are the ideological and bureaucratic constraints on newsmaking, which events are not covered, which categories and models of causality are used to explain deviance in the media, what are the dominant and taken-for-granted models presented in the news, or what myths are used by the media. Although these categories are predominantly social, they are based on media content analysis, and it should not be too difficult to find equivalent notions for a systematic discourse analysis of the news, both at the thematic and at the stylistic and rhetorical levels. Much other work in the 1970s remains focused on the coverage of social protest, deviance, crime and law and order in the news (e.g., Chibnall, 1977). Much as in the later study by Fishman (1980), previously discussed, Chibnall shows how the daily contacts of crime reporters with the police leads them to a nearly inevitable reproduction of official and informal police definitions of crime, and conversely, a confirmation through the media of police action.

Most of this work could be categorized as a mixture of macrosociology and microsociology. Although not carried out within an ethnomethodological framework, the interest for interpretation and representation processes in the news runs through all these studies. The macrocomponent in this case is the special interest for the sociopolitical control structure, the organizational constraints, and especially the class dependent nature of news production and news discourse. This is also the characteristic of much of the work done at the Centre for Contemporary Cultural Studies (CCCS) at Birmingham, then directed by Stuart Hall (see e.g., Hall, Hobson, Lowe, & Willis, 1980). Their media analysis is more directly influenced by French structuralist thinkers and Gramsci, and it more explicitly embodies a Marxist perspective on ideologies in news production. Here, we also find the more explicit formulations of the distinction established with dominant American or empirical studies of the news and the media. (Hall, 1980). One of the elements in the break with the dominating empirical, behaviorist media studies was the recognition that media messages are not transparent, as they are treated in quantitative content analysis, but rather they have a complex linguistic and ideological structure. Thus, Connell (1980) shows that TV news should not simply be seen as ideologically biased or distorted. Such a view presupposes that the distorted image can simply be compared to some kind of objective reality or with some kind of neutral or correct image. Yet, this reality represented in or through the news is itself an ideological construct, based on the definitions given by the accredited sources of journalists, such as the government or the union leaders. In other words, the media are not a neutral, common-sensed, or rational mediator of social events, but essentially help reproduce preformulated ideologies. A similar position is illustrated at length in the Hall, Critcher, Jefferson, Clarke, & Roberts (1978) study of mugging in the British press. They show that there is not simply a new crime wave of mugging, which the media simply report, whether correctly or in a distorted, exaggerated way. Rather, it is the definition of mugging as provided by the authorities, such as the police, that is reproduced in the news. This means, for instance, that mugging is preferably attributed to members of ethnic minority groups, viz. young black, West-Indian males.

Well-known in recent British media research are the bad news studies of the Glasgow University Media Group (1976, 1980, 1982). Their work focuses on the strategies used by TV newsmakers in the coverage of strikes or industrial disputes. By a close analysis of news programs, they are able to show that dominant interpretations of such strikes are subtly favored in the news, e.g., by shot length and perspective, interview techniques, or other strategies. This means that the point of view of the workers is seen less on the screen or embedded in less credible circumstances. Thus, strikes are mainly represented as problems for the public (the TV news viewers): they cause delay and inconveniences, while at the same time contributing to the socioeconomic problems of the country. Wage claims in such a construction of strikes can only be interpreted as unreasonable behavior. In their second, follow-up study (Glasgow University Media Group, 1980), the group pays even more attention to the text and the visuals of TV news about industrial disputes. Thus, an analysis of lexical style shows that workers are systematically presented as making demands and industrial managers as making offers. In this and other ways, even the language of the news expresses subtle positive and negative associations with the respective news actors involved.

Downing (1980) shows that similar processes are at work in the representation of women or ethnic minority groups. Much in the same way as the news pays more attention to industrial disputes than to industrial accidents, the news has little systematic attention for negative actions against women (such as rape), or place such actions in a sensational and sexist framework. Also, many other topics are not found at all in the news about women, such as their history, political struggle, or their role as cheap labor in industry, offices, or at home. In this and many other subtle ways, the male dominance in the media reproduces the male dominance in society at large. Ethnic groups or immigrants in the media are presented in a similar way. As was already shown by Hartmann & Husband (1974), the British media, and especially the popular press, represented the immigration of black citizens as an invasion and their presence as a problem for the autochthonous population. Minority groups are often associated with crime (see the mugging wave studied by Hall, et. al. 1978), whereas crimes against them, such as racism or violent attacks, is underrepresented. Much like women, their opinions are not asked: White males (ethnic minority specialists) speak about or for them (van Dijk, 1983a, 1987d).

Despite theoretical and ideological differences of approach, the studies briefly reviewed above show several common characteristics. They provide a critical analysis of the media in general and of the news in particular. Unlike most American studies, though, they do not primarily formulate this critique against the background of civil right claims or in terms of bias and distortion. Rather, they pay attention to the basically ideological nature of the media reconstruction of social reality as a form of reproduction of the dominant forces and ideologies in society. That is, such a reproduction is not just the result of the news values and especially the journalistic routines and practices that underlie the production of news (see also Golding & Elliott, 1979). Next, there is marked attention for the representation of deviance and deviant or marginal groups, and it is shown that the dominant definitions of deviance or marginality are reproduced in the news.

Although such analyses are implicitly or indirectly based on a critical reading of news articles or programs, only the work by the Glasgow University Media Group attempts to go into the details of news discourse structures and production to illustrate these processes. On the whole, therefore, the approach remains sociological (Gurevitch, Bennett, Curran, & Woollacott, 1982). Close discourse analysis remains an exception or is reduced to ideological analysis as is the case also for the work of the CCCS group. Yet, there is growing attention for the language of the news and, thus, for the ways the dominant ideologies are actually formulated (Davis & Walton, 1983). This linguistic or grammatical approach is particularly well illustrated by Fowler, Hodge, Kress, & Trew, (1979). In a systematic analysis of the representation of incidents during the West-Indian carneval in London, these authors show that the very syntax of sentences in the news may express or dissimulate the main agent of positive or negative acts. Finally, a more systematic semiotic approach to news analysis is formulated by Hartley (1981), who studies both the language and the visual dimension of news and the media. These few linguistic and semiotic studies are first steps towards the full-fledged discourse analytical approach advocated in this book. We show later that such an approach is an important step towards a systematic discourse analysis, but that at the same time the semiotics of mass media news also has its limitations as an explicit method.

Other News Studies in Western-Europe

Where relevant, news studies in other countries of Western Europe are referred to in the next chapters. Although there are valuable studies of the news in many Western European countries, studies in West Germany are particularly important. The German approach, in a sense, is closer to the British studies we have already reviewed. Besides systematic analyses in mass communication and linguistic terms, much attention is paid to the socioeconomic and ideological implications of the news. Thus, Strassner (1975) edited a collection of papers that clearly shows the interdisciplinary nature of German approaches to news discourse. Economic studies of news production as a market commodity, the comprehensibility of news for viewers and readers, as well as linguistic studies of headlines or ideological content can be found side by side in this collection. Several years later, Strassner himself published what might be one of the most voluminous studies of television news (Strassner, 1982). This study has an interdisciplinary setup and deals with production, reception, and the product, i.e., the news programs themselves. Besides the usual analysis of the sources and news agencies that supply news to TV news programs, this book also offers pragmatic analyses of news communication (e.g., in terms of Grice's well-known "cooperation principles", Grice, [1975]), semantic and stylistic processing of agency dispatches, an analysis of the various discourse genres in news shows, and a study of the relations between news text and visual information. More than any other study to date, this monograph shows the possibilities of an interdisciplinary, discourse analytical approach to the news.

Other German studies exhibit a linguistic, semiotic, or discourse analytical approach to news discourse and news language. Kniffka (1980) provides a detailed sociolinguistic analysis of headlines and leads of American newspapers in their reports about the Angela Davis trial. Lüger (1983) presents a brief introduction to the language and discourse of the press and shows how a linguistic, stylistic, and rhetorical analysis works. He also provides a typology of press discourse. Bentele (1981) is more broadly semiotic, which means that a systematic study is also made of pictures and films in the media. However, the language and meanings of news discourse receive most explicit attention as, for instance, in a discussion about new methods of systematic content analysis. Due to the widespread attention in West Germany for the various branches of discourse analysis ('Textwissenschaft'), such studies are prominent in the establishment of a new, discourse analytical approach to content analysis. And much like some isolated work in Britain (e.g., Heritage, 1985), such a collection may also pay attention to subtle details such as the ways interviewed politicians try to influence dialogical interaction (Schwitalla, 1981).

These few recent books follow many other German studies about the media in general and of the news in particular. We mentioned earlier that often these studies have a critical goal, paying attention especially to ideological dimensions. Thus Schmidt (1977) compared newspaper news with TV news, paying special attention to the notion of "complementarity." Bechmann, Bischoff, Maldaner, & Loop (1979) provide one of the many critical studies of German Bild-Zeitung, in which the content analysis is organized around some fundamental Marxist notions for the analysis of socioeconomic life.

We have merely mentioned these studies here to show that much of this work provides necessary complements to most American and to some English studies of the news. In addition, the German work on news is closest to what we understand by a linguistic and discourse analytical approach. Although there is also substantial work in France about mass communication, and French structural analyses of the media have become well known and applied elsewhere (see our reviews of British work), there are few specialized studies about news. The well-known journal *Communications* remains a central forum for various approaches, from the early structural analyses of stories in the 1960s to a multitude of other semiotic studies (see Gritti, 1966, for an analysis of a news story, as well as the work of Violette Morin, e.g., Morin, 1966). Barthes' (1957) classical study of the "fait divers" remains a good example of ideological (mythological) analysis of the account of mundane events in the press (see also Auclair, 1970). Against the background of his earlier work on the ideological implications of the mass media, Véron (1981) provides a detailed analysis of the coverage of the accident in the nuclear plant at Three Mile Island in the French news media. This and the other French studies of news show that it is possible to integrate a structural analysis of news discourse with a study of news production constraints and their underlying ideologies. We may conclude, therefore, that much of the British, German, and French work about news discourse provides a rather different picture from the prevailing mass communication studies in the United States. Common to most European studies, whether linguistically/semiotically inspired or sociologically oriented, is their systematic attention for the ideological dimensions of news and news production.

Conclusion

In this chapter, we have outlined the goals of the studies reported in this book. Against the background of much other work about the structures and the functions of news in the media, we have advocated that a new approach should be taken. This new direction of research is essentially interdisciplinary, combining linguistic, discourse analytical, psychological, and sociological analysis of news discourse and news processes (van Dijk, 1985b). In a succinct review of other work about news in the press, we found that the news itself was often neglected and treated as an unanalyzed variable between newsmaking organizations or journalistic routines, on the one hand, and to the reception by, or the influence on, the reading public, on the other hand.

After the earlier anecdotical approaches to the study of news, and after the classical methods of content analysis, which still characterize much

American work, we witnessed increasing attention for the ideological, microsociological, linguistic, and discourse analytical study of news, especially in European work. Yet, we also found that this work is still in its early stages. A systematic theory of news discourse, as well as an account of the relationships between news structures and production and reception processes, is yet to be developed.

2

STRUCTURES
OF NEWS

DISCOURSE ANALYSIS

This chapter presents a structural analysis of some major dimensions of news discourse. As an introduction, we first give a brief summary of the aims, development, and methods of the new cross-discipline of discourse analysis. The subsequent sections specify the various theoretical notions by applying them to news discourse in the press.

The Development of Discourse Analysis

Discourse analysis is a new, interdisciplinary field of study that has emerged from several other disciplines of the humanities and the social sciences, such as linguistics, literary studies, anthropology, semiotics, sociology, psychology, and speech communication. It is striking that the development of modern discourse analysis took place more or less at the same time in these respective disciplines, at the end of the 1960s and the beginning of the 1970s. Whereas at first these developments were more or less autonomous, the last decade has seen increasing mutual influences and integration, which has led to a more or less independent new discipline of text or discourse studies.

Historical Background: Rhetoric

Historically, discourse analysis can be traced to classical rhetoric. More than 2,000 years ago, rhetoricians like Aristotle specified the various structures of discourse and indicated their effectiveness in processes of persuasion in public contexts. From a large body of normative concepts, however, the legacy of rhetoric in our age has often been restricted to the study of figures of speech, which can still be found in traditional textbooks of speech and communication. Only in the 1960s was it realized that classical rhetoric had more to offer. Rhetoric was redefined as new rhetoric and began to play a role in the development of structural analyses of discourse, for example, in literary studies (Lausberg, 1960; Barthes, 1970; Corbett, 1971). Given the focus of rhetoric on persuasion, however, not only speech style but also argumentative structures were addressed in these contemporary developments of rhetoric (Kahane, 1971).

From Russian Formalism to French Structuralism

For other disciplines, the development of discourse analysis is closely tied to the emergence of structuralism. A first branch of this structuralist enterprise grew from anthropology, linguistics, and literary studies, later often unified under the label of semiotics. Thus, part of the structuralist approaches that emerged in the 1960s, mainly in France, are rooted in so-called Russian Formalism (Erlich, 1965). The Russian Formalists, who started publishing abound the time of the Russian Revolution, counted among them important linguists, such as Roman Jakobson, and literary theorists, such as Šklovskij, Tynjanov, and Eixenbaum. Elsewhere, structuralist linguistics, after Saussure's influential book (Saussure, 1917), soon developed its own methodology and proposed a systematic approach to language sounds in the form of phonology, but literary and other discourse forms were only addressed much later.

Across several disciplinary boundaries, it has especially been the work of Propp (1958 [1928]) on the morphology of the Russian folk tale, which provided the main impetus for a first systematic analysis of narrative discourse after the translation of his book three decades later. More than anywhere else, France was the scene of this structuralist endeavour, where Propp was introduced by the anthropologist Lévi-Strauss and where the literary Russian Formalists were translated by Todorov (1966). This common interest among anthropologists, linguists, and literary scholars for narrative, both in discourse and in film or comics, was one of the perspectives taken in the new discipline of semiotics (*Communications* 1964, 1966; Barthes, 1966; Todorov, 1969; Greimas, 1966; see Culler, 1975, for survey and introduction).

At the same time, this semiotic-structuralist movement (in which many different approaches should be distinguished) received important guidelines from the hitherto independently developed discipline of structural linguistics. Indeed, more than any other discipline, linguistics came to play the pivotal methodological role for semiotics and structuralism in general, whether in literary studies, in anthropology, or in other disciplines (including new ones such as film studies). The linguistic model of that moment distinguished between the language system (langage) and the use of language (parole), and between an expression and a content level of the basic units—signs—of the language system. Phonology, morphology, and syntax describe abstract sound patterns, their combination into words (morphemes), and the possible combinations of words (word or word group categories) into sentences. Semantics, developing only in the later 1960s, reconstructs content or meaning by building up the meaning of words and sentences from elementary word meaning elements or dimensions (Greimas, 1966).

Interesting for us is the fact that this branch of European structuralism did not necessarily stop at the sentence boundary, as much earlier and later American structuralism usually did (with the exception of the rather isolated work of Harris, 1952). Rather, similar methods were applied to the analysis of discourse in general and of narrative in particular. Thus, Greimas (1966) defined the well-known narrative functions and units of Propp in terms of a structuralist semantics. This was possible because his analysis of sentence meaning involved the distinction between different roles of participants (agent, patient, etc.), which can also be distinguished at more global levels of analysis, e.g., within the plot of a story. Later developments in linguistics and semantics on 'case grammars' made similar functional analysis of sentence meanings, which were subsequently also used to characterize the overall meanings of discourse (Fillmore, 1968; Dik, 1978; van Dijk, 1972). After various renewals and extensions of the earlier work of Propp (e.g., Chabrol, 1973), semiotic structuralism soon addressed many other forms of discourse, such as poetry, "faits divers" in the newspaper, and especially various folk genres such as myths and folk tales and their modern variants, such as crime stories.

Many of the later developments in discourse analysis, as well as in other disciplines such as psychology, had undergone direct or indirect influence from these various approaches in French semiotic structuralism. As we saw in the previous chapter, this also holds for the analysis of news and other media discourse, mainly in England. In France itself, the 1970s brought various developments of so-called poststructuralism, influenced by psychoanalysis, Marxism, and history. Much of this work, however, is restricted to literary criticism (Harari, 1979; Culler, 1983). The more general earlier attention for discourse analysis (Pêcheux, 1969) unfortunately did not develop into an independent branch of research.

Sociolinguistics and Ethnography of Speaking

Most other developments of discourse analysis remain close to linguistics and anthropology and have only indirect links with this semiotic structuralism. Much discourse analysis emerged from the structuralist anthropology, exemplified in the analysis of myths or folk tales of Propp and Lévi-Strauss, and the same may be said about the development of anthropology and ethnography in the United States. More or less at the same time as in France, Hymes published an impressive collection of articles from anthropological linguistics (Hymes, 1964). This volume already contains the first articles from the new discipline of sociolinguistics and also features the first articles that deal with the structural analysis of texts and talk. Both sociolinguistics and ethnography have engendered the more interesting empirical, sociocultural branches of discourse analysis in the 1970s. Thus, Labov (1972a, 1972b), in his studies of the Black English Vernacular, not only examined phonological or syntactic variations in Black English but also narrative style and other discourse forms, such as verbal duelling. His earlier work with Waletzky (Labov & Waletzky, 1967) was taken up again in several of his own articles on narrative analysis (Labov, 1972c, 1982). Contrary to most previous structuralist work on narrative, this approach dealt with oral, spontaneous stories and not with fixed or written narrative genres such as myths, folk tales, or crime stories. The interest in spoken, spontaneous discourse forms in naturalistic contexts will later turn out to be the prevailing new development in the 1970s, not only in sociolinguistics and ethnography, but also in linguistic and sociological analyses of conversation. The ethnographic approach, under the label of the "ethnography of speaking" or the "ethnography of communication," soon came to be interested in many informal and formal discourse genres in cultural contexts (Gumperz & Hymes, 1972; Bauman & Sherzer, 1974; Sanches & Blount, 1975; see Saville-Troike, 1982, for survey and introduction).

Conversation Analysis

A third development in this more socially oriented approach to discourse was more independent, as was inspired by new directions of research in microsociology, mainly within so-called ethnomethodology (Garfinkel, 1967; Cicourel, 1973). This work focused on the details of everyday interaction and in particular on everyday informal talk, that is, on conversation (Sacks, Schegloff, & Jefferson, 1974; Sudnow, 1972; Turner, 1974; Schenkein, 1978; Atkinson & Heritage, 1984; van Dijk, 1985a, vol. 3). Much like linguists of earlier structural grammar, these analyses sought to uncover the basic rules and units of everyday conversation, such as those of turn taking, sequencing, and strategic moves. Analyses were based on close examination of detailed transcripts of naturalistic talk, including pauses, repairs, intonation, and other properties of talk hitherto neglected in linguistics. Just as in sociolinguistics, the emphasis thus shifted from abstract, formal, and invented sentences to real language use in the social context. This focus was not restricted to everyday talk but was soon extended to other forms of dialogue or spoken discourse, for instance classroom talk (Sinclair & Coulthard, 1975; Mehan, 1979; Sinclair & Brazil, 1982). In the last decade, these various branches of conversation analysis have been very influential in discourse analysis and have even been identified as discourse analysis *tout court*, as opposed to other forms of textual (written discourse) analysis (for introduction, see Coulthard, 1977; and for a recent survey, see McLaughlin, 1984).

Text Linguistics

Among the many other branches of discourse analysis that emerged in the 1960s was a more linguistic approach to mostly written texts, a development taking place mainly in continental Europe, primarily in East and West Germany and surrounding countries. Methodologically, this so-called text linguistics, and especially its more specific direction called text grammar, first sought its inspiration in generative transformational grammars, as developed by Chomsky. Much like most other discourse analysts in other disciplines, they rejected the artificial boundary of the sentence and argued that linguistic competence and its rules should also extend to textual structures beyond the sentence (Petöfi, 1971; van Dijk, 1972, 1977; Dressler, 1972; Petöfi & Rieser, 1973; de Beaugrande & Dressler, 1981). It was argued that many properties of syntax, and expecially those of semantics, were not limited to one sentence but rather characterize sequences of clauses, sentences, or whole texts: pronouns; definite and indefinite articles; demonstratives; many adverbs; connectives of various types; and phenomena such as presupposition, coherence, and topicality. From a somewhat different perspective, similar points were made by other linguists (Halliday & Hasan, 1976; Longacre, 1977). In more strictly syntactic and semantic sentence grammars, it was soon realized that many properties of sentence form and meaning require at least a discourse perspective (Givón, 1979). And although many directions of current linguistics and grammars are still focusing on sentence structures, it becomes more and more accepted that a systematic description of language, whether in abstract grammatical terms, or in terms of theories of language use, should also incorporate discourse forms. It should be added, however, that text grammar, other directions of text linguistics, or any other linguistic approach to discourse have merged with other branches of discourse analysis in recent years.

There may be differences in historical developments and influences or interest for different discourse types and phenomena, but all have at least one common central aim—to elaborate an explicit theory of the various structures of spoken or written discourse (see de Beaugrande, 1980; Tannen, 1982; van Dijk, 1985a for an integrated presentation of several directions of research).

Integration and New Developments

Since the initial steps taken in the mid-1960s and the publication of several influential books in 1972, discourse analysis has shown increasing cross-fertilization and integration. Linguistics, which came to modern discourse analysis rather late, but whose explicit methods and theories have played an important role in the background, is certainly no longer the major source of inspiration for discourse analysis. The special categories, units, and phenomena studied in semiotics, rhetoric, ethnography, sociolinguistics, and microsociology could no longer all be framed in the traditional terms and methods of analysis of sentence grammars. Many phenomena, such as rhetorical strategies or narrative structures. received attention in many different branches of discourse analysis, though often from different perspectives. Despite these theoretical and methodological differences and conflicts, therefore, we may speak of growing integration of discourse analysis as a new cross-discipline. Of course, this discipline has its own specializations and subdisciplines, and those working on intonation, for instance, might not always be interested in or know about what is being done on semantic connectives, interaction strategies, or cognitive dimensions of discourse understanding (for introductions, surveys, and examples of discourse analysis from several disciplines and directions of research, see van Dijk, 1985a).

Psychology and Artificial Intelligence

In the meantime, other disciplines also became engaged in the discourse analytical enterprise, and even a succint review of these developments is too involved for presentation here. As we will see in more detail in Chapters 3 and 4, for instance, a major development took place in cognitive psychology and Artificial Intelligence (AI). From an experimental and simulative point of view, respectively, these disciplines were especially interested in the modeling of discourse production and understanding by language users. Such a cognitive approach is formulated in terms of memory structures and processes involved in the interpretation, storage, and retrieval of discourse and in the role of knowledge and beliefs in these processes of understanding (Schank & Abelson, 1977; Graesser, 1981; Sanford and Garrod, 1981; van

Dijk & Kintsch, 1983). There are several links between this research and earlier work in text linguistics or narrative analysis.

Other Disciplines

Similarly, special attention for specific discourse forms or social contexts led to a discourse analytical approach to legal discourse (Danet, 1984) and thus established a link with law studies. Disciplines such as speech communication and interest in rhetoric and persuasive language also became integrated in the wider context of discourse analytical approaches (Roloff & Miller, 1980). Finally, the study of the media and mass communication was increasingly involved in a discourse analytical approach to various media genres. Contributions in this last field have already been reviewed and will be detailed in following sections.

Conclusions

From this brief review of the historical development and the various directions in discourse analysis, we may first conclude that discourse analysis is no longer the concern of a single discipline. The original focus on linguistics and grammar has been widened, especially towards the social sciences. Second, the first structural analyses of texts, especially of narrative, have not only been made more explicit due to new formal methods of description, but have also been complemented with a description of cognitive, social, and cultural dimensions of language use and discourse. In other words, both text and context are the actual field of discourse analytical description and theory formation. Third, after the initial interest in fixed and written types of text, we have witnessed increasing attention for spoken, dialogical types of talk in a variety of social situations, primarily informal, everyday conversation. Fourth, the earlier emphasis on only a few discourse genres, such as talk and stories, now becomes broadened to many other discourse genres, such as law, official discourse, textbooks, interviews, advertising, and news discourse. And finally, the theoretical framework has been enriched with new developments in formal grammars, logic, and computer-simulated AI programs. Hence, both methodologically, theoretically, and empirically, we have a rapidly developing full-fledged discipline, ready for new applications in unexplored areas. Despite these rapid advances, there are of course also limitations. The field is only 20 years young, with most of its substantial work having been done in the last decade. For many levels and dimensions of analysis, we still lack the theoretical instruments. Thus, we still know little about the precise structures and processes of media discourse. This chapter, therefore, is meant to contribute to such a discourse analysis of one type of media discourse and makes explicit some textual structures of news.

Principles of Discourse Analysis

In this section we give an elementary introduction to some of the basic notions and principles of discourse analysis. The next sections elaborate these notions in more detail while at the same time applying them to news discourse.

Discourse analysis is an ambiguous concept. In the previous section, it was used to denote a new discipline, one that studies text and talk or language use from all possible perspectives. In this section, discourse analysis denotes a theoretical and methodological approach to language and language use. In that sense, it is also defined by the object of analysis, namely discourses, texts, messages, talk, dialogue, or conversation. Linguistics in general, and especially grammars, usually focused only on abstract sentence structures, and considered discourse as an aspect of actual language use. This distinction between theories of grammar, accounting for the abstract underlying rules of language as a system and theories of actual language use is misleading, however. Sociolinguistics and pragmatics in the past decade, for instance, showed that many properties of what was usually considered to be language use also had a systematic nature, which could be explained by rules. This particularly holds true for the description of discourse. Much like sentences, discourse may exhibit structures that have a systematic, rule-governed nature, whereas—again much like sentences—discourse also may display properties that are very much ad hoc, individual, and context-bound. This means that if we want to distinguish between more abstract, grammatical structures and various properties of language use, we can do so both for sentences and for discourses. In earlier work, therefore, we proposed to distinguish systematically between the formal object text, on the one hand, and actually occurring discourse(s), on the other hand (van Dijk, 1972, 1977). Here, we won't make this distinction, but simply use text and discourse interchanageably. However, it is further understood that text or discourse may have general, abstract, or context-free properties, which might be accounted for by some kind of discourse grammars and properties that are variable across different contexts (situations, speakers, etc.) in the same culture. Of course, in a strictly empirical theory of language and language use, such a distinction is merely a metatheoretical artifact. In actual usage, we only have cognitive representations of discourse rules and strategies of their application in discourse production and comprehension. In other words, in a cognitive or sociological approach to discourse, the system-use distinction may be less relevant.

Text and Context

The major aim of discourse analysis, then, is to produce explicit and systematic descriptions of units of language use that we have called discourse. Such descriptions have two main dimensions, which we may simply call textual and contextual. Textual dimensions account for the structures of discourse at various levels of description. Contextual dimensions relate these structural descriptions to various properties of the context, such as cognitive processes and representations or sociocultural factors. Thus, structurally, language systems feature various pronominal forms of address, which may be different for different languages. But an aspect of the communicative context, such as the degree of formality of the situation or the familiarity of the speech partners, may determine whether a more formal or a more informal form should be chosen (such as French "vous" instead of "tu"). Cognitively, there may be other constraints in discourse, such as the use of full definite descriptions instead of pronouns in those cases where memory processes of retrieval require more than just the information from a pronoun.

Levels of Description: Grammar

Textual descriptions are usually differentiated as to their levels or dimensions. According to traditional distinctions in the theory of grammar, for instance, we distinguish between phonological, morphological, syntactic, and semantic descriptions. (for introduction, see e.g., Lyons, 1981). We thus describe sound forms, word forms, sentence forms, and meanings, respectively, both of sentences and of textual sequences of sentences. For written discourse, we may not want to account for actual realizations of sound forms in terms of phonetics but rather in terms of theories of graphical realization, which is crucial to describe the layout of news discourse. Here, we focus mainly on syntax and semantics. In general, syntax describes which syntactic categories (such as noun or noun phrase) may occur in sentences and in which possible combinations. Thus, syntactic rules specify which sentence forms, consisting of syntactic categories, are well-formed. We also use this notion of syntax in a wider, nongrammatical sense, for instance when we want to describe the overall forms of discourse. We may even use it to account for forms in the expressions of other semiotic systems, such as film, music, dance, or nonverbal gestures in talk. Semantics, next, deals with meanings of words, sentences, and discourse. It formulates the rules that assign interpretations to units and that combine interpretations of units into interpretations of larger units. Although this kind of meaning-semantics has prevailed in much of linguistic theory, it is only half of the story. In philosophy and logic, semantics also deals with interpretations, but in that case it is not only meaning which is assigned to expressions, but rather truth, or in general referents (or extensions, or denotations). A sound account of discourse requires both: Its semantics deals with meaning and reference, that is, with concepts and the things (objects, persons, events, etc.) in some situation we may refer to. It will be shown later, for instance, that to describe the fundamental discourse notion of coherence, we must specify not only how meanings of subsequent sentences are related but also how the facts these sentences refer to are related. To distinguish between these two aspects of semantics, we sometimes use the terms intensional (for meaning aspects) and extensional (for reference aspects).

Pragmatics: Speech Acts

The levels of description mentioned thus far are those familiar in linguistic grammar. In the last decade, and more or less parallel with the development of discourse analysis and sociolinguistics, it has been shown that we also need a pragmatic component of description. Here, we do not merely describe the forms or the meaning (or reference) of verbal utterances but rather the social act we accomplish by using such an utterance in a specific situation. Such acts are called speech acts (Searle, 1969). Promising, accusing, congratulating, and asserting are examples of such speech acts. These are social acts accomplished by the use of words, that is, by verbal utterances or parts of discourse. A pragmatic description then specifies what kind of speech acts exist in a given culture and the rules that determine under what conditions such speech acts are appropriate relative to the context in which they are used. Since news discourse nearly exclusively consists of assertions (and not of promises or threats), a pragmatic description in the strict sense would not yield much more than the conditions necessary for the appropriate accomplishment of assertions.

From Micro- to Macrostructures

We are now able to characterize three major aspects of discourse: sentence forms, meanings, and speech acts. Indeed, a theory of language is basically aimed at descriptions of these three components and their interrelations. There are, however, other aspects of discourse that cannot simply be defined in terms of the usual syntax, semantics, or pragmatics as applied mainly to isolated sentences. That is, we seem to operate only on what may be called a microlevel of description: sounds, words, sentence patterns, and their meanings. We also need a description at a more comprehensive, global level, that is of whole parts of discourse, or of entire discourses. For instance, discourses are usually said to have a theme or topic, and this semantic aspect cannot simply be accounted for in terms of the semantics of isolated sentences. Thus, we need some kind of macrosemantics, which deal with such global meanings to allow us to describe the meanings of whole paragraphs, sections, or chapters of written discourse. Similarly, we also need some kind of macrosyntax to characterize the overall forms of a discourse, which we will call schemata or superstructures. Stories or conversations have such overall organizational patterns, consisting—just as in sentence syntax—of a number of conventional categories, such as various forms of Opening or Closing a discourse, a Setting in story, or Headlines in news discourse. These overall schematic forms are filled with the overall, macrostructural meanings or topics of a discourse. The category of headline in a news discourse, thus, is merely an empty form, in which we may insert different meanings (as long as this meaning is a topic or summary of the meaning of the whole text). Similarly, a pragmatic description may be given such a macrocomponent, accounting for larger sequences of speech acts, or for the global or macrospeech act accomplished by a whole textual utterance. A news discourse as a whole may have the function of a macroassertion, and an advertisement the function of a macroadvice or macrooffer. A ransom note would typically be a macrothreat (van Dijk, 1980a, 1981a).

We now have form, meaning/reference and action, both at the local or microlevel and at the global or macrolevel. And just as forms, meanings, and action are systematically related, so are related microlevels and macrolevels. For instance, the meanings of whole text parts or entire texts are derived from the local meanings of words and sentences, which is a fundamental principle of semantics. This derivation takes place by macrorules, which will be discussed when we deal with the thematic structures of news discourse.

Style

There are still other dimensions of discourse description. First, we may want to describe the style of a discourse. Stylistic descriptions are usually located at the boundaries of linguistics, although they presuppose linguistic structures of discourse. Unlike the other properties already briefly introduced, style is not simply a distinct level but a dimension that cuts through various levels. Style is the result of the choices made by the speaker among optional variations in discourse forms that may be used to express more or less the same meaning (or denote the same referent). Saying 'physician' instead of 'doctor,' for instance, is an element of lexical style. We may also vary our pronunciation, and this may result in talk having a specific phonological style. And finally, more or less the same meaning may be expressed in sentences having different syntactic structures. Stylistic variation is not simply free or arbitrary, however. On the contrary, style is a major indication of the role of the context. It may signal personal or social factors of the communicative context, such as the speakers' impatience or familiarity between speaker and listener. Thus, specific social situations, such as a classroom lecture or a trial in court, may require specific sets of lexical or syntactic options from the speech participants. News discourse must also be formulated in a specific, formal style, which is characteristic for printed media. Hence, style is the trace of the context in the text. This trace consists of constraints on the possible variations in formulation.

Rhetoric

Another dimension of discourse, rhetoric, deals with both formulation and context. Earlier, we saw that both classical and modern rhetoric deals with the persuasive dimension of language use and, more specifically, with the account of those properties of discourse that can make communication more persuasive. These rhetorical structures of discourse, featuring for instance the well-known figures of speech, are also based on grammatical structures but are not themselves linguistic or grammatical. Thus, an alliteration presupposes identity of initial phonemes of morphemes, parallelism requires identity of syntactic patterns, and metaphor may involve partial meaning identity and referential identity of expressions. But the transformations involved, such as deletion, repetition, substitution, or permutation, are not as such grammatical. They do not express differences of meaning, nor do they always indicate differences in social context. Rather, the speaker uses them to enhance the organization, and hence the attention, the storage, and retrieval of textual information by the listener/reader. Whereas style is a necessary property of discourse in context, rhetorical structures are optional. Note that rhetoric is often understood in a broader sense as the discipline that deals with all aspects of persuasive speaking or writing. In that sense, it becomes nearly identical with at least a large part of discourse analysis. Here, we use rhetoric in a somewhat more restricted sense, namely as the theoretical subcomponent of discourse analysis that explicates very specific, rhetorical structures only. Like syntax, semantics or pragmatics, such a rhetoric also has a more empirical dimension, which studies the social psychological aspects of persuasion based on the use of specific rhetorical structures. Similarly, overall formal structures such as those of stories or news discourse are not called rhetorical, as such, but require description in terms of schematic superstructures. To put it simply, a well-formed story is not necessarily a persuasively effective story.

Summary

We now have a more or less complete picture of the various structural levels and dimensions studied in discourse analysis and the various subtheories that should account for them. Figure 2.1 sketches this picture in a more schematic form.

Note that not all cells are filled. That is, we take phonology and morphology as typical microlevel disciplines. Macrosyntax refers to the overall schematic forms or superstructures of discourse. It is doubtful whether we can speak about semantic or pragmatic style, since style characterizes formulations given the same meanings or speech acts. Rhetoric may be defined for all levels of description. Of course, if we take morphology in a broader sense, we might also use the term macromorphology, for instance to charac-

	Micro	Macro	Style	Rhetoric	Superstructure
Phonology	x		x	x	
Morphology	x		x	x	
Syntax	x	(x)	x	x	
Semantics	x	x		x	x
Pragmatics	x	x		x	x

Figure 2.1. Schematic representation of the levels and dimensions of discourse analysis.

terize the overall layout of printed text. Similarly, we may use the term macrophonology to describe overall coherence in pronunciation or printing type throughout a text or to deal with intonational patterns beyond sentence boundaries, as, for instance, those that characterize paragraphs. Finally, if we account for the fact that people have thematical options as defined by the situation, we may also have something like semantic style. The same would hold for specific contextual variations in the use of speech acts. In other words, if we do not take the various notions in a too narrow, linguistic or grammatical sense, we have examples of discourse analysis at all levels and dimensions. From this brief discussion of the various aims and methods of discourse analysis, we may also conclude that in several respects, no standard terminology or canonical method of description has been developed. There may even be dimensions of discourse that cannot be integrated into one of the cells of Figure 2.1. However, for the description of news discourse in this book, our framework will have to do as a provisional plan for the analysis of news discourse.

Text and Context

Discourse analysis does more than just describe textual structures. In the previous section it became clear that in pragmatics action is also involved. The same holds when we describe structures of dialogues. That is, discourse is not just text but also a form of interaction. A plea in court is not only a sequence of coherent sentences that define a discourse type but also a particular juridical form of action, which only specific participants may perform at specific moments. In other words, a full-scale analysis of discourse involves an integration of text and context in the sense that the use of a discourse in a social situation is at the same time a social act. Similarly, the interpretation and production of a text involves the mental processes of interpretation and formulation, the retrieval and use of knowledge, and other strategies of the cognitive dimension of discourse. Meanings of discourse, therefore, are merely an abstraction from these cognitive interpretation processes, much in the same way that utterances and speech acts are only abstractions of real social actions in social situations. Hence, a complete empirical account of discourse also requires a description of cognitive processes of discourse production and understanding and of social interactions in sociocultural situations. Engaging in discourse means engaging in interpretation processes and social interaction, and a description of the cognitive and social contexts, therefore, is not a task that lies outside of discourse analysis. This does not mean that discourse analysis has as its proper task the full description of cognitive processes and social situations, which are objects of research for psychology and sociology. Rather it is interested in the systematic relationships between text and context. That is, it wants to know how cognitive processes specifically affect the production and understanding of discourse structures and how discourse structures influence and are influenced by the social situation. Thus, it was already suggested that style can be appropriately analyzed only when it is taken as an indication of the personal and the social contexts. Many aspects of discourse meaning, such as macrostructures and coherence, can be fully understood only if we know which cognitive representations of discourse and knowledge are involved during interpretation.

The questions asked here address the uses, effects, or the functions of discourse in contexts of communication. This carries discourse analysis into various social sciences, which also include social psychology and mass communication, and shows that the study of discourse analysis must indeed be interdisciplinary. Issues such as the change of knowledge, beliefs and attitudes, therefore, also belong to the discourse analytical inquiry when they involve the uses of discourse. Yet, the theoretical instruments must be borrowed from other disciplines. A full account of news discourse, then, requires both a description of textual structures of news and a description of the production and reception processes of news discourse in communicative situations and sociocultural contexts.

THEMATIC STRUCTURES

Theoretical Introduction

Perhaps even more than for other discourse types, the thematic organization of news discourse plays a crucial role. Therefore, this systematic analysis of the textual structures of news begins with an explication of notions like theme or topic. Intuitively, a topic or theme is what the discourse is about, globally speaking. Similarly, the topic of a lecture or a book is more or less equivalent with what we understand by its subject or subject matter. We then refer to the most important, central, or dominant concepts of a lecture or book. The same is true when we speak about the topic of a conversation. Such a topic is a summary or the gist of a conversation. We see that in English we have several terms to denote more or less the same concept. In this chapter we alternatively express this concept by the words "topic" or "theme."

Macrostructures

Topics are a property of the meaning or content of a text and, therefore, require theoretical analysis in terms of a semantic theory. Topics, however, are not defined as the meaning of individual words or sentences. We only speak about the summary, gist, upshot, or most important information of an utterance when we are dealing with larger stretches of talk or text. Hence, topics belong to the global, macrolevel of discourse description. The theoretical notion we use to describe topics or themes, therefore, is that of semantic macrostructures (van Dijk, 1972, 1977, 1980a).

Propositions and Macropropositions

Like meanings at the local level, macrostructures are characterized in terms of propositions. Roughly speaking, propositions are the smallest, independent meaning constructs of language and thought. As we have seen in the previous section, however, semantics not only deals with meanings but also with reference. Along the referential dimension, then, propositions are also the smallest semantic units that can be true or false. Propositions are typically expressed by single sentences or clauses, as in "Mary is a lawyer" or "Sandra fired her manager yesterday." Complex sentences, on the other hand, may express several, single or complex propositions, as we see in "Sandra fired her manager because he was incompetent." A single concept like "Sandra" or "manager" is not such a proposition. Used in isolation it cannot be true or false. We need at least two concepts, namely, a predicate like "is a lawyer" or "fired," and one or more arguments, which may denote things, persons, or events. Some predicates require several arguments: we(1) may rent a flat(2) from somebody(3), or we(1) pay somebody(2) 20 dollars(3) for a book(4). So, we may have 1-place, 2-place, 3-place and n-place predicates, and a full proposition is obtained by such a predicate together with at least one of these arguments (of which several may remain implicit, as in "He never paid"). Instead of saying that propositions, referentially speaking, may be true or false, we will simply say that propositions may be used to denote facts. Truth values seem relevant only when propositions are used and expressed in speech acts of assertion, but we also need a semantics for questions, commands, promises or threats. "I will kill your son . . . ." denotes a fact in the future, usually conditional upon the refusal of payment of a ransom, for instance. Similarly, accusations may involve past facts. And finally, facts need not exist in our own real, historical world but may also make up alternative worlds, such as dream worlds, counterfactual worlds, fictitious worlds, and so on. Thus, fiction consists of propositions which denote facts in another possible world.

These few elementary concepts define the semantics of discourse in general and the nature of macrostructures in particular. Thus, macrostructures are organized sets of propositions. Yet, unlike the propositions expressed by clauses or sentences, they are only expressed, indirectly, by larger stretches of talk or text. For ease of reference, we simply call propositions that are part of macrostructures 'macropropositions,' and we will henceforth assume that each topic of a text can be represented as such a macroproposition.

Macrorules

Longer discourses usually contain several topics and, therefore, have a macrostructure consisting of several macroprositions. Some topics are more general or abstract than others, so the whole macrostructure has a hierarchial organization, in which each sequence of macropropositions can be subsumed under a higher level macroproposition. These hierarchical relationships can be defined by macrorules, which represent what we intuitively understand by summarizing. Formally speaking, macrorules are semantic mapping rules or transformations, which link lower level propositions with higher level macropropositions. This means that topics or themes are derived from the meanings of a text by such summarizing macrorules. These rules define the upshot, gist, most important information, and hence the theme or topic for each sequence of propositions of a text, for instance, those of a paragraph. One way to represent the macrostructure of a text is by means of a tree-diagram (Figure 2.2).

Macrorules essentially reduce information. This reduction can take place in three different ways. First, we can simply delete all information that is no longer relevant in the rest of the text, such as local details. Second, we can take a sequence of propositions and replace them by one generalization. Instead of saying that we have a cat, a dog and a canary, we can more succinctly say that we have pets. Third, we can replace a sequence of propositions that denote the usual conditions, components, or consequences of an act or event by one macroproposition that denotes the act or event as a whole. Going to the airport, checking in, walking to the gate, etc. can be aptly summarized by the macroproposition "I took a plane to . . . ." We construct an overall event by its constituent details and, therefore, call this the construction rule. Deletion, generalization, and construction, then, will be taken as the three major macrorules that reduce information of a text to its topics. These rules are recursive. At higher levels, they may apply again.

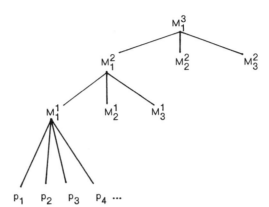

Figure 2.2. Schematic representation of the semantic macrostructure of a text.

We may summarize a page in a novel by a few macropropositions; and the sequence of macroprositions of several pages, or of a chapter, may again be summarized by the same macrorules, until we get at the highest level, where one or two macropropositions resume the text as a whole. The overall macrostructure thus assigned to (or derived from) a text defines not only what we call the thematic organization of the text but also its global coherence. Topics guarantee that a text or talk has semantic unity. If a speaker expresses propositions that cannot be subsumed under a given or new topic in a conversation, we may say that the speaker is incoherent or does not stay with the topic we were talking about.

The Subjectivity of Macrostructures

Thus far, our account of topics in terms of semantic macrostructures and rules has a rather formal flavor. Much like linguistic semantics, it approaches topics as if they were properties in or of the meaning of a text. Nevertheless, such an abstract approach has its disadvantages. Empirically speaking, meanings are assigned to texts in processes of interpretation by language users. They have a cognitive nature. The same is true for macrostructures. People assign a topic to a text, or infer it from a text, and these processes are a constituent part of understanding (Kintsch & van Dijk, 1978; van Dijk & Kintsch, 1983). This also enables them to construct their own personal macrostructures. After all, different language users may find different information in the text more important, and therefore, we may expect at least slightly different summaries of a given text. So, cognitively speaking, topics may be subjective, even when a minimum of overlap exists to guarantee mutual comprehension. To convey the topic(s) a speaker assigns to a piece of text or talk, attempts will be made to clearly signal them, e.g., by summaries or expressions such as "the most important thing is . . ." or "the

topic of my lecture will be . . . " The listener or reader may or may not pick
up these signals and may assign a more personal topic, depending on individual interests or relevancies.

Macrostructures and Knowledge

Another reason for a more cognitive complement to the theory of macrostructures is that macrorules require knowledge of the world, such as
frames or scripts (Schank & Abelson, 1977). We can only subsume information such as "I went to the airport, checked in my luggage, went to the
gate . . .," under the macroproposition "I took a plane to . . " if the component details of the macroaction are known by the language user, for instance
as part of a flying script. The same is true for our ability to generalize cats
and dogs as pets or when we have to decide whether or not information in a
text is an irrelevant detail. The details of these cognitive representations and
processes are explained in Chapter 3. It is important to stress here that
macrorules cannot operate simply on propositional input from the text.
They also require propositions derived from our knowledge of the world
and, as we just saw, from our personal beliefs and interests.

Strategic Macrounderstanding

Cognitive assignments of topics, that is the global interpretation of a text by
language users, do not take place when the language user has interpreted all
the words and sentences of the whole text. Rather, the reader starts to make
expedient guesses about the most probable topic(s) of a text, aided by the
thematic signals of the writer. Initial summaries, the explicit reference to
topics, or titles are examples of such signals (Jones, 1977). Instead of formal
rules, then, language users apply effective strategies in the derivation of
topics from a text (van Dijk & Kintsch, 1983). As soon as we have heard a
first sentence, we may already try to guess what the overall or initial topic of
a text or talk fragment may be. This is vitally important because the topic
acts as a major control instance on the further interpretation of the rest of
the text. When we already know the topic, it is easier to understand the
respective sentences of the text. This is an example of what psychologists
call top-down processing.

Summary

We may now summarize the theoretical account of themes or topics in this
section and thus express the semantic macrostructure of this section. A topic
of a text is a strategically derived subjective macroproposition, which is
assigned to sequences of propositions by macroprocesses (rules, strategies)
on the basis of general world knowledge and personal beliefs and interests.
Such a topic is part of a hierarchical, topical, or thematical structure—the

semantic macrostructure—which may be expressed by a summary and which defines what is subjectively the most important information, gist, upshot of the text. Topics may be signaled by speakers in several ways, so that the listener is able to make a quick guess about the first or major topic. Topics are crucial in the overall understanding of a text, e.g., in the establishment of global coherence; and they act as a semantic, top-down control on local understanding at the microlevel. Topics in a text indeed play a central role. Without them it would be impossible to grasp what the text is about globally; we would only be able to understand local fragments of the text, with no understanding of their overall relationships, hierarchy, and organization.

The Derivation of Topics from News Discourse

In principle, the theoretical introduction given in the previous section also holds for the description of themes or topics in news discourse in the press (van Dijk, 1983b, 1985c). The first aim of the rest of this section, therefore, is to illustrate, test, and refine this theory of semantic macrostructures for this specific type of text in the mass media. Our second aim is to show whether there are specifics in the thematic organization of news discourse. Topics in the news may be organized, realized, expressed, or signaled in a specific way. Perhaps the overall coherence defined by them is somewhat different from other types of printed text.

To begin, let us examine a few examples. The *International Herald Tribune*, of July 12, 1984, published the following small item on its front page:

UN HEAD IN MOSCOW FOR AFGHAN TALKS

MOSCOW (Combined Dispatches)—Javier Pérez de Cuellar, secretary-general of the United Nations, arrived in Moscow on Wednesday with Diego Cordovez, a UN special representative on Afghanistan, for talks with Soviet officials on prospects for ending the Afghan conflict. The two men were met at the airport by Foreign Minister Andrei A. Gromyko. Thex will be in Moscow until Friday. Babrak Karmal, president of Afghanistan, flew to Moscow Monday evening.

Mr. Pérez de Cuellar had indicated that he also might discuss the issue of the dissident Soviet physicist Andrei D. Sakharov, who is in exile in the city of Gorki. (Reuters, AP)

This small routine item of international news about the visit to an important country of an important politician who is about to discuss an important issue has a clear main topic, namely, the one just summarized. This topic is also summarized in the headline. Here, we find a first important feature of newspaper discourse: Topics may be expressed and signaled by headlines, which apparently act as summaries of the news text. The headline expresses a macroproposition: It has an implicit predicate (to be), and a number of arguments, viz., an agent (UN Head), a location, and a goal. To derive this macroproposition from the text, information must be eliminated according to the previously discussed rules. In the first paragraph, this information is the time of arrival, which is no longer relevant, and the identity of a companion visitor. These are details, and may be abstracted simply by deletion (the information is not necessary to understand the rest of the text). That de Cuellar arrived in Moscow may be omitted because a visit to a foreign town, or being there, presupposes the normal condition of arriving there, and normal conditions may be integrated by the construction rule to yield the overall macroact, given our general knowledge about international travel, about the concept of visiting and our knowledge about international politics (see Carbonell, 1979). This also applies to the information about talks with Soviet officials, which is also implied in the general concept of political talk and the location of the talk. Knowledge about the protocol of international meetings allows us to integrate the information that the UN Secretary was met by a high-ranking politician, the Minister of Foreign Affairs. The precise length of the stay is a detail, not part of the main topic, and may be deleted. That Karmal is also in Moscow is not part of the theme itself, but his presence in Moscow is related to the topical element talks about Afghanistan. It is a subordinate topic here, not elaborated, and as such may function as information about previous news events. Interesting is the final paragraph, which cannot be subsumed under the main topic of the news item. It also presupposes knowledge about previous news events, specifically about the fate of Sakharov, and may be connected to the current event only because Western leaders have been concerned about the fate of Sakharov. Thus, it could be expected that de Cuellar would bring up this other delicate matter along with the other critical issue (Afghanistan).

From this simple example, we may conclude first that topics of news discourse may be routinely expressed in headlines, which apparently have summary function. Second, this topic may be obtained by deleting information that can be considered as detail, which means that it is not directly relevant for the understanding of the rest of the text. Technically, this means that deleted propositions are not presuppositions of subsequent propositions. Third, information may be subsumed by a macroproposition if it refers to normal conditions or components of the macroevent. This subsumption takes place on the basis of our general knowledge of the script about international politics (political events, acts, politicians, political talks, visits, etc.). Fourth, the news event may feature information that is not subsumed by the main topic, but is an independent subtopic (talks about Y being a subtopic of talks about Z if the speech participants are the same and, similarly, visit of A to B is also thematically related to the visit of C to B if the goals of these visits are related). Fifth, part of the implied or presupposed information that can be deleted, or subsumed by construction, is about previous news events, which were topical in previous news reports. In general, then, macrorules operate rather straightforwardly by reducing details and normal components of political macroacts and by the application of general and particular political knowledge. That this is the case may be tested by trying to expand the topic based on that knowledge: Given the topic alone, we may, with some confidence, predict what stereotypical things may happen when one knows the political situation. This means that in the derivation of topics from news text, semantic rules go hand in hand with vast amounts of cognitive representations. Even the text itself, therefore, may be incomplete and presuppose much information. This brief news item could itself be a summary of a longer news item, but the reverse is also true: The *Times* that same day published a small item hardly longer than the summary we have given above. The only information added in that item is that diplomats doubted de Cuellar's visit would be successful.

The (London) *Times* of July 12, 1984, also printed a news item in the Overseas section about East Timor, under the heading EAST TIMOR'S PLIGHT. SHULTZ JOINS CRITICS OF INDONESIAN RULE. As a further example, let us try to derive a macrostructure from this text fragment by fragment, that is by assigning a macroproposition to each paragraph, at a first level of macrostructure (M1)

M1. 1. Shultz, U. S. Secretary of State, raised the issue of congressional concern about Indonesian military actions in East Timor, during a meeting with Foreign Minister Mochtar Kusumaatmadja.

2. Shultz carried a letter from members of Congress, saying that the plight of East Timor was of concern to the United States.

3. The letter urged free access to the area by independent organizations and expressed concern with the actual situation after new actions of the Indonesian army.

4. The letter used materials from the East Timorese apostolic delegate about the death of many people.

5. Shultz's declaration coincided with an Australian Labour Party resolution.

6. The resolution expressed grave concern about the new fighting in East Timor.

7. The Australian left and the press were the most vocal critics of Indonesian policy, whereas the United States regrets lack of self-determination while accepting Indonesian sovereignty.

In this somewhat longer news article, we first observe that the application of macrorules on each paragraph does not necessarily reduce the text directly to the highest topical level. It is as if each paragraph is itself a

East Timor's plight

Shultz joins critics of Indonesian rule

From Our Correspondent, Jakarta

Mr George Shultz, the US Secretary of State, yesterday unexpectedly raised the issue of congressional concern over continuing Indonesian military activity in East Timor in a meeting with the Foreign Minister Professor Mochtar Kusumaatmadja.

Mr Shultz, who is here to attend an expanded Asean (Association of South East Asian Nations) foreign ministers' meeting, carried with him a letter of concern signed by a bipartisan group of 123 Congressmen. The letter said that the plight of East Timor, annexed by Indonesia after bloody fighting in the middle and late 1970s, was very much the concern of the United States as long as America continued to supply arms used in the territory.

The letter urged Jakarta to give unrestricted access to relief and humanitarian organizations, journalists and independent observers, and expressed concern over reports of the situation worsening since the Indonesian Army launched a new operation – still continuing – in the area last August.

Much of the source material used by the Congressmen came from the East Timorese apostolic delegate, Mr Carlos Felipe Belo, who said in a letter that about 100,000 of an estimated 600,000 people in East Timor had died since the conflict began.

Diplomatic sources pointed out that Mr Shultz had raised the subject with Professor Kusumaatmadja on the same day the ruling Labour Party in neighbouring Australia passed a strongly worded resolution. This was considered a narrow victory for the moderate faction in the Australian Government in that it did not call for self-determination for East Timor.

The text of the Canberra resolution, however, expressed grave concern in remarkably similar terms over the renewed fighting

The Australian press and left wing of the Labour Party have been the most vocal critics of Indonesian policy in East Timor, while the United States has expressed its regret over the lack of an act of self-determination, while accepting Indonesian sovereignty.

Mr Shultz: A message from Congressmen.

THE TIMES, July 12, 1984

38

summary of events, and further reduction hardly seems possible. This means that larger sections of text, that is several paragraphs at the same time, might be reducible to more abstract topics. Second, the headline only covers part of the information in the text. It is an elite politician of an elite country (U.S. Secretary of State) whose action is summarized in the headline, although the predicate "to join" presupposes other criticism of the situation in East Timor. Neither the U.S. Congressional letter nor the Australian Labour resolution are mentioned in the headlines, although they are high level topics. Third, the first paragraph of this news item is a somewhat larger summary of the text and, hence, functions as a lead section.

The information reduced in each paragraph is as follows: (1) time and manner of Shultz's declaration; (2) the context of his presence in Indonesia and further details about the authors of the letter and about East Timor; (3) details about the letter; (4) numbers of victims, (5) political background of Labour resolution; (6) detail of resolution; (7) no reduction. In other words, macroreduction may apply to details about time, place, manner of an act, irrelevant background, precise numbers, and properties of persons and objects mentioned. This means that deletion is one of the more powerful rules of macroreduction in this example. The construction rule, based on common political knowledge, hardly allows for much reduction in this case: There are few traditional scripts involved, except for the international protest script, in which a representative of country (or countries) A criticizes the leaders of country (or countries) B for the treatment of its own citizens.

We may try to further reduce the first level of macrostructure informally as follows:

M2. 1. U.S. Secretary of State raised the issue of Congressional concern about East Timor in a meeting with the Indonesian Foreign Minister.

2. U.S. members of Congress urged for access to East Timor.

3. There are many victims in East Timor because of army actions.

4. Australian Labour Party also expressed grave concern with the situation in East Timor

At this level, we have reduced across paragraph boundaries, such that the first paragraph can be used as the first Lead paragraph, allowing reduction of information in several subsequent paragraphs. Identification of actors is no longer necessary, since their roles are more important. The context of the action (Asean meeting, etc.) remains irrelevant and the Congressional letter and resolution of the Australian Labour Party are no longer relevant since their messages become more important. The last paragraph can be fully deleted because it merely reminds the reader of the Australian and American policies about East Timor.

Further reduction of level M2 might yield the highest level M3, which is the shortest theoretical summary of the news item:

M3. 1. U.S. members of Congress and Shultz and the Australian Labour Party criticized Indonesian policy in East Timor.

At this level, we only keep (1) the major actors involved; (2) the macroactions and events (criticizing and policy); (3) and the specific subject or issue involved (East Timor). This reduction is possible only if we presuppose knowledge about the situation in East Timor and about the ways international protests are formulated and delivered. Criticizing presupposes negatively-evaluated actions; and world knowledge as well as evidence from impartial sources and requests for independent assessment of the facts provide the possibility that persecution of many victims may be involved. We observe again that macroreduction in the press is based on deletion of irrelevant local details, and on the script-based subsumption of normal conditions, components, or consequences under a higher level macroaction, in which actors may be represented only by their role designations. A more or less representative headline for this article, then, could have been: NEW ACTIONS INDONESIAN ARMY IN EAST TIMOR as superposed headline and U.S. AND AUSTRALIAN PROTESTS AGAINST INDONESIA as main headline.

From this rather informal discussion of topics in news discourse, we may provisionally conclude that the main principles of macrostructure interpretation are also relevant for news discourse. We find several levels of macropropositions, which may be obtained by applying semantic reduction rules that delete irrelevant details or that subsume components under higher level action or event concepts. It was observed, however, that these rules also have more specific application conditions. Thus, information about previous topics may function as a reminder and is not directly relevant for the actual news. The same holds for context and backgrounds of the actual events. Then, reduction presupposes vast amounts of general and particular political knowledge, often of a stereotypical, script-related nature. Finally, main topics are signaled by the news item in headlines and leads. They define the overall situation and indicate to the reader a preferred overall meaning of the text. In the article about Shultz and East Timor, for instance, the U.S. actors are more important than the Australian ones, and these two western actors are more important than direct, local participants and their actions or declarations. Also, the emphasis of the news on the actual events can be inferred by macroreduction of context and background. The topics as signaled in the news, then, are macrostructural from the point of view of the newspaper or the journalist. Readers in Indonesia or East Timor may assign other relevancies to the events. Similarly, critical readers in the West may assign more relevance to the information that the U.S. still supplies arms to

Indonesia or to the fact that the U.S. government has actually done very little to prevent Indonesia from occupying East Timor and from massacring its population (Chomsky, 1981). News events, therefore, necessarily embody a point of view, and so does their description in a news discourse. This point of view also shows in macrostructural organization and signaling.

It should be noted, finally, that our analysis was informal. A purely formal, algorithmical application of the rules would have involved the precise formulation of script-related and textual information in terms of propositions and the specification of the precise rules and their constraints in the derivation of the macropropositions. In this study, however, we avoid such formal analyses and definitions, and rely on systematic but intuitive observations (for details of theory and application, see van Dijk, 1980a, and for application on a news article and explanation of the cognitive mechanisms involved in the macrounderstanding of news, see van Dijk & Kintsch, 1983).

Thematic Structure

The topics of news discourse are not simply a list; rather, they form a hierarchical structure. In our analysis of two examples in the previous section, this structure has not been dealt with explicitly. How exactly are the topics organized in an overall topical or thematic structure? Theoretically, we only assumed that a higher level macroproposition can be derived from a sequence of lower-level macropropositions or micropropositions. This means that the macroproposition is entailed by the propositions from which it is derived. The ordering of macropropositions at each level is implicitly defined by the ordering of expressed propositions at the lower level(s), that is by the order of propositions and sentences in the text. This, however, may lead to problems for the representation of news discourse, where the ordering of the text is defined rather by relevance of topics (first, main topics come first) than by some logical order of topics. In the news item about Shultz and East Timor, for instance, the information about Shultz's critique is given before the information about the letter from members of Congress, although we may assume that this letter preceded the critique of Shultz. In other words, antecedents of news events may well be expressed later in news discourse, compared to their semantic position with respect to the main news event.

Thus, macrostructures, much as any semantic structure, may be further organized by a number of fixed categories, including Causes, Antecedents, or Consequences. A simple thematic structure for the Shultz/East Timor item, then, could be represented as in Figure 2.3.

In this simple schema we have indicated that macropropositions may have different semantic functions, whether intensionally or extensionally. That is, the protests of Shultz are conditioned by the letter from members of

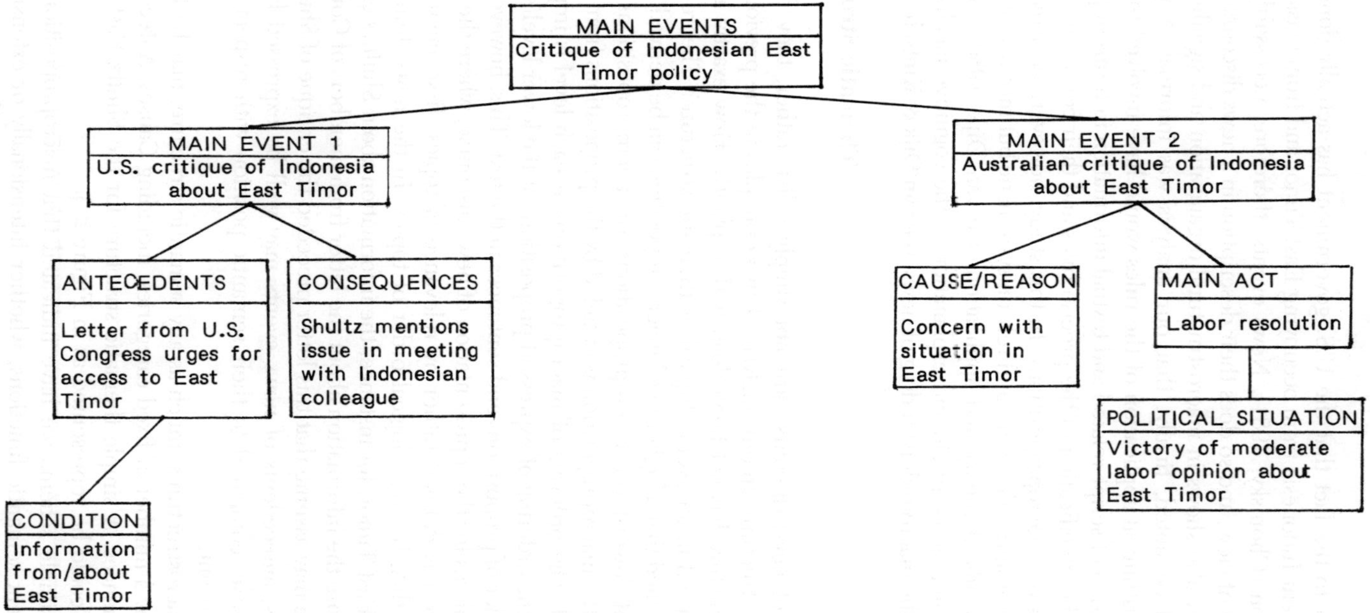
MAIN EVENTS
Critique of Indonesian East Timor policy
MAIN EVENT 1
U.S. critique of Indonesia about East Timor
MAIN EVENT 2
Australian critique of Indonesia about East Timor
ANTECEDENTS
Letter from U.S. Congress urges for access to East Timor
CONSEQUENCES
Shultz mentions issue in meeting with Indonesian colleague
CAUSE/REASON
Concern with situation in East Timor
MAIN ACT
Labor resolution
CONDITION
Information from/about East Timor
POLITICAL SITUATION
Victory of moderate labor opinion about East Timor

Figure 2.3. Representation of the simplified thematic structure of the news report about Shultz/East Timor.

the U.S. Congress, a letter which is again conditioned by new information about victims in East Timor. Hence, condition/cause or consequence relationships, which characterize the facts referred to (and not the propositional links themselves), seem to be an important organizing feature of thematic structure. Similarly, for each theme or theme level, we may specify context or situation, participants involved, the maor events or acts, and so on. Chapter 3 explains that this kind of thematic organization is also determined by the cognitive representation language users have about the situation, the so-called situation model. Thematic structure may be used by the reader to construct such a new model of the actual news events or to update old models. Conversely, previous models about the news situation (e.g., the situation in East Timor) may be used to construct the actual thematic structure of a news discourse. We have witnessed this interplay between textual structures and cognitive information before, when we argued that macrostructures depend on scriptal knowledge. The same holds for the internal structure of this macroorganization: It is determined by our beliefs about the structures of events and actions in general and about the political events in an actual situation in particular.

Thematic Realization: From Macrostructure to Microstructure

Topics can be topics of text only when they are actually realized, directly or indirectly, through propositions expressed in the respective sentences of the text, that is, in episodes (van Dijk, 1982a). Whereas the derivation of topics seems to simulate the understanding processes of the reader, the analysis of the reverse process seems to simulate how a given topic is expressed, detailed, or elaborated by the speaker or writer. The reader must infer topics, given detailed input from headlines, leads, and respective sentences; whereas the author already knows at least the main or first topics and must express, signal, and fill them. This section analyzes the structural nature of the process in terms of textual organization.

One of the most conspicuous and typical features of topic realization or elaboration in news discourse is its installment character. That is, each topic is delivered in parts, not as a whole, as is the case in other discourse types. This structural characteristic is caused by the top-down principle of relevance organization in news. This principle says that news discourse is organized so that the most important or relevant information is put in the most prominent position, both in the text as a whole, and in the sentences. This means that for each topic, the most important information is presented first. When the important information of other topics has been expressed, earlier topics are reintroduced with lower-level details. Thus, instead of a left-right realization of topics from a thematic structure, a top-down realization occurs, if this top-down organization of general to particular also coincides with the important—less important dimension (which is not always the case: sometimes a semantic detail may have more relevance than the higher-level proposition by which it can be subsumed).

Specification Rules

In formal terms, the realization of topics in news discourse takes place by the application of inverse macrorules, which we may call specification rules. High-level, abstract information is specified so that for overall events or actions, detailed descriptions are given as to the identity and properties of the participants, conditions, components and consequences of the action, time, place, or manner of the events and various kinds of circumstances. Specification takes place in cycles in news discourse: High-level specifics are given first, followed by lower-level details. This structural feature of news is also the result of a production strategy that considers relevance constraints and possible reading strategies, so that readers will get the important information first. Partial reading in that case will not result in partial understanding but only in missing a few, lower-level details. Finally, traditional news production has size constraints. Top-down organization allows editors to cut the final paragraphs of a news story without the loss of essential information.

To illustrate this particular feature of news discourse, let us take a report from the *International Herald Tribune* (July 12, 1984) about the current events in Lebanon. In our case study of the international coverage of the assassination of Bechir Gemayel of Lebanon (van Dijk, 1984b; 1987b) we analyze in more detail the backgrounds of the Lebanon story. The main topic of the article as suggested by the headline is LEBANESE COMMITTEE NAMED TO SECURE RELEASE OF MOSLEM, CHRISTIAN HOSTAGES. Let us go through the respective paragraphs to categorize the details specified for this and other topics. We thus hope to obtain more insight into the specification rules and strategies of news in the press.

1. This is the lead paragraph, giving the full macrostructure of the main topic. It specifies the Agent (Lebanese Cabinet), Time, the roles of the political groups (rivals), and a further Goal set for the committee (investigate fate of others missing).
2. This paragraph is the specification of the contents of a statement by the main Participant (premier) of the Cabinet meeting and of length of the meeting (Time).
3. This paragraph does not provide specification; rather it gives a generalization: the actual decision is part of a larger issue. Such a generalization is important in the specification of context or backgrounds to a story.

Lebanese Committee Named to Secure Release of Moslem, Christian Hostages

New York Times Service

BEIRUT — The Lebanese cabinet appointed on Wednesday a special committee to secure the release of hostages held by rival Moslem and Christian militias and to investigate the fate of other missing persons.

Prime Minister Rashid Karami said after a four-hour cabinet meeting that he hoped all hostages would be freed soon. He did not, however, mention a fixed date for any release.

The issue of abduction victims has become a major challenge to the cabinet's efforts to re-establish peace in Lebanon.

Families of missing Lebanese, who have blocked crossing points between the Christian and Moslem halves of Beirut and cut off access to the city's port and international airport, agreed to suspend their protest temporarily, pending measures by the government to deal with the situation.

Of thousands of Lebanese reported missing in the past few years, the International Committee of the Red Cross has been able to account for only 200. The Red Cross teams who visited the hostages in recent weeks said they were being detained by both Moslem and Christian militias.

Earlier Wednesday, gunmen attacked and blew up part of a building in West Beirut housing the Libyan Embassy, formally known as the Libyan People's Bureau. A Shiite Moslem faction, calling itself the Imam Sader Brigades, claimed responsibility for the action.

The raid occurred shortly before daybreak, when a group of masked gunmen arrived at the embassy building. They overpowered the Lebanese and Libyan security guards.

After making sure there was no one else in the four-story structure, they planted an explosive charge estimated by Lebanese investigators at about 55 pounds (about 25 kilograms) of TNT, then detonated it by remote control, causing extensive damage but no casualties.

An anonymous caller telephoned

(Continued on Page 2, Col. 4)

Beirut Names Group to Get Hostages Released

(Continued from Page 1)

the French news agency Agence France-Presse in Beirut to claim responsibility for the attack on behalf of the Imam Sader Brigades.

The group, believed to be comprised of Shiite radicals, has been conducting a campaign against Libyan diplomats to protest the disappearance six years ago of Imam Sader, the spiritual head of the Lebanese Shiite community. He disappeared at the end of a visit to the Libyan capital, Tripoli.

The same group claimed credit for two separate incidents recently in which Libyan diplomats were kidnapped in West Beirut and subsequently released.

The attack on the embassy is believed to be timed to a visit to Lebanon by the Libyan foreign minister, Ali Treiki, who was scheduled to hold talks with government officials in Beirut on Wednesday.

Shiite religious leaders added their voices to those who called for the visit to be canceled. They said the government of Lebanon should receive Libyan emissaries only if they disclose the fate of Imam Sader.

President Amin Gemayel and the cabinet met at the presidential palace in Baabda, a Christian suburb overlooking the capital. The meeting was the cabinet's first in Baabda since its formation 10 weeks ago. Previously, it convened at the presidential residence in the mountain resort of Bikfaya about 12 miles (about 20 kilometers) northeast of Beirut. Moslem ministers had refused to go to Baabda, citing security reasons.

They dropped their reservations in the past few days, after the Lebanese Army applied a security plan in and around Beirut that opened crossing points between the Moslem and Christian sectors. Mr. Karami and Minister of State Nabih Berri, both Moslems, flew to Baabda from Moslem West Beirut by helicopter, while the public works and tourism minister, Walid Jumblat, the Druze leader, arrived by car.

The new committee on the hostages includes two cabinet members, Interior Minister Joseph Skaf and Education Minister Selim Al Hoss. They are to be assisted by army and police officers.

Red Cross officials declined to say where the kidnapped Lebanese were being held. Government officials and political leaders believe that most of those who disappeared were killed by their abductors.

Relatives have been called upon to provide the committee with all available information about the abduction victims.

Mr. Karami said the cabinet formed a second committee to consider ways to reopen the southern coastal highway, which links Beirut and Sidon. The identity of those members was not given.

The highway has been closed since February, when a Druze militia seized the coastal plain between Beirut and Damour. A section south of Damour to the Awali River is held by the Lebanese Forces, a Christian militia. The Israeli Army's outposts are located near the Awali, just north of Sidon.

4. This paragraph is the specification of a direct Consequence of the decision to name a special committee: blockade suspended. Also reminding specification of a previous event, namely participants, reasons and goals of the blockade.

5. Details are given about main Participants (hostages): Numbers, Time, Sources of the information, and details about acts of Participants (Moslems, Christians, Red Cross).

6. This paragraph opens a new story, not signaled by the headline, which in other papers gets a separate article: the raid of Shiites on the Libyan embassy in Beirut. This story is summarized here featuring Time, while at the end of the paragraph the Moslem faction is identified.

7. The second topic (topic B) is further specified: Time, details of action (preparation, etc.), other Participants (guards).

8. This paragraph presents specification of bombing action, preparatory moves, specification of weight of bomb (Number), and immediate Results of the action.

9. Paragraph overflow from front page to p. 2. Contains specification of stereotypical Consequences: Actors phone news agency to claim responsibility.

10. This paragraph presents Specification of identity of the group and of the historical background (Motivation) of their action.

11. This paragraph is the specification of two previous events in which the same group was involved.

12. This paragraph returns to the actual political context: the actual timing and hence Reasons for the bombing (visit of Libyan Foreign Minister to Beirut).

13. This paragraph gives details of the context: Shiite protests against this visit, i.e., introduction of further Participants and possible Reasons and Motivations for the bombing.

14. Suddenly, the article reverts to topic A, the cabinet meeting, of which several details of Location are given: first meeting in Baabda, instead of the previous meeting in Bikfaya (further Properties of Location are given). General motivation of Moslem Cabinet members not to go to (Christian) Baabda.

15. Presented here are the causes of dropping reservations to meet in Baabda. Details about Manner of travel of named Participants to get to the meeting.

16. This paragraph names Participants in committee, with their major Roles.

17. This paragraph gives the specification of Location of Participants

(hostages) and Source (Red Cross). Official statement Contents about the fate of the hostages.

18. This paragraph gives the preparatory actions (give information) for committee by further Participants (relatives).
19. A new topic (C) is addressed: the formation of another committee (preparing reopening of highway).
20. This paragraph is the specification of main Object of topic C: Time and Cause and Participants (Agents) of closure, and groups now involved in the control of the highway.

We have gone into some detail in the description of the specifications of the various topics discussed in this news report. We first observed that a news item may feature high-level topics not expressed in the headlines or the lead. Especially topic B would usually have required a separate news item, as we also found in other newspapers. Here it is embedded in the main topic of the formation of a committee by the Lebanese cabinet. Second. we find that this main topic A is delivered in installments throughout the article. The lead gives the general macrostructure, and the next paragraphs have specifications of the following type:

1. Main Participant (in meeting; Premier).
2. Contents of declaration (Act of main Participant).
3. Generalization describing the general Background.
4. Immediate Consequence of committee formation of the Conditions of the cabinet decision (acts by other Participants: relatives of hostages).
5. Numbers of Participants (hostages) and Sources of this information.
6. Details about Location of cabinet meeting.
7. Motivations of Participants not to meet in Location.
8. Manner of Act (travel) of Participants to Location.
9. Identity of Participants (committee members).
10. Information about properties of main Participants (hostages).

Specifications for topic B are:

11. Main Action and Participants (Topic).
12. Time, other Participants (Opponents) and Preparatory Actions.
13. Preparatory Actions, Number (weight of bomb) and direct Results and consequences.

14. Motivations or Reasons for action and existence of special group.
15. Specification of previous events of similar type with same Participants as Agents; Comparison.
16. Context of the attack: visit of other Participant.

These specifications show that the general summary expressing the highest topic in full (main Act, main participants, etc.) is followed by further details about the identity of participants, their further properties, reasons or motivations for actions, immediate and indirect consequences of the actions, specification of the links with previous news events (often in terms of conditions or comparisons), details of Time and Location, Preparatory actions if politically relevant, the Context of the events or actions, Goals, numerical information (number of participants, weight of bomb, etc.) and Contents of Participant declarations. These specifications may follow a specific order. Thus, specification of the contents of the declaration of the main participant (the Premier) comes long before a specification of the identity of the members of the committee (who, internationally, are less known and less relevant). Also the political causes and consequences of the decision to form a special committee are mentioned rather prominently: the protests of the population against the abduction and retention as hostages of relatives is presented as a possible condition that may challenge the peace efforts in Lebanon. Before further details about the cabinet meeting and the committee are specified, we first get information about the second main Topic, the bomb attack on the Libyan embassy.

From this analysis, we conclude that news discourse may exhibit a thematical realization structure that is basically (1) top down; (2) relevance controlled; and (3) cyclical (in installments). That is, main acts and participants that are politically relevant come first, followed in each cycle by details of main participants, identity of secondary participants, components/conditions/consequences/manner of acts, Time and Location details, etc. Political relevance as a criterion for thematic realization means that those conditions or consequences and participants are mentioned first that are compatible with the newspaper's and readers' model of the situation in general (peace efforts in Lebanon, nature of actual government, delicate balance of power, etc.), and of the recent events in particular (blockade of green line transition points by relatives of missing persons). Indeed, in this example, an early paragraph even explicitly states why this issue is so important politically. Further theoretical and empirical work is necessary to establish the precise constraints on the ordering and nature of thematic expression and elaboration in news discourse, but we seem to have uncovered some of its basic principles.

NEWS SCHEMATA

Textual Superstructures

The overall meaning (macrostructure) of discourse has more than its own organizing principles. It also needs some kind of overall syntax, which defines the possible forms in which topics or themes can be inserted and ordered in the actual text. That is, we need at a global level what has been customary in traditional sentence grammars, where semantic representations are mapped onto syntactic structures of sentences. This global form of discourse can be defined in terms of a rule-based schema. Such a schema consists of a series of hierarchically ordered categories, which may be specific for different discourse types and conventionalized and hence different in various societies or cultures.

Let us give some well-known examples of discourse schemata. Stories, for instance, have a narrative schema, consisting of conventional categories such as Summary, Setting, Complication, Resolution and Coda (Labov & Waletzky, 1967; Labov, 1972c). This means that stories may begin with a sequence of sentences that, as a whole, functions as the summary of the story, followed by a sequence of sentences that functions as a setting for the events of the story. Such a Setting category may contain information about the initial situation (state of affairs, time, place), in which events or actions may take place or information about main participants and their properties, and so on. In other words, there are parts of a text that have a specific function and that require specific meaning information. A Summary for instance must contain the macrostructure of a story.

Everyday conversations also have schemata. These may also be functionally analyzed in global units that may be conventionally categorized. Many conversations, for instance, begin with some kind of Greetings exchange, and may be terminated by a sequence of Closing turns and Leave-taking formulas (Schegloff & Sacks, 1973). Scientific discourse, such as journal articles or lectures, may also have a conventional form, which often features an argumentative schema: a number of Premises followed by a Conclusion. Psychological articles may even have a fixed, normative form, which requires an Introduction or Theory section, an Experimental section that itself has subcategories such as Design, Materials, Subjects, and a final Discussion section (Kintsch & van Dijk, 1978). In this way, many discourse types in our culture have a more-or-less fixed schematic organization. Language users learn such schemata during socialization, although for some schemata, such as those used in professional discourse, special training may be required.

The theory of discourse schemata is still in its infancy. Most work deals with the organization of specific discourse types, such as stories and arguments. A general metatheory is still lacking. In such a theory, the precise nature of the categories, rules, and constraints should be specified for schematic structures in general. It should also explain how schemata are linked with other structural dimensions of discourse, such as the overall, global meaning (thematic structure) and the local structures of a text.

Story Grammars

There is currently a fierce debate in psychology and AI about the nature of story schemata (see e.g., Rumelhart, 1975; Mandler & Johnson, 1977; Mandler, 1978; Black & Wilensky, 1979; van Dijk, 1980b; and the discussion following Wilensky, 1983). On the one hand, we have the so-called story grammarians, who hold that story schemata can be specified by a rule system or grammar, featuring a number of typical narrative categories. On the other side, mainly in AI research on stories, are those who maintain that the structures of narrative can simply be accounted for in terms of a general theory of action, featuring terms such as goal, plan, and result. We have formulated an intermediary position that states that abstract schematic structures, also of stories, can in principle be described or generated by a rule system or specific type of grammar. However, such a grammar should consist of conventional narrative categories and rules and not feature general action theoretical notions (as we find both in story grammars and in AI models) (van Dijk, 1980c; van Dijk & Kintsch, 1983). General action theoretical notions are not specific for the description of stories but belong to the semantics of action discourse in general. Narrative categories must have a more formal, abstract nature and must be conventional. One should distinguish between the structure of action and the structure of action discourse. After all, the way we describe actions need not be structurally equivalent with the organization of action sequences: Actions need not be described in chronological order, for example. Stories may be preceded by a summary, and, of course, an action sequence cannot have an initial summary. Also, although each story is a type of action discourse, not each action discourse is a story. Actions may also be described in reports, manuals, or sociological discourse. Hence, stories have specific constraints, such as an interesting complication.

Our view can be characterized abstractly in terms of (1) a set of conventional narrative categories; (2) a set of narrative rules that specify the hierarchy and the ordering of the categories into schematic forms; and possibly (3) a set of transformation rules that may change underlying canonical narrative structures into various forms of actual narrative schemata. Such transformations may include, for instance, deletions of categories or premutations that change the canonical order.

Superstructures

Theoretically, we account for discourse schemata in terms of so-called superstructures (Van Dijk, 1980a). These are global structures of discourse, defined by specific superstructure categories and rules, in a similar manner as for stories. The necessary link with other discourse structures is established through semantic macrostructures (topics). That is, in order to assign a global form or schema to a text, we have to relate it to a global meaning that can fill this form or schema. Thus, each superstructure category is associated with a macroprosition (topic) from the semantic macrostructure. This category assigns a specific discourse function to the macroproposition and consequently to the sequence of sentences or propositions summarized by that macroproposition. A narrative category like Setting, for instance, may be filled by one or more macropropositions that, together, describe the setting of the story. This link between superstructure and macrostructure enables us to formulate specific mutual constraints. In a Setting only information that describes the initial situation and participants may be inserted. The Complication and the Resolution in a narrative schema also require specific information. Once we have linked the overall form with the overall content of the text, we also have a link with the microstructures of the actual text, namely, via the macrorules or specification rules. Each macroproposition is related to a sequence of propositions, which in turn is related to a sequence of clauses and sentences. This also means that the schema determines how the topics of a text could or should be ordered and, hence, how sequences and sentences should appear in the text. Finally, local coherence rules will then address the detailed meaning relations between sentences (see The Microstructures of News Discourse). Figure 2.4 presents a summary of this theoretical approach:

In this simplified schema, S1, S2, . . ., represent superstructure categories; M1, M2, . . . represent macrostructure categories; p1, p2, . . . represent propositions, which are finally mapped on an ordered sequence of sentences. For simplicity, we have assumed that each superstructure category is filled with only one macroproposition. Of course, each category may be filled with a complex set of macropropositions, that is, by a fragment of the thematic structure. For example, the Setting of a long story in a novel may be summarized by several macropropositions at several levels. This theoretical approach avoids the problems that arise when we link superstructure categories directly with sentences of a text, as do most other approaches that have dealt with story structure and that are often based on the analysis of very short stories, where microstructures and macrostructures coincide. We cannot go into the formal technicalities of our theory of superstructures and macrostructures, but the overall picture of the role of schemata in a text should now be clear (for detail, see van Dijk, 1980a).

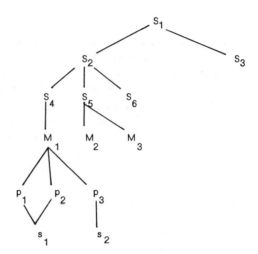

Figure 2.4. The link between
schematic superstructures and other
textual structures.

Finally, it should be added that this theory of superstructures is still
rather abstract. That is, it is not a theory of how language users go about
producing or understanding such schemata. A cognitive theory of superstructures, as we have seen for macrostructures, must have a more process
oriented nature. Instead of fixed rules and categories, it should also feature
flexible strategies (van Dijk & Kintsch, 1983). Such strategies may be used
by a reader to detect and understand the specific textual categories involved. Specific signals may indicate when a piece of text may be interpreted as a Setting or a Complication in a story for instance, even when
only a fragment of such a piece is given. Since language users have conventionalized knowledge of textual schemata, they are able to use them top
down in the strategic construction of the actual schema of a given text. The
same holds for the establishment of the links between superstructure and
semantic macrostructure. These and other cognitive processes involved will
be discussed in Chapters 3, and 4.

News Schema Categories

Not all discourse types must have fixed conventional schemata. Classical
poetry is rather strictly categorized at a prosodic level, but modern poetry
need not have such schemata. Similarly, there are constraints of a semantic
and pragmatic nature on advertisements in the press, but they do not seem
to have a fixed, conventional form. So, if we now turn to news discourse, we
cannot be sure a priori whether or not news in the press exhibits a fixed,
conventional schema. Let us, therefore, examine whether we can establish a
set of news discourse categories and formulate rules or strategies for their
ordering (see also van Dijk, 1986).

Summary: Headline and Lead

Intuitively, a few news discourse categories seem to impose themselves. Each news item in the press has a Headline for example, and many have a Lead, whether marked off by special printing type or not. We also have an elementary rule for them: Headline precedes Lead, and together they precede the rest of the news item. Their structural function is also clear: Together they express the major topics of the text. That is, they function as an initial summary. Hence, as in natural stories, we may also introduce the category Summary, dominating Headline and Lead. The semantic constraint is obvious: Headline + Lead summarize the news text and express the semantic macrostructure. Notice that the news categories we discuss here are formal, schematic categories. Thus, the Headline category in a news schema should not simply be identified with the physical headline (which we write with lower case initial) as it is printed in large bold type. Headline merely defines a special sequence in a news text, in which variable global content (a topic) may be inserted. The formulation of this content in a sentence and the expression of this sentence in concrete words realized in specific (bold, large) type lead to the expression of the Headline category in an actual headline. Such an actual headline, for instance, may consist of several parts (decks or banks), such as a main headline, a superheadline (a kicker, snapper, or eyebrow; Garst & Bernstein, 1982), and a subheadline. Similarly, as we suggested before, Leads may be expressed in separately and boldly printed leads or may coincide with the first, thematical sentence of the text. Conversely, the typical expression markers of a news category may of course yield specific signals that may be used by the reader to infer that a specific category is being used. First position, on top, possibly across several columns, large and bold type, etc. are, for instance, the properties of headlines that signal the schema category of Headline. In other languages and cultures, such as Japanese or Arabic, these signals may be somewhat different, but the category of Headline is the same.

Episode: Main Events in Context and their Backgrounds

In the analysis of the thematic structures of a few news items, we have found suggestions for further news schema categories. Some of these are also explicitly known by journalists and readers. For instance, a news text may feature Backgrounds or an Evaluation of the news events, and we may indeed take such categories as constituents of news schemata, although they are not exclusively appropriate only for news. Usually, Backgrounds follow later in a news discourse, that is, after the section that deals with the actual or main news events. Therefore, we also need a category of Main Events. Similarly, the information given in the Main Events category may be embedded in what we earlier called Context. Such was the case when the

54 NEWS SCHEMATA

protests of Shultz against the situation in East Timor was given in the context of an Asean meeting. Information in the text about this meeting, thus, functions as Context for the main event, which consists of information about the East Timor issue. Context is often signaled by expressions such as "while," "during," or similar expressions of simultaneity. Semantically, Context information must denote the actual situation, consisting of other concrete news events, and not a general structural situation, such as the situation in the Middle East. Often, Context is main event in other or previous news items. Context in this respect is different from Backgrounds, which have a more comprehensive, structural, or historical nature. Indeed, part of Backgrounds may include the history of the actual events and their context. In the article about Shultz's East Timor protests, for instance, we find a brief historical section about the policy of Australia and the United States in the East Timor issue. Of course, in actual cases, it may sometimes be difficult to distinguish between Backgrounds and Context. Such would be the case with the category of Previous Events, which is often used to remind the reader of what has happened before (and what was probably reported earlier in the same newspaper). The Previous Events category is taken as part of the actual circumstances to which we also include Context, but it also has a historical dimension. By History, then, we understand only the section of a news text that deals with nonrecent past history of actual situations and their events. In practice, this means that a History section cannot be main event in news items that have appeared recenty. Since, semantically, History denotes events that embrace years, not days or weeks, the differences between previous events, context, and history are marked by different verbs, verb tenses, or temporal adverbs.

Consequences

Consequences is another category that routinely occurs in news discourse. The newsworthiness of social and political events is partly determined by the seriousness of their consequences. By discussing real or possible consequences, a news discourse may give causal coherence to news events. Sometimes, consequences are even more important than the main news events themselves. In that case, topics in the Consequences category may have the same hierarchical position as the Main Events topics, or they may even become the highest level topic and be expressed in the headline.

Verbal Reactions

Verbal Reactions is a specific news schema category that may be seen as a special case of consequences. Most important news events follow a standard procedure for asking the comments of important participants or prominent political leaders. The rationale for such a Verbal Reactions section is ob-

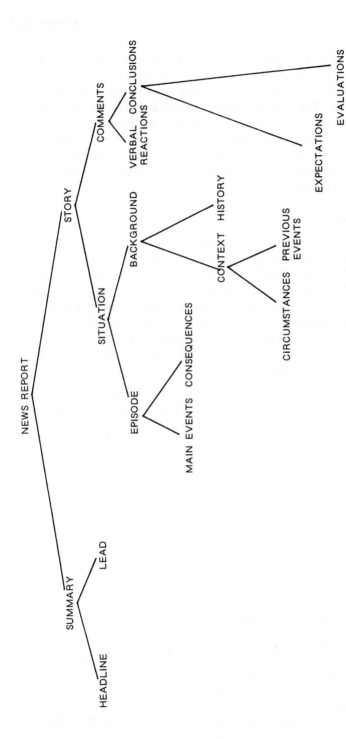

Figure 2.5. Hypothetical structure of a news schema.

vious. It allows journalists to formulate opinions that are not necessarily their own, but which nevertheless are objective because they have actually been stated. Of course, the selection of speakers and of quotations need not be objective. The verbal reactions category is signaled by names and roles of news participants and by direct or indirect quotes of verbal utterances. This category usually comes after the Main Events, Context, and Background categories, towards the end of the news discourse, although important reactions may be mentioned earlier in the item, under the additional constraint of relevance ordering.

Comment

Finally, a news discourse has a category that features the comments, opinions, and evaluations of the journalist or newspaper itself. Although many newsmakers share the ideological view that fact and opinion should not be mixed, this final Comments category frequently appears in the news, albeit sometimes in an indirect form. The Comments category consists of two major subcategories: Evaluation and Expectations. Evaluation features evaluative opinions about the actual news events; Expectations formulates possible political or other consequences of the actual events and situation. It may for instance predict future events.

These major news schema categories together define possible news discourse forms. Their linear and hierarchical ordering is determined by rules or strategies and may be represented in a tree-like form schema (Figure 2.5).

Notice that the schema proposed in Figure 2.5 is theoretical in the sense that all categories are mentioned, although it is obvious that many news texts only have some of these categories. Strictly speaking, only Headline and Main Events are obligatory in a minimally well-formed news discourse. Categories such as Backgrounds, Verbal Reactions, and Comments are optional. Some categories may be recursive, that is, they may be repeated several times. For example, several main events may be subsumed under a higher level episode node. Note also that the same text sequences may have several functions simultaneously.

Ordering of News Categories

By definition, the news schema also determines the overall ordering of topics in the text and thereby organizes the topics and the realization of the thematic structure, as discussed earlier. Under specific constraints, such as those of relevance, transformations are possible, (e.g., those supposing moving Consequences, Verbal Reactions, or Comments to earlier positions) [which usually come towards the end of a news item]. Since topics may be realized cyclically in installments, this is also the case for superstructure categories. That is, a Main Event category may be expressed in several positions throughout the text. We have already shown the production strategies used for such a discontinuous realization of global news categories. The basic strategy is top down: realize high level information of each category/topic first, working from left to right; and then express lower level information of each category/topic. However, the general relevance principle is so powerful that it may overrule this strategy. This means that in some cases, semantically minor details are nevertheless expressed in prominent (first, signaled) positions, e.g., in the headline or lead. This salient detail move in news production strategies can be directly influenced by fundamental news values such as negativity, unusualness, unexpectedness, etc. These news values and their cognitive role in the processes of news production are discussed in Chapter 3. Here, it is merely relevant to stress that other factors may influence the realization and expression of underlying topics and news schema categories. This is also why we take thematic and schematic structures as abstract, underlying structures: They may be realized in the text in different ways.

We may however conclude that news schemata indeed exist, and that both journalists and readers at least implicitly use them in the production and understanding of news. Although the categories we have identified have a hypothetical nature, extensive empirical research (van Dijk, 1984b) has shown that news discourse routinely features such categories. Similarly, several rules determine their ordering in a canonical schema, and various cognitive strategies make use of that schema to effectively express news information in a concrete news discourse.

An Example

Finally, let us try to apply the theoretical analysis to the Lebanese hostages item analyzed previously. We have indicated in this article the schematic category functions of each sentence or paragraph. Although the category assignments are self-explanatory, some comments are in order.

The Headline and Lead categories are straightforward and, according to rule, express one main topic of the text. Note though that only the first main topic is expressed in the summary and not the second topic (attack on the Libyan embassy), which is summarized in paragraph 6. The lead is only signaled by first position. Note also, that both Headline and Lead, given their summarizing function, also feature the main event, but are not part of the Main Event category because in biased news discourse this may not be the case. Paragraph 2 may be taken as a Verbal Reaction of an important participant, but such a declaration is a rather normal component of the political meeting script and, therefore, simply part of the Main Event category, summarized by the topic "The Lebanese Cabinet decided to appoint a committee to investigate the fate of the Moslem and Christian hostages and other missing persons." Paragraph 3 is a good example of a Context sequence because it denotes a dimension of the actual political situation and problems in Lebanon: The decision to appoint a committee is functionally embedded and made intelligible in that context. The actions of the victims' relatives are a good example of Previous Events. These actions were indeed topic in previous news discourses, preceded the actual events by a few days, and are causally or conditionally related to the actual event of forming a committee.

The next paragraph gives both historical information (past few years) and information about some recent events. This is an example of historical background for the actual problem of the release of the hostages. This background is structurally related to the more embracing background of the civil war in Lebanon (van Dijk, 1984b, 1987b).

Paragraph 6 opens a new topic, not signaled before in the headline or in the first lead. This indicates that a new Main Event begins, and/or that we must admit a second lead section (or a discontinuous lead) in the expression of the summary of the whole news text. Paragraphs 7, 8, and 9 are typical Main Events sections. They express normal conditions, components, results, and consequences of a bomb attack. The next paragraph gives the usual historical background about a political group. Similarly, the following paragraph features information about recent events and, therefore, should be taken to form a Previous Events category. The information about the visit of the Lebanese foreign minister is characteristic for a Context category (see the indication of time simultaneity).

Next, the article returns to information about the first main event, the meeting of the Lebanese cabinet. Part of that paragraph, however, also gives information about previous events, this time not about the causes that have led to the formation of a committee but about a situation that led to the location of the actual meeting. This shows that there may be multiple and independent causes, expressed in different Previous Events categories. After further Main Event information (members of the committee), we find further Context information about the actual hostages issue.

Finally, the article closes with a third, smaller topic, for which Summary and Main Event coincide, followed by a paragraph with some historical information about the issue ("since February") and further details about the actual situation ("who occupy the highway").

Note that this news article has no separate, final Comment and Verbal Reactions section (except perhaps for the declaration of the Premier). Yet, there is an indirect combination of these categories in the section about the Red Cross (who refuses to say something). This satisfies the general constraint that independent sources should be mentioned. The assumptions of the Red Cross about the fate of the hostages are also an indirect form of the Expectations category. Since the events as such have a rather local nature, no international reactions need be given here.

In this example we find that most categories of the news schema are indeed present and can be identified rather easily. We saw that several topics may be expressed, but that only one is signaled as the main topic by the headline and first lead. Some categories appear to be realized discontinuously, but others, such as Background and Context for each Main Event, are continuous. Several categories are properly signaled by position, layout, verb tenses, and temporal adverbs. Finally, it also appeared that two rather different stories about different main events may be mingled, even in such a way that the second story is embedded in the first story: Details about the first story are given after the second story has been presented. Although one news discourse often features several topics, they are rarely semantically full independent. Strictly speaking, a separate news item should have been dedicated to the story about the bomb attack on the Libyan embassy, as we find in other newspapers. Integration of several stories in one item is possible, however, if the events take place in the same country and the same news situation. This actual news situation might be defined as "difficulties of peace efforts in Lebanon."

THE MICROSTRUCTURES OF NEWS DISCOURSE

Some Elementary Notions of (Local) Semantics

After our analysis of the global structures of news discourse in terms of semantic macrostructures and schematic superstructures, we now turn to the analysis of the local or microstructures of news. We have repeatedly observed that the abstract, overall structures need to be realized or expressed at a more concrete local level of words and sentences. At this local level, we also distinguish between meaning and its expression in surface structures, such as word, phrases, clause, and sentence forms. After a brief discussion of some elementary notions of semantics, including proposition, presupposition, and local coherence, we address some more specific features of news discourse.

Propositions

Formally speaking, local semantics deals with propositions, objects similar to the macropropositions previously discussed. Recall that propositions are built up from a predicate and a number of arguments. These arguments may be variables, such as x, y, and z or constants such as a, b, and c, or Mary,

Peter and my old cat. Overall, a proposition may be modified by operators of different kinds. These operators make propositions out of propositions. Well-known operators are for instance "it is necessary (possible) that," "it is obligatory (permitted) that," "A knows (believes, thinks, etc.) that," or "Now (Past, Future)." Thus, we are able to represent the semantic structure of the sentence "Perhaps John believed that Mary would have to give her new book to Peter" as follows: Possible (Past (John believes that (Mary is obliged (Future (give (Mary, book, Peter)))))). The various arguments in such a proposition have different semantic roles or cases. Thus, John and Mary have agent role, Peter has beneficiary role, and book has object role. Although this analysis is extremely brief and incomplete, it gives an impression of the possible formal structures of propositions (see e.g., Keenan, 1975; Dowty, Wall, & Peters. 1981). In addition, since many meaning properties of natural language have not yet undergone adequate formal analysis, we do not even try to give a formal account of local meanings in this section. Instead, we introduce some basic concepts applicable for our analysis of news discourse.

Propositions may be of various levels of complexity. They may be atomic, such as "f(a)" or "This is a cat;" but in natural language discourse they are usually more complicated, consisting for example of a single nonatomic proposition such as "John loves Mary," several connected propositions as in "John loves Mary and Peter loves her too," or in "Because she is so smart, John loves Mary and Peter loves her too," etc. That is, propositions may be coordinated by a conjunction or disjunction; or they may be subordinated by connectives such as *when, because,* or *despite.* These relationships between propositions may also show in the clausal structure of the sentence, where we find similar distinctions between simple, compound, and complex. That is, there are systematic relationships between the semantics and the syntax of sentences. Most sentences of texts in natural language, thus, express several propositions, organized in sometimes complex structures.

Proposition Sequences

Obviously, we need more than isolated propositions to account for the meanings of discourse. Meaning may also consist of several propositions, expressed in several sentences in a sequence. Thus, more or less the same meaning may be expressed in the following examples:

1. John loves Mary because she is smart.
2. John loves Mary. She is smart.

There are several reasons for this difference in the actual expression of underlying meanings. In the first example, the speaker makes one assertion of a complex proposition and may focus on the last part of the sentence. This sentence may be expressed in a situation where the listener already knows that John loves Mary, and in that case the sentence may be used to specify John's reason for loving Mary. The second example expresses two separate assertions of single propositions. This means that the speaker assumes that the listener does not yet know about John's love for Mary or about his reasons for loving her. Hence there are pragmatic and cognitive differences between the uses of these two examples. Notice that a connective between the propositions expressed in the respective sentences of example two is not necessary: The listener will interpret the second sentence as a possible explanation of the fact denoted by the first sentence. This inference is based on the listener's world knowledge about the reasons people may have for loving each other.

Local Coherence

The second example also is characterized by local coherence (van Dijk, 1977). The sentences in the minitext are not an arbitrary list, but somehow they belong together. The information in the second sentence may be used as an explanation of the information of the first sentence. In this way a next sentence may not only give an explanation, but also an addition, a correction, a contrast, or an alternative to the first sentence. These are examples of functional coherence (van Dijk, 1981b). This means that a proposition B has a specific function relative to a previous proposition A.

Another type of local coherence is known as conditional. In this case, the coherence is not based on relations between propositions or sentences, but rather on relations between the facts denoted by them. Thus, it is not the proposition or the information that Mary is smart that causes the proposition or the information that John loves her. Rather, it is the fact that Mary is smart that causes the fact that John loves her. We speak of conditional coherence between propositions when they denote facts that are conditionally related. It is now clear why we stressed earlier that semantics is not only about meaning but also about reference. Facts are the referents of propositions. Conditional relationships may be of different degrees of strength. Causality, for instance, is fairly strong and involves empirical necessity. Often, however, the link may be weaker and involve probability or just possibility. Thus, the fact that Mary is smart may have John's love for her only as a possible consequence (although the condition may well be a necessary condition for John's loving her, which is not the same thing as saying that John will love any smart woman). In other words, conditionality has two directions, forward and backward, and each direction may have different degrees of strength: We have necessary (probable, possible) consequences of a fact, and conversely, we may have necessary (probable, possible) conditions of a fact.

Topic and Knowledge as Controls of Local Coherence

Local coherence between propositions in a sequence is controlled by the topic dominating that sequence. Thus, the sequence "John bought a ticket. He went to his seat." only makes sense given a topic like "John went to the movies." It is less meaningful under a topic like "John went to the swimming pool," in which a next sentence like "He undressed, and took a dive" would be fine but strange in a story about John's visit to the cinema. In other words, propositions cohere locally only if they both match the topic. This means that they should denote facts in an episode that is consistent with the knowledge or beliefs of the listener. This knowledge is represented in socially shared scripts about the usual sequence of events in the "going to the movies" and the "going to the swimming pool" scripts. To be correct, therefore, we should say that local coherence is established relative to the current topic and knowledge or beliefs (e.g., scripts) of the speech partners.

Cognitive Strategies and the Subjectivity of Coherence

Since beliefs may be different for speaker and listener, local coherence may also be subjective: Propositions may cohere for the speaker but not for the listener. Obviously, this is crucial in the analysis of news discourse, in which vast amounts of social and political knowledge and beliefs are presupposed by the journalist. Our analysis shows that semantics is not only micro and macro and not only intensional (meaning) and extensional (reference), but it is also cognitive and not merely linguistic. Discourse coherence requires description at all those levels. Although this chapter focuses on the abstract, structural nature of local coherence, Chapter 4 demonstrates that, empirically speaking, discourse does not *have* coherence, but is *assigned* coherence by language users. This assignment is strategic: People begin establishing coherence when they hear the first words of the next sentence and do not have to wait until the end of a sequence of propositions. Thus, a reader of example 2 given in Proposition Sequences may strategically hypothesize that "she" in the second sentence refers to the same person as "Mary" in the first sentence, even when the rest of the second sentence has not yet been read. This guess about referential identity may sometimes be wrong; "she" may refer to John's wife who is smart enough to know that John is in love with Mary. Hence, what is grammatically ambiguous, is usually made clear by text and context.

Entailment, Presupposition and Implicitness

When we consider the amount of knowledge and beliefs necessary to interpret sentences and sequences of sentences, actual discourses are much like the proverbial icebergs: Only the top of the information is visible as expressed information in the discourse itself. Most other information is personally or socially shared and cognitively represented by the language users and, therefore, may remain implicit in the text and presupposed by the speaker. Yet, this hidden information may be signaled in the text. Well known is the use of the definite article "the." When a sentence features an expression like "the boy," we may conclude that the speaker assumes that the listener knows which boy is meant, e.g., because this boy has just been introduced as "John" in a previous sentence of the discourse. This is not always necessary. In a story about events in a restaurant, a waiter may be introduced directly by the phrase "the waiter," simply because it is assumed that a restaurant may have a waiter. The same holds, more generally, for the introduction of unique concepts such as "the queen" or "the moon."

These concepts are very important in discourse analysis and, theoretically, are rather complex. In semantic terms, a presupposition B of a sentence A is a proposition that is entailed by A and by non-A (Petöfi & Franck, 1973; Kempson, 1975; Wilson, 1975). Thus, the proposition "Shultz was in Indonesia" is a presupposition of the sentence "I knew that Shultz was in Indonesia" because it is implied by that sentence and by the negated sentence "I didn't know that Shulz was in Indonesia." Apparently, predicates like "to know" preserve the presupposition of their that-clause. Similarly, other words also have specific presuppositions. If we say, "Even Shultz was in Indonesia," we usually presuppose that we didn't expect Shultz to be in Indonesia. Thus, some presuppositional phenomena are tied rather closely to word meanings or other grammatical signals. In cognitive terms, the definition of presupposition—the set of propositions assumed by the speaker to be known to the listener—is easier but more general—this may include all relevant knowledge (scripts, etc.) necessary to understand a text but also, more specifically, the few propositions necessary to interpret one sentence or to establish one coherence relation. In our earlier example about John's love for smart Mary, for instance, we must assume that, for John, smartness may be a good reason to love a woman. This information is not expressed but presupposed if we want to understand the local coherence of such a sequence.

Presuppositions involve entailment, which is also a difficult notion to define (Anderson & Belnap, 1975). Here, it is synonymous with semantic implication. A semantically implies B, if when A is true, B is also true, in all possible situations (or in terms of facts: if the fact denoted by A is the case, then the fact denoted by B is also the case). Here, the meaning of B is contained in the meaning of A: "Shultz is Secretary of State" entails "Shultz is a politician," simply because the concept 'Secretary of State' includes the concept 'politician.' Besides this form of conceptual (or necessary) implication, we may also have weaker forms, as we saw earlier for local coherence relations. For instance, the sentence "Shultz was in Indonesia for an Asean meeting" implies many things, given our knowledge of Shultz, secretaries of state and their duties, Indonesia, the Asean countries, and meetings. Thus, relative to that set of knowledge and beliefs, we may safely infer that Shultz would have talks with other politicians. Thus, a semantically implied or entailed proposition is any proposition we may infer from another proposition, given a set of presupposed knowledge. All propositions of a text that are implied or presupposed by information in the text and which are not directly or fully expressed (formulated) in the text, will be called the implicit information of the text.

We have shown that relations between propositions may vary in strength, both in conditional coherence and in implicational relationships. Thus, in some cases we may safely infer certain propositions from a text, simply because they follow from general shared knowledge. This is, however, not always the case. Sometimes, our inferences may have a weaker and more subjective basis. Here we enter the realm of notions such as suggestion, association, and other intuitive concepts used to describe what we may infer from texts. Thus, Shultz's visit to Indonesia may only suggest that he will discuss a current issue of concern such as East Timor, but this is certainly not implied by information about his visit. Yet, both in diplomatic discourse and in news discourse, frequent use is made of such weak implications (sometimes called "implicatures," Grice [1975]), in order to suggest information not explicitly expressed in the text. These inferences are of course not arbitrary. Nor are they based on general scripts or shared political knowledge but rather on more particular beliefs, opinions, and knowledge of some concrete situation. Again, this gives us an instrument to analyze ideologically relevant inferences of news discourse. In such cases, we shall use the terms "suggest" (A suggests B), or "weakly implies," to distinguish this kind of propositional link and inferences from stronger implication and entailment.

The Relevance of Local Semantics

We have focused on various dimensions of local coherence in discourse because they may reveal many interesting properties of discourse in general and news discourse in particular. Since coherence also requires assumed knowledge and beliefs, the intelligibility and the actual understanding of a text may depend on the ideology of the speaker or writer. This knowledge and beliefs usually remain implicit, precisely because they are supposed to be socially shared. An examination of local coherence links between propositions, then, enables us to make explicit the tacit assumptions and beliefs of the speaker/writer. This provides us with a subtle instrument for the ideological analysis of news discourse. Semantics is a rather divided discipline, but we have tried to integrate notions taken from linguistic (meaning) semantics, formal or logical (truth functional) semantics, and cognitive semantics. All are needed to explain the many facets of interesting discourse phenomena such as coherence and implicitness and are not yet well known in mass communication research. We have discussed only the most general outlines of the local semantics of discourse. Technical intricacies and formalities have been omitted; the reader is referred to the literature in the various fields for these details.

The Local Coherence of News Discourse

According to the principles of local discourse semantics, propositions expressed in the news should be conditionally or functionally connected, relative to the topic and relevant world knowledge of an item or paragraph. However, these general principles may have a special form for news discourse. Unlike everyday stories, news does not usually present events in chronological order. It does not start at the beginning or end with the last of a sequence of events or acts. We have discovered earlier that news, at least globally, displays a top-down, schema-driven and relevance-dependent realization of information. That is, important information comes first.

This fundamental constraint upon news discourse also has consequences for local structures. For instance, conditional relations of cause/consequence or the associated temporal relation of before/after, which are essential in storytelling, may be replaced by functional relations of specification: A higher level statement about a global event or action may in a subsequent sentence be further clarified with details. Also, we have seen that topics in news discourse may not be expressed continuously. This means that because of topic shifts subsequent propositions may not always be directly connected. In other words, according to this preliminary picture of what to expect about the local organization of news, the reader must unscramble bits and pieces throughout the text and fit them into the appropriate topics and schematic categories.

Let us examine a few arbitrary examples to illustrate and further elaborate these assumptions.

Example 1

The photographer and sculptor Brassaï, 84, renowned for his studies of nighttime Paris, of Picasso and of other members of the artist colony of prewar Montparnasse, died Sunday in Nice, his family said Wednesday. He died of a heart attack and was buried Wednesday in a private ceremony morning in Montparnasse Cemetery. (*International Herald Tribune*, July 12, 1984, p. 1).

Notice first that news discourse sentences may be rather complex. The first (lead) sentence and paragraph of this news item about the death of Brassaï expresses several propositions, appended to the main proposition

"B. died Sunday in Nice," which is in turn subordinated to the source statement placed at the end of the sentence (a syntactic feature discussed later). The main participant of the first propositions is placed in initial, so-called topic position: The sentence is about him. Sentential topics differ from the discourse topics previously discussed. They indicate a special function of semantic units, for instance the function of being in focus of attention, having been mentioned just before, and similar notions that denote the distribution of information across sentence boundaries or the cognitive status of semantic information in memory. Sentential topics are not quite independent of overall discourse topics, however. "Brassaï" is also put in topical position because he is the main argument of the discourse topic or theme "Brassaï died," which is expressed in the headline BRASSAI, 84, IS DEAD. Second, notice that the first complex sentence has a number of descriptive or qualifying propositions attached to the main, topical argument, even before the information about his death is repeated in the lead. This semantic style of (left) embedding several propositions into main propositions is rather typical for news discourse. If one complex sentence is to express the macrostructure of the text, as is the case in lead sentences, then a minimum of identification for discourse participants must be given if the participant is not generally known to the reading public.

Local coherence, thus, is not limited to subsequent sentences, but is already operating within the same complex sentence. In the first lead sentence, the descriptive clauses express propositions that function as specifications of the information that Brassaï is a photographer and sculptor. The relationship between the declarative clause and its complex embedded clause could be called a content relation. The next sentence, which forms the next paragraph, gives specifics of the cause of death and a normal consequence of death (burial) with its specifics. This example shows that information may have several simultaneous functions. Cause of death is on the one hand conditionally related to dying, but at the same time it is a specification of the kind of death. However, the cause of death is specified after the information about the death in the first paragraph. We saw earlier that postpositioned cause information may also be interpreted as an explanation relation (answering questions such as why and how). This second sentence also starts with topical "he," which is a conventional pronominal signal of coreferential identity for discourse referents. Most paragraphs of this news item in fact start with the name of the artist. In an obituary, however, several propositions are usually ordered temporally, thus indicating the life history of the artist. This type of natural ordering is common in everyday stories but less typical for news reports.

Example 2

Under the main headline PRETORIA EDGES TOWARDS REFORM and a smaller upper headline SEX ACROSS THE COLOUR BAR, the Times (July 12, 1984) published a report from its correspondent in Cape Town that begins as follows:

> The South African Government has opened the way for the repeal of two of the basic apartheid laws—the bans on marriage and sex between black and white—once the new multi-racial parliament, to be set up in September, is operating.
>
> Mr. F. W. de Klerk, the Minister of Internal Affairs, told the existing all-white House of Assembly here that the Government has agreed to widen the brief of the all-party select committee examining the laws to enable it to consider the option of repeal.

This example contains two complex sentences, each featuring several propositions. The most important information of the lead is expressed first, followed by specifications of the laws, the time/conditions of the main action of the main actor (the South African government), and a specification of the opening time of the new parliament. The next sentence opens with a new argument/actor, a minister, which is a particular member of the government. The predicate assigned to him is a declaration, which specifies the way the action of the government is announced. The content propositions detail how the government "opened the way" for reforms of the apartheid laws. Specification takes place by mentioning a member of a collectivity, and the details (decision, instructions. goals) of the overall action of opening the way for repeal. That is, the specification of actions may consist of mentioning the normal conditions of such actions. After further details about the committee and the laws, the last sentence of this article runs as follows:

> Fundamental as the two laws are to the whole philosophy of apartheid and its long-term survival, their abolition would not, in one sense, make much immediate difference.

The coherence link of this sentence with respect to the previous fragments of the article can be inferred from its function as a final comment from the correspondent. It expresses a conclusion about the possibility of abolition, and at the same time indicates a hypothetical consequence of the abolition. Hence, we do not have a real condition/consequence relation here, but merely a prediction or expectation, which functions as a conclusion of the news events. This conclusion, by the way, is not further substantiated, and arguments for it seem to have been deleted. Notice also that the first, concessive proposition of this sentence is itself related by a relation of generalization and evaluation to the preceding information.

Example 3

Finally, let us analyze systematically a brief news item taken from *USA Today* (July 12, 1984). Instead of the original text, we give a list of propositions and the local coherence relations that link them:

PERSIAN GULF: MISSILES FIRED AT BRITISH TANKER

1. Shipping officials said 2.:
2. A warplane fired two missiles at a British
   oil tanker in neutral waters Tuesday.   °Content(2,1)
3. (Warplane was) believed to be Iranian   °Specification(3,2)
4. Lloyds of London said 5.:   °Specification(4,1)
5. Both missiles hit the 133,000-ton   °Content(5,4)
   British Renown in the forward cabins   °Specification(5,2)
6. 5. caused a small fire: &Consequence(6,5)
7. (the fire) was quickly extinguished   &Consequence(7,6)
8. None of the 26 crewmen was injured   &Consequence(8,6/5)
9. And damage was minor   &Consequence(8,6–5)
10. In Washington, Richard Murphy said 12:   °Addition (10,1)
11. (Murphy is) assistant secretary of state   °Specification(11,10)
12. The supply of arms to Saudi Arabia has   °Content (12,10)
    reduced the possibility of a U.S. mili-   &Cause
    tary role to keep oil flowing through the   &Consequence
    gulf.

In this example we have represented each expressed proposition on a
separate, numbered line, indicating dependent relations with semicolons.
Functional relationships are marked with '°' and conditional ones with '&'.
Line numbers in parentheses identify the propositions related by the coherence links. We first find the usual specification relations. These may
involve an identification of a plane and ship and the role specification of an
individual (Murphy). The conditional relationships give a more narrative
flavor to part of the article. They link the detailed events of a main event
section and indicate the consequences of the attack: a fire and lack of
injuries and damage. They are coherent relative to the world knowledge we
have of missile attacks. Therefore, a negative statement must be made to
contradict plausible expectations derived from the script. The discourse-
based nature of much of the news can be gleaned from the frequent reference to sources and their declarations. These are linked by content to the
declarative statements. Interestingly, the last sentence is not directly coherent with the rest of the text. It cannot be subsumed under the same topic
and it is not summarized in the headline. The only link between the whole
sentence and the rest of the text may be called addition because it simply
adds new information. The internal links are somewhat closer: The location
(the Gulf) is the same as in the previous propositions. A similar strategy of
news discourse was shown in earlier example: Small news items about a

topic A may be attached to a larger news item about topic B if there is partial coherence between A and B, often identity of actor or location. Although we have represented proposition 12 as a single, complex, proposition, the many nominalizations, which are typical in news discourse, in fact express several underlying propositions. In this case, for example, there is a cause-conse- quence relation embedded within the proposition.

With this slightly more systematic analysis of local coherence links in news discourse, we may conclude this section by the provisional assumption that news discourse makes frequent use of various specification relations. These were already studied earlier in our analysis of the macro-micro rela- tionships of specification. In other words, the vertical links that relate mac- rotopics with local details here find their linearization (Levelt, 1982) in local specification links between subsequent sentences and their underlying propositions. The description of concrete events follows the conditional coherence links of a narrative style, and the source quotation routines of newspapers find their expression in numerous content links.

Implications in News Discourse

Much like other discourse types, news leaves many things unsaid. These must either be inferred for full comprehension or are routinely presupposed as general or more particular taken-for-granted information. Several types of the unsaid semantic implications, presuppositions, suggestions and asso- ciations have been described. These may be inferred from single lexical items, which would bring their analysis into the field of lexical stylistics, or from propositions and proposition sequences. Thus, if USA Today writes on July 14–16, 1984, under the headline FERRARO BOOSTS UNITY HOPES, thereby referring to presidential candidate Walter Mondale's choice of a woman as candidate for vice-president, that "Threats by women's organiza- tions to nominate their own vice-presidential candidate—and possibly to walk out—collapsed with Mondale's choice of New York Rep. Geraldine Ferraro as a running mate," the use of the nominalized initial clause "Threats . . .," presupposes that indeed such threats had been made. Sec- ond the very choice of the predicate "threat" has negative implications. It pragmatically implies that noncompliance with the demands involved in a threat will result in negative acts against the person being threatened. The information might have been expressed, announced or even promised, which have less negative associations.

Similarly, when the Times reporter in Washington, Nicholas Ashford, writes about the other presidential candidate, Jesse Jackson, that "The Rev Jesse Jackson, living up to his reputation for shooting his mouth off, has lashed out at Jews, white women, the press and his Democratic presidential rival Mr Walter Mondale," he presupposes that Jackson often shoots off his mouth, a presupposition hidden in the use of the predicate "reputation." Similarly, "lashes" is more negative and more violent than for instance "criticizes." Jackson, too, is represented as having "reiterated a warning that blacks may not support actively Mr Mondale's campaign if their demands are not satisfied." It has been discovered by the Glasgow University Media Group (1976, 1980) in their analysis of the language used in TV news about industrial strikes, that strikers are routinely associated with predicates that are associated with violence, intransigence, aggression, or similar negative concepts. The "threat", "warning," "reputation for shooting one's mouth off," and "lash" of Jackson and of the women's group, seem to satisfy the same type of description.

The same item in the Times (July 12, 1984), carrying the headline JACKSON LASH FALLS ON JEWS, THE PRESS, WOMEN AND MONDALE, which alone rather pervasively characterizes Jackson as racist, sexist, and antipress, uses the phrase the "black presidential candidate." In the same article, Jackson's critique of the press for using such phrases while not identifying Mondale as the "white candidate," which he calls "cultural racism," is mentioned with the usual quotes. These quotes suggest that 'these are his words,' and are used routinely when the journalist wants to distance himself from such an expression. Indeed, Jackson's reputation for shooting his mouth off is not put in quotes.

These are just a few random examples of lexical choices that have specific semantic implications or associations. That lexical selection in the article about Jackson is not incidental may be inferred from the complete list of verbal acts attributed to him:

> lash, shooting off his mouth, lashed out at, made clear that Convention would be a far from tranquil affair, reiterated a warning, pique, accused Jewish leaders, used derogatory terms, claimed, disparaging about women, assailed the press, his latest diatribe

Obviously, both at the macrolevel, as suggested by the very headline, and at the microlevel we may infer from these descriptions that Jackson is not represented very positively in this news item (see van Dijk, 1983a, 1984a, 1987a, 1987b, 1987d, for details about representation of ethnic groups in the press and the ways people use media styles of reporting in their own conversations about minorities).

Implications and presuppositions may also be found subtly in clausal relations. Let us take the same *Times* article again and consider the following complex sentence:

> Much of Mr Jackson's pique seems to derive from the fact that Mr Mondale has not considered him actively as his vice-presidential running mate, although he

has interviewed two other blacks for the job, Mr Tom Bradley, The Mayor of Los Angeles, and Mr Wilson Goode, the Mayor of Philadelphia.

The interesting connective is "although," which is normally used to denote a concessive relationship between propositions. In this case, the use is not only grammatically confusing (it does not relate the last clause with the main clause but with the preceding embedded clause) but suggests that Jackson did not have a valid reason for being angry because after all Mondale considered (interviewed, that is) "two other blacks" for the job. This means that Jackson's claims (and hence the reasons for his "pique") are considered only in terms of his being black and not in terms of his bid for the presidency during which he won many votes. From this example, we may conclude that implications and presuppositions may be rather subtle and indirect. Moreover, their analysis also requires substantial amounts of political and social background knowledge. A significant use of indirectness not only expresses ideological positions but also requires from the analyst the ability to make such ideologies explicit.

Whereas negative implications are often associated with politically or socially defined them-groups, neutral or positive implications may be associated with the acts of those considered as we-groups. Thus, both the *Times* and the *Herald Tribune*, refer to the Israeli highjacking of a ferryboat from Cyprus to Beirut as "reroute" and "divert." The concept of 'piracy,' used in the *Herald Tribune*, is credited to an accusation by the Lebanese. Similarly, people from the boat were said to be "detained" or "held in custody," which suggests normal legal procedure of authorities. On the other hand, two persons thus kidnapped are said to be accused by the Israeli authorities of "seaborne terrorist attack." And whereas the Israeli army is regularly said to carry out "raids," their Palestinian foes are credited with "terrorist attacks." These few examples show how lexical and semantic implications may involve evaluations based on the point of view and the ideology of the reporter.

NEWS DISCOURSE STYLE

Discourse Style as Context Marker

At the beginning of this chapter, we suggested that style is a property of language use that is difficult to define in precise terms. Traditionally, style and its discipline, stylistics, were closely associated with personal uniqueness and the esthetics of language use, for instance in literature (Chatman, 1971; Freeman, 1981). More thorough were linguistic approaches to style (Sebeok, 1960; Crystal & Davy, 1969; Enkvist, 1973; Hendricks, 1976; for a survey, see Sandell, 1977). Yet, an adequate contextually defined notion of style was developed only at the end of the 1960s, with the attention in sociolinguistics for variations of language use in the social context (Labov, 1972b; Scherer & Giles, 1979). Here, style was defined as an indication or marker of social properties of speakers and of the sociocultural situation of the speech event. Thus, age, gender, status, class, or ethnic background were the social factors that also determine language use variations. These variations were examined primarily at the levels of surface structure, such as phonology, morphology, syntax, and the lexicon. Depending on various social dimensions, language users may have recourse to different sound patterns, sentence patterns, or words to express a given meaning. Similarly, more-or-less independent of speaker dimensions, the context of communication has its own stylistic constraints. In court or in a public lecture, speakers tend to make use of a more formal style than in everyday conversations with friends or family members. Similarly, written or printed language may be associated with a more formal style than spoken language.

This is what style is about. Yet, before we begin with a brief account of news discourse style, some clarifications are in order. First, the crucial notion of language variation needs some comment. Variation presupposes that something is indeed variable. Yet, while we may pronounce certain phonemes in different ways and may use different syntactic patterns, such variation is not arbitrary but takes place within given boundaries. Style variation seems to involve notions such as selection or choice. The possible selection of a given variant results in a given style feature, only if there are alternatives. Next, style implicitly presupposes comparison. The specific style profile of a person, a communicative context, or a social dimension or group can be said to be specific only when compared to the language style of other situations or people. In a normative study of language use, it was frequently maintained that there was neutral style (or no style) on the one hand and deviations from this style on the other hand. While this view is now obsolete and all language use is now recognized as having style, it remains true that most descriptions of style have an implicitly comparative perspective. If we want to speak about the specifics of legal discourse, for example, its lexical jargon and its syntactic peculiarities are at least implicitly compared with the way similar meanings would be expressed in nonlegal discourse types (Danet, 1980, 1984).

Second, we should know what exactly may vary. We suggested that variations usually pertain to linguistic surface structures such as sounds, words, and sentence patterns. If variation could be stylistically relevant at the semantic level, it would result not in a stylistic feature but simply in a different meaning. Therefore, implicit in a characterization of style, in a narrow sense, is the assumption that something does *not* vary, that something in the linguistic utterance is constant and allows for comparison. Indeed, as we indicated earlier, while surface structures may vary, it is the underlying meaning or reference that must be kept constant. Style, thus, seems to be captured by the well-known phrase "saying the same thing in different ways". While this is basically correct, there is some room for a broader definition of style invariability. We may call it a typical or characteristic feature of a person's talk when he or she makes a specific selection of possible topics. If, according to stereotype, men tend to speak more often than women during informal talk about cars, computers, taxes, politics, and women, such thematic choices would be examples of what could be called "thematic style." The stylistic dimension would then reside in the notions selection from a set of possible topics in a given situation. Invariability, then, is not semantic, but pragmatic, textual, or contextual. A given range of possible topics is typical for a specific discourse type (conversation) and a specific context or situation (e.g., a party). The choice of a particular topic in that situation then may be a marker of the social dimension of male interests. Similarly, when performing a specific speech act, such as a request, the meaning of the utterance may also vary, involving polite meaning implications for example. In that case, the invariability is pragmatic: The same speech act is performed in a similar situation. From these few examples, it is clear that there is also some possible variation in the very use of the notion of style. Instead of a marker of the social context, it is in such cases also a characteristic of a person or a group, a sort of a linguistic fingerprint. Therefore, in a general sense, style is the total set of characteristic, variable structural features of discourse that are an indication of the personal and social context of the speaker, given a semantic, pragmatic, or situational invariant.

Thus, while style may also be a marker of specific personal features of language use and may express ad hoc cognitive or affective states of the speaker such as happiness or rage, this discussion is concerned with its social dimensions. That is, we focus on stylistic variations as systematic markers of the speech of social and cultural groups and as signals that a discourse is seen as characteristic or normatively appropriate for speakers that are members of such groups. Although linguistic options are of course not strictly deterministic, this social dimension suggests that style is also not the result of completely free choices among alternatives. Speakers of a sociolect often do not have or do not actually make a choice, let alone a conscious choice, among various phonological possibilities. A sociolectic style, thus, is rather a sociolectic variant of a given language and not style in the sense previously defined. Similarly, a specific legal style may be appropriate in court, but again there is hardly a choice in such cases: The situation requires specific forms of language use. In this case, there is a specific discourse genre and a specific social context; the stylistic dimension is defined only in its grammatical peculiarities or differences with respect to nonlegal discourses and situations. Hence, the comparative perspective of social styles, which states that in a different situation people of different social groups would say the same thing in a different way.

Since there are apparently different notions of style, we henceforth specify them by various descriptors. Thus, personal style is the set of stylistic features of an individual person's language use (discourse) across different situations. Ad hoc or momentaneous style is characteristic of the discourse of a person in a single situation. Group style is the situation independent style of most members of a social group. Contextual style is the set of language use features that are associated with a particular social context type (such as in court, in the classroom, etc.). Functional style is the set of language characteristics of social members as speakers in a social situation while acting in a given functional role (chairperson, doctor, patient, etc.). Medium style is the set of language features associated with a specific communication medium (written, printed, spoken). Sociolectal style is the language variant of a specific sociocultural group or community. Discourse type style is the set of specific stylistic features that are associated with a specific discourse genre (conversation, everyday story, a law, or a public address). These various styles may be combined. Social contexts may require special discourse types, as is the case in court, at an auction, or when seeing the doctor. And functional styles are often closely associated with a given social context, which they in fact help define through the verbal acts of the speech participants.

General Constraints on News Style

Style of news reports in the press, like any style, is controlled by its communicative context. As a type of written discourse, it must meet the general constraints of monological, written, or printed text. Readers as communicative partners are present only indirectly and implicitly in news discourse. They are not even addressed, as may be the case in written manuals or textbooks: There is no "you" in the news, except in quotations or sometimes in feature articles or editorials. There are no reader-addressed speech acts such as specific promises, threats, or accusations: If they do occur, they are addressed to third parties. Hence, stylistically, we may expect distance towards the usually implicit reader.

News is not only written but also public discourse. Contrary to personal letters or special-purpose publications, its readers are large groups, sometimes defined by similar political or ideological allegiance, but usually undifferentiated at a more personal level. This applies to any type of mass-mediated discourse. Socially and cognitively, this means that a considerable amount of generally shared knowledge, beliefs, norms, and values must be presupposed. Without such taken-for-granted information, the news would not be intelligible. More specific is the tacit presupposition of a vast political database, which the news regularly intends to update. News style must bear the marks of these shared presuppositions.

Third, news discourse is also impersonal because it is not produced and expressed by a single individual but by institutionalized organizations, whether public or private. That is, not only is a "you" generally absent, but also a really individual "I." News stories, then, are not stories of personal experiences, and they do not routinely express private beliefs and opinions. According to the prevailing news ideology, they are intended as impersonal statements of facts. The "I" may be present only as an impartial observer, as a mediator of the facts. If news stories are signed the names are not intended as the signals of personal expression but as secondary identifications of an institutional voice (Lindegren-Lerman, 1983). Of course, there are style differences within and among newspapers and among types of newspapers, countries, and cultures. In the Netherlands, for example, until recently quality newspapers rarely had signed news stories, except for an identification of the desk they came from (city, national, foreign, arts, etc.). Background features and opinion articles could be more individual, especially when attitudes were concerned. This did not imply that they were purely personal, as were the case for columns, letters to the editor, or eyewitness type reporting. Note that the institutional voice of the newswriter is impersonal only according to the everyday routines and their underlying ideologies. That is, impersonality is a normative accomplishment, not a descriptive one. The signals displayed merely suggest impersonality and impartiality. Clearly, underlying beliefs and attitudes are not so easily suppressed, and they may appear indirectly in the text in many ways: selection of topics; elaboration of topics; relevance hierarchies; use of schematic categories; and, finally, in style, such as the words chosen to describe the facts. In our brief analysis of the *Times* item about U.S. presidential candidate Jesse Jackson, examples were found of such an evaluative description of news actors, even if explicit signals such as "I think that" or "according to me" are absent.

Fourth, news style is controlled by the possible topics of news discourse. These topics may belong to major categories like national politics, international politics, military affairs, social life, violence and disasters, sports, arts, science, and human interest. Topics, by definition, control local meanings and hence possible word meanings and, therefore, lexical choice. The boundaries of topics and of possible lexical variance are set in advance, even when there is personal and newspaper variation in the description of the same things. In general, though, the style of a report about a pop concert is less formal than that of a report about an international summit of political leaders.

Fifth, news style displays the usual features of formal communication styles, which has been partly explained by the impersonal and institutional nature of mass-mediated discourse in the press. This means that everyday colloquialisms, spoken language style, and specific lexical registers are inappropriate and admitted only within quotations. Indeed, as we saw earlier, quotes are a powerful strategy for the journalist to avoid the constraints on impersonality, opinions, point of view, and formality. Colloquialisms, then, appear either in inverted commas or as quoted expressions of news actors. Formal style is associated with long and complex sentences with frequent embeddings and selected lexical registers featuring technical words, jargon, and in general the languages of the elite that are the prime news actors in our newspapers. The language of politics and social relations is the major source for such lexical news registers, and, unlike other discourse types, it is full of new coinages, new words to denote new developments, or new ways to look at old affairs.

Finally, whereas the features informally described in the previous paragraphs already signal many dimensions of the news production process, we also find more direct stylistic marks of news production. Deadlines require fast writing and editing; and, to avoid too many grammatical errors, stylistic inappropriateness or semantic nonsense, the syntax and lexicalization must also be routinized. We may expect fixed patterns of sentences, strategically effective schemata that can be used frequently to describe recurrent properties of news events. Journalism textbooks teach part of this news grammar in normative terms (Metz, 1979; Baker, 1981). They tell the new journalist about effective headline and lead sentences. Then, there are space constraints, which necessitate compact writing style. To avoid repetition, sentences are packed with much information contained in relative clauses. Full propositions are simply condensed to nominalizations, which also may be used to carry the bulk of presuppositions and brief back reference to previous events of the actual news.

We have examined a few general constraints on the style of news discourse. Its printed medium, public and mass mediated nature, institutional impersonality, formality and topic selection, and production demands lead to a complex set of style features easily identified as the characteristic news style of the press. Specifics of printing and layout also contribute to this style. Finally, there are feedback constraints from assumed readability and intelligibility. Journalists routinely take into account what they assume the average reader will understand, and this assumption influences their style. Yet this feedback is seldom direct. Newsmakers write according to their intuitive beliefs about middle-class readers. Experimental results about readability are usually less heeded than sales figures. Close participants in the domains and communication styles of which they write, their feedback seldom comes from readers, except in the indirect way of economic market factors. It is not surprising, therefore, that even the simple news style of TV appears to be understood only by part of the viewers, and we may expect that this is even more the case for newspaper items. Nor is there any feedback from results in the psychology of text understanding. Rather impressive evidence suggests that journalists tend to be reluctant to accept insights from any scholarly investigation into their art. Editing and correction of style, then, is mostly based on intuitive insights, professional routine, and common sense, which of course is often sufficient for the effective accomplishment of everyday routine tasks.

News Syntax

As already demonstrated, sentence syntax in news discourse may be fairly complex. Rarely do we find sentences consisting of a simple clause. Most sentences are complex, with several embedded clauses and nominalizations and, therefore, express several propositions. Let us examine a few examples.

> Walter F. Mondale opened his general election campaign with a sharp attack on President Ronald Reagan's record in office and promised a presidency of "new realism," dedicated to tough-minded economic policies and a strong but conciliatory posture abroad. In his acceptance speech wrapping up the Democratic National Convention, Mr. Mondale muted some of the liberal tones that have marked his political career and, acknowledging mistakes that led the Democrats to defeat in 1980, sought to make the fall campaign a referendum on the Republican record and on the future. (*Herald Tribune,* July 21–22, 1984, p. 1; Washington Post Service).

These two initial sentences of the opening story of the *Herald Tribune* about the Democratic Convention in 1984 are not only complex, they coincide with the two first paragraphs of this news item. The first lead sentence is a compound, coordinated structure, in which the first has an embedded nominalization (attack), and the second an embedded relative clause (dedicated to . . .). This summary sentence expresses four different topics: that Mondale opened this campaign, that he attacked Reagan, that he promised a "new realism," and that his policy would be "tough." The second sentence, which is both a specification of content of the first and which opens new topics, is even more complex. Again, we have a conjunction of two main clauses. The first clause has relative clauses appended to its two major noun phrases, and the second main clause has an embedded temporal or implicitly concessive clause ("acknowledging . . ."). Notice also that the noun phrases themselves are fairly complex. Each head noun is modified several times: (general election) campaign, (President, Reagan's, in office) record, (tough-minded, economic) policies, (strong, but conciliatory, abroad) posture. In this way, one single sentence may express at least ten propositions. As we shall see in Chapter 4, this is a rather heavy cognitive load for immediate processing in short-term memory. Full understanding of such sentences is, therefore, rather difficult. The second sentence is similarly complex. Semantically, we find reference to the actual event, the closure of the convention with an acceptance speech, an evaluation of Mondale's political career, mention of earlier mistakes, and an announcement of the fall campaign's objectives. Schematically, this means that this single sentence alone features several fragments of superstructural news categories: Main Event, Evaluation, and History. In other words, we see that the sentential syntax of lead sentences must do several jobs: formulate the summary of the article, and thereby express the major topics; express several schematic categories; and organize this information such that it is syntactically well formed and understandable. Long prepositional and relative clauses result and are often further condensed to nominalizations.

The news item about the speech of Mondale's running mate Geraldine Ferraro in the same paper of the same day (taken from the *Los Angeles Times* service) also opens with such a complex sentence:

> Representative Geraldine A. Ferraro has proclaimed her nomination as the Democratic vice presidential candidate to be a historic step toward the defeat of President Ronald Reagan in November and toward greater opportunity for all Americans. (. . .) Ms. Ferraro, 48, the daughter of an Italian immigrant, accused the Reagan administration of undermining the traditional promise to American children that "if you work hard and play by the rules, you can earn your share of America's blessings."

Again, we find two rather complex sentences, the first consisting of a main clause with several embedded clauses and nominalizations ("nomination," "to be . . .," "defeat") and complex prepositional constructions (toward the defeat of Reagan in November). The nominalization *nomination* may function as a summary of a previous event category: It is presupposed that Ferraro was nominated. The second sentence is also typical, employing the usual descriptive relative clauses in coordinated position that give further information about a news actor, such as age and personal (here ethnic) background, before further specifying the present acts of the news actor. Similarly, the quoted content specification may be integrated into the current sentence structure. Such sentences are not restricted to reporting about political events, as we may see from the beginning of an (in)human interest story about a brutal killing that took place at the same time in California:

> The widow of [JOH], the gunman who killed 21 persons at a McDonald's restaurant, has issued a public apology in which she said that in recent days her husband had "started hearing voices and seemed to be talking to people who were not there." (*Herald Tribune*, July 21–22, 1984).

This sentence features a main clause, opening with a topical noun phrase, modified with an identification which itself maybe a summary of a recent event, and a declarative sentence, which may contain a complex quoted sentence (We only give only the initials of the gunman, whereas the newspaper gives the full name, because we do not want to repeat in a book even the name of a mass murderer, which is also the name of his family; the lack of respect for privacy in criminal reporting should not be copied in an analysis of the news as long as essential properties of the news are not missed by our editing of the original).

The kind of sentence complexity we have been examining is not limited to quality newspapers or to English. In our case study of the international reporting of the assassination of Gemayel (van Dijk, 1984b, 1987b), we found that both in First World and in Third World newspaper, average sentence length is about 25 words, and complexity approximately 2.5 (that is 2.5 embedded clauses to each main clause). The sentences in the previous example from the *Herald Tribune* about Walter Mondale and the Democratic National Convention are even longer (38 and 51 words) and have similar degrees of complexity. Hence, sentence complexity appears to be a rather general feature of newsreporting in the press. Sentences in TV news are substantially shorter (see e.g. Findahl & Höijer, 1984). To give an impression of a complex lead sentence in another language, we have taken the front page report of Italian *Corriere dell Sera* (July 20, l984) about the same convention, translating it more or less literally into English:

> After having easily obtained the "nomination" [in English in the original, TAvD] on the first ballot (with 2191 votes against 1201 for Gary Hart, 466 for Jesse Jackson and 68 divided among minor candidates) Walter Mondale has immediately raised the attack against Reagan and in his acceptation speech at the end of the proceedings of the Convention of San Francisco, indicated the setup and the themes of his electoral campaign for the White House.

The overall structure of this lead sentence resembles those in the English language newspapers: two main clauses, the first being preceded by a temporal clause with a long parenthesis, and featuring the same nominalization (attack), and the second also with a long prepositional phrase ("at the end of . . .") and a complex noun phrase. Popular newspapers often make use of similar syntax, but this is not always the case, as we may read from *USA Today*'s report about the closure of the Democratic Convention:

> Former Vice President Walter Mondale and his history-making running mate, Geraldine Ferraro, launched their 1984 presidential campaign Friday after accepting nomination Thursday with pledges to "fight for the future" (*USA Today*, Int. ed., July 21–23, 1984, p. 1).

Although this sentence has only one main clause, this clause also contains an embedded temporal clause referring to a previous event, a complex NP and a complex prepositional phrase with a declarative statement. The use of the adjective "history-making," which appears in many of the reports about the convention, shows the routine phrasing of semantic content and the use of stereotypes in the news.

As a summary of this brief syntactic analysis of news sentences, we may represent one frequent structure we have often met in the following structural formula:

$$S < NP \ (N(Srel) \ \& \ N(Srel)), \ VP \ (NP(Srel), \ PrepP(Rel)) > \& \ S < >.$$

That is, the sentence may be complex (consist of several Ss, coordinated, or subordinated), and each S may feature complex noun phrases with appended relative clauses (often more than one for each head noun) and/or a complex prepositional phrase. Relative clauses may be substituted by nominalizations, prepositional phrases, adjectivals, or other modifiers. Of course, this is merely an example of the kind of structures we may find in news discourse; variations are possible. The formula is meant only to give an impression of the kind of syntactic complexity we may find in sentences in the news. We earlier explained this complexity by the overall constraint of formal discourse and communication, in general, and those of news production processes, in particular. Relatively brief reports must pack large amounts of information into sentences to keep the text as short as possible, to establish links between events, to integrate previous events and background, and to identify news actors. Lead sentences especially are intended as summaries of the whole article. Towards the end of news items, we occasionally find shorter sentences among the longer, complex ones.

The Role of Word Order and Syntactic Functions

Although there is more to sentence syntax than its overall complexity, this analysis will not address the details of word order, special constructions (such as the use of passives, cleft sentences, and relative clauses), and other important properties of sentential organization. Regarding word order, noun phrases often function as sentential topics that are also discourse topic arguments. That is, a news actor like Mondale, who is part of the top macroproposition of the previously analyzed reports will also often appear as sentence topic throughout the text. This does not merely contribute to the usual on-line, local coherence, and is not only a result of macrostructural control, but also signals the relevance structure of the text: Mondale is thus marked as the main actor of the news events and the news story. Despite Ms. Ferraro leading political role during the convention and in the campaign, she is mostly mentioned in second position in sentence structure. In this way, syntactic structures of the news may signal an interpretation of Ms. Ferraro's formal role as candidate for the vice presidency, after Mr. Mondale as candidate of the presidency. Yet, it may also signal routine sexist attitudes in which the place of women, especially in politics, is after men. There is substantial evidence for this annihilation of women in the news (Tuchman, Kaplan, Daniels, & Benét, 1980; Downing, 1980). Syntactic analysis is merely an indirect, but subtle and therefore often reliable, source of evidence for such an analysis. Similar results were obtained by Fowler, et al. (1979) in their syntactic analysis of press reports about the West Indian carneval in London. As was suggested in Chapter 1, these authors found that the use of active and passive sentences, and the agent or subject position of news actors in sentences, revealed much about the newspaper's implicit stance towards these news actors. If authorities, such as the police, are agents of negative acts, they tend to occur less in agent position. They may then be made less conspicuous in a prepositional phrase of a passive sentence ("by the police") or remain implicit in an agentless sentence structure ("Many demonstrators were injured"). In our study of minorities and squatters in the press (van Dijk, 1987b), we show that such syntactic signals are indeed relevant in news discourse.

Lexical Style of the News

The choice of words, even more than syntactic patterns, is usually associated with the style of discourse. Lexical stylistics is not only central to a stylistic inquiry, but it also forms the link with semantic content analysis. The choice of specific words may signal the degree of formality, the relationship between the speech partners, the group-based or institutional embedding of discourse, and especially the attitudes and hence ideologies of the speaker. Whether the newspaper selects *terrorist* or *freedom fighter* to denote the same person is not so much a question of semantics as an indirect expression of implied but associated values incorporated in shared-word meanings. Besides this standard example of ideologically-based lexical variation in the news media, such opinion-controlled lexical choices abound, although many are more subtle.

Other lexical choices do not originate in sociopolitical ideology but are part of professional registers used to denote specific event characteristics, such as the use of stereotypical *historical* in the examples of the previous section. Finally, lexical style may be controlled by rhetorical strategies, e.g., those of understatement. Mitigations, especially used when describing negative acts of important news actors, are a routine procedure, used also to avoid charges of libel. The stereotypical term "controversial," for instance, is used routinely to denote characteristics of a person that are considered negative by the journalist or other important reference groups. Point of view is crucial in this case. What for one journalist is "tough" or "strong" action or policy may be "aggressive" or "offensive" for others. In our earlier example of the *Time*'s reporting of Jesse Jackson's criticism of Mondale and others, a series of lexical items consistent with an aggressive image was demonstrated.

THE RHETORIC OF NEWS DISCOURSE

Rhetoric and the Effectiveness of Discourse

Much like style, the rhetoric of discourse has to do with how we say things. But, whereas news style is heavily constrained by various contextual factors deriving from the public, mass-mediated, and formal nature of news, the use of rhetorical structures in the news depends on the goals and intended effects of communication. Stylistic choices indicate the kind of discourse for a particular situation or the presupposed ideological backgrounds. The recourse to rhetoric is not dictated by context in this way. It may be freely engaged in, if only to make the message more effective. Discourses used for esthetic functions may thus organize surface structures in such a way that rhyme, special intonation and rhythmical structures, alliterations, and other sound patterns result. The same holds for special uses of syntactic patterns, such as parallelisms, or the use of semantic operations such as comparisons, metaphor, irony or understatements. Yet, what is esthetically functional may also be used for persuasive ends. At the cognitive-semantic level, we want people to understand what we say about some event or situation. That is, we want to get a message across. We have seen before that this means that the reader or listener is expected to build a textual representation and a situation model as intended by the speaker/writer. Pragmatically, we also intend that something similar happens for the speech act(s) we perform by the expression of such underlying meanings: We want our speech partner to understand that what we say was intended as an assertion, a request, or a threat.

So far so good. But even if the listener or reader has understood perfectly well what we meant—semantically or pragmatically—this is half of the intent of communication. We also want him or her to accept what we say, that is, believe our assertion, perform the actions requested, and execute our commands. In traditional pragmatic jargon, our speech acts should not only have illocutionary functions but also perlocutionary effects. In terms of rhetoric or of the study of speech communication, this means that we are involved in a process of persuasion.

The Effectiveness of News: Suggesting Factuality

Persuasion has a very specific aim and function for news discourse. Unlike advertising in the press, news does not primarily aim at promoting goods or services coming from a special firm or institution. Of course, economically, news is also a market commodity that must be promoted and sold. Ideologically news implicitly promotes the dominant beliefs and opinions of elite groups in society. Pragmatically, however, it is not primarily the type of global speech act that pertains to the actions of the speaker (like promises or threats) or to those of the reader (as in accusations). Rather, the bulk of our everyday news is an instance of the speech act of assertion. For such speech acts to be appropriate the writer must express propositions that are not yet known to the listener/reader and which the writer wants the listener/reader to know. The perlocutionary or persuasive dimension that sustains such intentions in practice, then, is the formulation of meanings in such a way that they are not merely understood but also accepted as the truth or at least as a possible truth. Rhetorical structures accompanying assertive speech acts like those performed by the news in the press should be able to enhance the beliefs of the readers assigned to the asserted propositions of the text. Persuasion in this case, therefore, need not involve a change of opinions or attitudes. Assertive persuasion is the zero level of persuasive processes: Without at least believing what the other says, it can hardly be expected that we change our opinions based on such beliefs. We are not easily persuaded to march in a protest demonstration against a new nuclear plant unless we believe that nuclear waste products are dangerous for people and the environment in the first place.

The acceptance of knowledge and belief propositions is a complex process. It presupposes some minimal coherence, if not consistency, with the other knowledge and beliefs we already have. High level, topical, propositions in our schemata, models, and attitudes especially should not be inconsistent with the newly accepted propositions. If so, we should not only accept a new proposition but also change our basic beliefs. We know and experimental research confirms that this is not easy. Without good reasons and evidence, we do not discard fundamental beliefs constructed from years of understanding, experiences, and action. No wonder that the persuasive dimension of talk and text often involves argumentation. Explicit or implicit arguments are meant to influence the cognitive work we engage in when considering for acceptance a proposition, asserted by the speaker. Let us simply call this the content aspect of rhetoric. Argumentative structures, their organization, and cognitive relevance, however, require separate treatment.

Rhetoric also has a form aspect, which regulates the ways or manners of our formulation of the propositions or arguments. More or less independent of the content or substance of the persuasion process, these formal aspects may help (1) represent the textual information in memory; (2) organize this information better; (3) enhance the chances for its retrieval and use; and finally, (4) influence intended belief and opinion changes.

Both aspects are relevant for news discourse: It should express the propositions that may be added coherently to the models the readers already have of the world, and at the same time, it should make such propositions memorable. News discourse does not work routinely along the second dimension: We do not expect fancy sound patterns, complex syntactic patterning, or artificial metaphorizing in regular news items. They are reserved, at most, for special background pieces and for editorials. Everyday reporting has no time for sophisticated, original, creative writing. Rather, emphasizing important content is accomplished fully by the various relevance structures of the news, such as hierarchical organization, ordering, schematic structures, and corresponding layout (headlines, leads, size, frequency, etc.). In this sense, a huge headline is similar to the specific phonetic organization involved in rhetorical exclamations and exaggerations. In other words, the form aspect of news rhetoric is not primarily based on grammatical levels of phonology, morphology, or syntax, as may be the case in esthetically functional discourses (see, however, Roeh, 1982; Roeh & Feldman, 1984). It is fully geared to the goal of putting specific content in evidence by the various relevance or prominence enhancing features of the news.

Persuasive Content Features

The content itself needs further organization, in order to be noticed, understood, represented, memorized, and finally believed and integrated. If propositions are to be accepted as true or plausible, there must be special means to enhance their appearance of truth and plausibility. News discourse has a number of standard strategies to promote the persuasive process for assertions (see also Tuchman, 1972):

(A) Emphasize the factual nature of events, e.g., by
   1. Direct descriptions of ongoing events.
   2. Using evidence from close eyewitnesses.
   3. Using evidence from other reliable sources (authorities, respectable people, professionals).
   4. Signals that indicate precision and exactness such as numbers for persons, time, events, etc.

5. Using direct quotes from sources, especially when opinions are involved.

(B) Build a strong relational structure for facts, e.g., by:

1. Mentioning previous events as conditions or causes and describing or predicting next events as possible or real consequences.
2. Inserting facts into well-known situation models that make them relatively familiar even when they are new,
3. Using well-known scripts and concepts that belong to that script.
4. Trying to further organize facts in well-known specific structures, e.g. narratives.

(C) Provide information that also has an attitudinal and emotional dimensions:

1. Facts are better represented and memorized if they involve or arouse strong emotions (if too strong emotions are involved, however, there may be disregard, suppression and hence disbelief of the facts).
2. The truthfulness of events is enhanced when opinions of different backgrounds or ideologies are quoted about such events, but in general those who are ideologically close will be given primary attention as possible sources of opinions.

Part of these rhetorical conditions are well known in cognitive and social psychology (van Dijk & Kintsch, 1983; Bower, 1980; Roloff & Miller, 1980; Schulz, 1976). They derive partly from the inherent news value system that underlies news production. Attention for the negative, the sensational, sex, and violence, even in quality papers (though more subtly), satisfies the rhetoric of emotions, which we also know from the reporting of accidents, catastrophes, disasters, and crime. These kinds of events report hard facts, which have witnesses and which require precise numbers (victims); they may be cast in narrative structures; they may reflect opinions (both of officials and participants); they allow for many direct quotations; they emphasize causes and consequences (how and why could that happen?). In brief, they satisfy the basic cognitive and emotional conditions of effective information processing. These events comprise the bulk of what most people in our Western countries consume as news. In England, the country with the highest newspaper consumption (Merrill, 1983), the tabloids that report this news practically exclusively, sell perhaps 10 times more than the so-called quality press (Spiegl, 1983). Their rhetoric seems to be very effective for many people.

The conditions relating to building a strong relational structure for facts (B) are familiar from such news value conditions as familiarity and ideological coherence. The exceptional and the unexpected in the news are to make events salient and hence more memorable, but this deviance should still remain within the boundaries of the understandable. An accident like a fire in our own street, supermarket, neighborhood, or town is not only a deviant, negative, or unexpected serious event that may be more interesting for us than a famine in the Sahel, it also is more understandable because we can fit it into well-known models. We can imagine, sometimes very concretely, the event and the consequences. These events at the same time update our everyday models. A distant famine does not satisfy these conditions, even when ethically the event may be more serious. In other words, news is more persuasive if it represents events that fit our models without being completely predictable.

Yet, these various rhetorical conditions that make specific news items or information more acceptable affect the very attention, focus, and selection of news events as newsworthy. The real rhetoric of the news seems to reside in conditions relating to Emphasizing the factual nature of events (A). Given a specific event, the use of these rhetorical features makes the information about that event more plausible and more acceptable.

Direct Description and Eyewitness Reports

One of the basic conventional conditions of truth is direct observation: "I have seen it with my own eyes" is the ultimate warrant of truthfulness. Within the limits of their financial budget, newspapers therefore try to get first-hand evidence from their correspondents or reporters and may even send a special envoy to places where dozens of other reporters already are present. The immediacy of the description and the closeness of the reporter to the events is a rhetorical guarantee for the truthfulness of the description and, hence, the plausibility of the news.

Similarly, eyewitness reports given in interviews may be used as necessary substitutes of the reporter's own observations. Reports of what people have seen with their own eyes are taken to be closer to the truth than hearsay, although of course not all eyewitnesses are qualified. That eyewitnesses may be wrong in their testimony, however, is only of marginal importance (Loftus, 1979). It is not so much the real truth as the illusion of truth that is at stake in the rhetoric of news. Again, it is the popular press that uses direct reporting and eyewitness interviewing extensively. And if ordinary people are participants and are interviewed, it is as if the ordinary reader himself or herself had seen the events. Descriptions of immediate events are also highly model dependent, concrete, and therefore imaginable, unlike more distanced, abstract, and schema-based representations of events. We have already seen that events closer to such models are more credible and memorable.

Sources and Quotations

Nevertheless, most of the news is about events that do not allow for direct observation or for description by eyewitnesses. Reporters get it from other media, from news agencies, or from reports of others. Their factuality must be assessed in different ways, and the rhetorical strategy used is a subtle use and quotation of sources. Primary sources are immediate participants, both for the description of facts (as eyewitnesses) and for the formulation of opinions. Yet, not all sources are equally credible (Hovland, Janis & Kelley, 1953; Cronkhite & Liska, 1980). There is a hierarchy of sources and associated degrees of their reliability. Elite sources are not only considered more newsworthy (as news actors) but also as more reliable as observers and opinion formulators. In a report about a strike, the director of a firm and the union leader will be quoted as sources much more often than the individual striker (Glasgow University Media Group, 1976, 1980). Similarly, in most social conflicts, authorities such as high ranking politicians, experts, or police officers are asked their description of and evaluation of the facts (Maddux & Rogers, 1980). A cabinet minister in that case ranks higher as a source than a parliament member. The social hierarchy seems to be reproduced in the rhetorical hierarchy of credibility and reliability.

Similarly, quotations or quasi-quotations are closer to the truth and more reliable than event descriptions by the reporter. Quotations not only make the news report livelier but are direct indications of what was actually said and hence true-as-verbal-act. Introducing participants as speakers conveys both the human and the dramatic dimension of news events. News actors are represented as real actors in that case, playing or replaying their own role. Finally, quotations are the reporter's protection against slander or libel, and the rhetorical illusion of truthfulness here finds its social and legal correlate in the veracity of representation (Tuchman, 1972). That quotations are seldom fully correct contextually is irrelevant. They should merely suggest that they are true, hence their rhetorical function and effect.

Numbers

Finally, the rhetoric of news discourse forcefully suggests truthfulness by the implied exactness of precise numbers. This is one of the reasons why news discourse abounds with numerical indications of many kinds: numbers of participants, their age, date and time of events, location descriptions, numerical descriptions of instruments and props (weight, size), and so on. Imagine a report about a demonstration without an estimate of the number of demonstrators, often a fact in dispute between the authorities (the police) and the organizers of the demonstration. Imagine a report about an accident or a disaster without an indication of the number of victims. Few rhetorical ploys more convincingly suggest truthfulness than these number games. In van Dijk (1981b) we illustrate this in our case studies of domestic and international news. Again, it is not so much the precision of the numbers that is relevant but rather the fact that numbers are given at all. They may be highly variable among news media, even when using the same sources, and if incorrect they are seldom corrected in follow-up news items. They are predominantly meant as signals of precision and hence of truthfulness.

Example 1:
16 Years Innocent in Jail

Let us try to briefly illustrate our points by analyzing a concrete example, indicating the rhetorical dimension of a common news item. In van Dijk (1987b), we provide more systematic and quantitative data about the uses of stylistic and rhetorical features of the news. Such concrete case studies can better compare newspapers and news items about the same events, so that variations in description and formulation become evident. Our present example is taken from a front-page article in the *Times* of July 21, 1984, headlined MAN SET FREE AFTER 16 YEARS. The most obvious rhetorical feature of this headline is of course the number of years this man spent in jail for a crime he didn't commit (or for which at least unreliable evidence was given during the trial). This numerical rhetoric continues in the text itself:

1. Eleven cases like this before the court of appeal.
2. The first case in which the judges upheld the appeal.
3. Two others earlier this week were rejected.
4. Sentenced in 1969.
5. Murder of a 84-year old woman.
6. Man will seek damages "although no amount of money can ever bring back what I have lost."
7. The record of compensation is 77,000 pounds.
8. Man can expect up to 150,000 pounds.
9. This was the man's second appeal.
10. His first was in 1970.
11. Man is aged 37.
12. His arrest was in 1968.
13. Eight more cases are waiting for appeal.
14. Scientist was suspended in 1977.

Man set free after 16 years

By John Witherow

A man who was sentenced to life imprisonment for murder on the evidence of the discredited Home Office forensic scientist, Dr Alan Clift, was freed yesterday after serving nearly 16 years in jail.

The case, one of 11 referred to the Court of Appeal by the Home Secretary because of Dr Clift's involvement, was the first in which the judges upheld the appeal. Two others heard earlier this week were rejected.

Mr Geoffrey Mycock, a landscape gardner, who was sentenced in 1969 for the rape and murder of a woman, aged 84, walked free from the court saying he intended to seek damaged, "although no amount of money can ever bring back what I have lost".

The record for compensation for false imprisonment is £77,000 but legal sources said yesterday that Mr Mycock could expect of receive up to £150,000.

It was the second appeal against conviction by Mr Mycock who has always protested his innocence. At his first in 1970 it was established that a policeman, now retired, had lied at his trial.

But the appeal judge decided that the scientific evidence from

Dr Clift was so strong that the conviction should be upheld.

Yesterday Lord Lane, the Lord Chief Justice, sitting with Mr Justice Glidewell and Sir Roger Ormrod, said: "It follows as night follows day that this court is driven to the conclusion that there is now reasoned unease as to whether this conviction is safe and satisfactory."

The Crown offered no opposition to the appeal with counsel, Mr Desmond Fennell, QC, saying that because of the dependence on Dr Clift's evidence it would be unsafe to do so.

Mr Mycock, aged 37, from

Mr Geoffrey Mycock: Will seek damages.

Macclesfield, Cheshire, was found to have scratches on his face after his arrest in 1968 for the killing of Miss Adeline Bracegirdle.

Scientific evidence about fibres found on Mr Mycock's clothing and fibres taken from the scene of the murder assured considerable importance in the case, but it had been impossible to verify independently his work and the conclusions he had reached.

Continued on back page, col 6

Court sets prisoner free after 16 years

Continued from page 1

Mr Mycock, who granted his freedom with a wave from the dock, said afterwards: "I am bitter about Dr Clift's evidence and that of the police. I am in no way responsible for the crimes committed against this old lady. The murderer could still be at large."

Eight more cases are pending before the Court of Appeal concerning evidence given by Dr Clift. He was suspended by the Home Office in 1977 and compulsorily retired in 1981 after the Scottish Court of Appeal concluded that he had been "discredited not only as a scientist but as a witness".

Earlier this year the Ombudsman criticized the Home Office for delays in investigating Dr Clift's work after his suspension. The review considered 1,500 cases in which Dr Clift had examined material and 129 instances when people were convicted after denying the offences.

Sixteen cases were referred by the Home Secretary to the Court of Appeal. Two did not want their cases reopened and three have not been traced.

A further two cases are to be heard this month and six in the autumn. The people involved have been released, including a man who was given a life sentence for murder in 1970. The convictions included rape, burglary, grievous bodily harm and manslaughter.

THE TIMES, July 21, 1984

15. Scientist was compulsorily retired in 1981.
16. Ombudsman has reviewed 1,500 cases.
17. Of which 129 cases in which people denied the offences.
18. Sixteen cases were referred to the Court of Appeal.
19. Two did not want their case reopened.
20. Three could not be traced.
21. Two cases will be heard this month.
22. Six (will be heard) this autumn.
23. The cases included a man who was given a life sentence in 1970.

In this brief article, thus, we find 23 indications of a quantities, amounts, dates, and similar numerical data. All these figures are not really interesting or even relevant, but their use suggests preciseness in reporting and seemingly direct access of the reporter to the data.

What other rhetorical devices may be found in this article? First, we find many quotes of those involved in the appeal and the release of the innocent man. The man's own words of course provide direct access to the opinions of the victim, as well as an emotional appeal, which is rhetorically effective in its own right. Not only can the innocent man not be paid back, but the decision implies that the real murderer may still be at large. The reference to several legal sources gives further credibility to the amount of damages the man may receive (it is not just a vain hope of the victim). The justification for the present decision is embedded in a direct quotation from Lord Lane, the Chief Lord Justice. Descriptive details about "scratches" and "fibres" earlier found on the accused make the story even more concrete (and not just a legal matter), and such details are rhetorically more effective than for instance a general statement about inadequate evidence. Besides the Court of Appeal judges, the authority of the Ombudsman is invoked in the preparation of these cases.

This news article is a regular everyday piece of crime reporting mixed with human interest. For an innocent man to be in jail for 16 years, however, is both shocking and incredible. This means that the story can or even should be presented with a number of rhetorical devices, the extraordinary amount of numbers being especially striking. In addition, we find direct quotations of the victim involving emotional reactions and appeals as well as a colorful (while metaphorical) statement of the highest official involved, which also represents an opinion. Finally, concrete descriptive details are given about the old case. The story is embedded in a well-known scriptal framework of legal process. The most interesting deviance—being convicted innocently and having served years of a jail sentence—is both understandable and remarkable from a rhetorical point of view. A person who is in jail innocently for a month or so would not arouse the interest of the press in this way. Nor would the structural problem of innocent convictions, wrong evidence, or lies by authorities, for that matter. In other words, an innocent man spending sixteen years in jail is itself a rhetorical exaggeration, a hyperbole of deviancies in legal process. The news exploits these rhetorical potentialities of the case and puts this dimension in evidence by the headlines and the nearly mimetic exaggeration of other numbers.

Example 2:
660 Polish Political Prisoners Released

Another example, taken from the *Daily Telegraph* of July 23, 1984, deals with the amnesty granted to political prisoners in Poland on the occasion of the 40th anniversary of the Polish liberation (represented in this newspaper as "40 years of Communist rule," which is not quite the same, but certainly very suggestive). Let us first examine the use of numbers. Most important, 660 political prisoners are said to have been released as well as 35,000 other (nonpolitical) prisoners. The political prisoners are of course most important, for the conservative Western press. The figure of 660 therefore receives much more prominence than the one of 35,000, which is mentioned at the end of the article. This differential attention for similar hard facts (numbers of prisoners released) can only be understood by the general tendency in most Western news media to represent the situation in Eastern Europe and especially in Poland from the point of view of Western interests. This includes any interest that is anti-communist. Any opponent of communist regimes, such as the Catholic Church or Lech Walesa, the leader of Solidarity, therefore receives special attention as prime news actors, if not as heroes for the good cause.

Of course, there may be good reasons for such a portrayal. After all, resistance against an oppressive state apparatus is undoubtedly heroic. What is relevant, however, is the differential treatment the same kind of opponents in our own Western countries receive by the same press, such as union leaders, strikers, peace activists, or demonstrators (Halloran, et al., 1970). It is unlikely that they would be the only ones quoted and referred to as reliable and important spokespersons or that only their opinion would be quoted in detail rather than those of the authorities. In the CAUTION IN WARSAW article, the converse is true. The reactions mentioned in the lead involve (1) Catholic Church leaders; (2) Western officials; and (3) Lech Walesa. They are also the only news actors whose opinions are directly mentioned or quoted, including diplomats (implied, Western diplomats), Poles in the street, a senior clergyman, and of course Lech Walesa. The objective fact of the amnesty, thus, is embedded in an ideological framework that characterizes the conservative Western press. Rhetorically, this

SANCTIONS ON POLAND MAY END

Amnesty welcomed by EEC and U.S.

THE Common Market and America may begin lifting their economic sanctions against Poland following the weekend announcement by the Polish Government of an amnesty for 660 political prisoners, including prominent members of the Solidarity movement.

In Brussels today, Sir Geoffrey Howe and other E E C Ministers will discuss easing restrictions on trade and financial aid. America is soon expected to lift its ban on Polish airline services.

Although the amnesty has been welcomed in the West, the Church and Solidarity in Poland have reacted cautiously, says OUR STAFF CORRESPONDENT in Warsaw. It is noted that the freed prisoners can be re-arrested for repeat offences and may be subject to other constraints.

Editorial Comment—P14

Caution in Warsaw

By ROBIN GEDYE in Warsaw

THE first of Poland's 660 political prisoners to released under a general amnesty leave today. But the amnesty, announced on Saturday, being greeted with guarded optimism by Cath church leaders, Western officials and Lech Walesa, leader of the banned Solidarity trade union.

They want to be certain that those released over the next 30 days are not forced to agree to conditions that could curtail their individual freedom or place them under political constraints.

The amnesty can be revoked for both political and criminal detainees who repeat offences within two years.

It coincides with official celebrations marking 40 years of Communist rule in Poland.

In 1944 the liberating Soviet Army installed a Communist government in the city of Lublin while still fighting Poland's Nazi invaders.

Low-level representation

An indication of what Poland's East Bloc neighbours thought of yesterday's occasion and the nation's recent record was obtained in the very low-grade official representation at ceremonies.

While the then Soviet leader, Mr Brezhnev, attended Poland's 30th anniversary celebrations, the Kremlin had only thought fit to send Mr Nikolai Tikhonov, the Prime Minister, to yesterday's events.

Hungary, Bulgaria, Czechoslovakia, Rumania and East Germany were all represented by lower level government and party officials.

Diplomats believed this represented reservations about the amnesty and, more generally, over the leadership of a Communist party whose failings had led to the emergence of Solidarity.

The feeling among Poles in the streets was characteristically of a "wait and see" ￭nature, brought about by a scepticism born out of their experiences over the last 2½ years.

A senior clergyman pointed out that while Cardinal Glemp, Poland's primate "received the amnesty great satisfaction," the still regarded the retu free trade unions as a p dition of a reconci between the state and p

Mr Walesa said the an "could be a great step to social agreement," but that it would not be ful ceptable if those freed forced to curb their pe activity.

He said the amnesty also have to include Mr B Lis, Solidarity's underg leader until his arrest on 8, who has been charged treason — an offence covered by the amnesty.

Mr Walesa said he wou hesitate to contact the union leaders and four arity advisers, known a

Continued on Back P, ￭

SANCTIONS

Continued from Page

solidarity eleven, on the lease.

"There are important m to be discussed and the after all, my friends," he ᵴ

The amnesty will also to some 35,000 people de or under investigation charges not officially desi as political.

Such offences can range traffic violations to the stones during demonstrat

Observers feel that tho leased will hesitate to themselves into clearly i fiable opposition groups, ferring to keep a low profi the time being.

At the same time, the G ment is expected to show leniency towards any of released who may choo speak out about their tin jail, at least until the Wes withdrawn its sanctions Poland.

The sanctions include ᵴ on fresh Government-fina loans and on high-level ￭ cal contacts as well as a su sion by the United State Poland's most-favoured-n trading status and a block ᵴ access to the Internat Monetary Fund.

embedding is important. The script associated with the notion of amnesty has positive connotations. Since the agent of the amnesty is the Polish government, and the beneficiaries most notably the political prisoners, there may be attitudinal incoherence: the despised they-group should not be associated with positive acts. The amnesty news itself, therefore, is played down and embedded in opinions that are at most cautious, involving nagative expectations about what might still happen. Similarly, the fact that other Eastern European governments seemed to protest against the amnesty by their low-level representation during the celebration of Polish liberation day receives rather extensive attention. Thus, the coherence of the picture is reestablished because it suggests (by drawing an inference from the acts of the communist countries) that communism and amnesty are incompatible. No authorities or sources are quoted that declare happiness with the decision of the Polish government to ease social conflict by releasing political prisoners. Quotation fragments that might be interpreted positively for the Polish government are always followed by "but" and a statement of negative conclusions and expectations.

This brief analysis shows a different rhetorical setup from the one described above for the-innocent-man-in-jail item. Numbers are cited (660 and 35,000), but they are used in quite a different manner: The higher number, which usually gets more prominence, is now played down. Other numbers are somewhat less prominent. Exceptions include the "40 years of Communist rule," followed by a historical flashback to the 30-year celebration when Brezhnev was present (implying a rhetorical contrast with the low-level representation from the USSR now), a reference to the last 2½ years (since the actions of Solidarity), and some small other details. More important from a rhetorical point of view is the mention and quotation of reliable observers or participants, that is, of those who are considered ideologically close. And finally, the attitudinal incompatibility between communism and leniency must be rhetorically emphasized by focusing on those aspects of a situation that suggest the opposite. Hence, the extensive attention for reservation, caution, warnings, negative expectations, special emphasis on remaining inequities, remaining sanctions from the West, and the negative reactions from other communist countries. In other words, this article should not be read primarily with a dominant amnesty script but with an anticommunism attitude schema (see Carbonell, 1979, for details about the structures and contents of such a schema).

Concluding Remark

Methodologically, we may conclude that news rhetoric is not limited to the usual figures of speech. Rather, strategic devices that enhance truthfulness, plausibility, correctness, precision, or credibility are used. We have illustrated these in somewhat more detail, though still rather informally, in two examples. These devices include the remarkable use of numbers; a selective use of sources; specific modifications in relevance relations (incompatible propositions are played down or fully ignored); ideologically coherent perspectives in the description of events; the uses of specific scripts or attitude schemata; the selective uses of reliable, official, well-known, and especially credible persons and institutions; the description of close, concrete details; the quotation of eyewitnesses or direct participants; and the reference or appeal to emotions. This means that a rhetorical analysis cannot be fully independent of a semantic and ideological analysis of news discourse. Indeed, as we suggested before, rhetorical operations may involve all levels of discourse analysis.

3

NEWS
PRODUCTION

NEWSMAKING AS DISCOURSE PROCESSING
AND SOCIAL COGNITION

News as Process

News discourse should not only be characterized in terms of its various structures, as we have done in the previous chapter. It must also be considered as part of complex communication processes. Chapters 3 and 4 focus on the process dimension of news. Processes and structures are integrated and mutually dependent properties of news discourse. Processes of production are a function of the structures of source texts but they also depend on the structural plans that underlie the news text to be written by the journalist. Similarly, processes of reading, understanding, and belief formation and use are conditioned by the structures assigned to news texts by the reader. One of the major aims of these two chapters, therefore, is to show how the processes of production and comprehension interlock with news discourse structures of various sorts.

This chapter deals with processes of news production and analyzes the respective steps or phases involved in the making of a news text. The analysis is restricted by focusing on an important dimension of production that hitherto has been neglected in the study of newsmaking, namely, the cognitive processes involved. In the last decade, several studies have been published dealing with the production process in sociological or economic terms (Roshco, 1975; Gans, 1979; Tuchman, 1978a; Fishman, 1980). These macrosociological and microsociological approaches have been discussed in Chapter 1 (see e.g., Siebert, Peterson & Schramm, 1957; McQuail, 1983). We try to integrate the relevant results of these studies into our own analysis. News production, obviously, involves journalistic activities and interactions, both among other journalists and among many other social members. Professional routines in the newsroom or during the beat of reporters have received extensive attention (Gans, 1979; Fishman, 1980) as has the institutional nature of newsmaking and the group characteristics of journalists (Tunstall, 1971; Hirsch, 1977; Johnstone, Slawski, & Bowman, 1976; Hardt, 1979). And finally, the socially-shared news values, ideologies, and goals of journalistic activities, which also underlie the production of news, have been studied in several recent monographs (Sigelman, 1973; Gans, 1979; Tuchman, 1978a; Golding & Elliott, 1979). Even is such an approach is still far from complete, we do not intend to contribute primarily to these various social dimensions of news production.

Most work fails to analyze closely what news production is all about, namely the production and writing processes of news texts themselves. What we know about such processes of actual writing comes from normative textbooks for the education of journalists. They tell us how headlines should be formulated and what a good lead should look like. They give rules of thumb for good stories about various topics. Or they specify what kind of information should be collected when, where, and from whom, and how it should be included in the news article (Dennis & Ismach, 1981; Garst & Bernstein, 1982; Baker, 1981; Metz, 1979). Such intuitive and normative rules are important, but they are not adequate as forms of analysis. Rather, they are empirical data that themselves need analysis.

News Production and the Processing of Source Texts

The key thesis of this chapter is that news production should be analyzed primarily in terms of text processing. This may seem self-evident, but often the obvious in the social sciences tends to be neglected in scholarly inquiry. By the phrase "text processing" we not only mean that a news text is being processed, i.e., written in various stages or phases. The phrase also implies that most of the information *used* to write a news text comes in discourse form: reports, declarations, interviews, meetings, press conferences, other media messages, press releases, parliamentary debates, court trials, police documents, and so on. Indeed, we have already observed in Chapter 1 that news events are seldom witnessed directly by journalists. Events usually become known through the already coded and interpreted discourses of others, most prominently through the dispatches of news agencies. Moreover, many of the discourse genres we just mentioned are themselves often news events. A declaration, press conference or interview of an important news actor, for instance the prime minister, the president or other leading politicians, are not just talk. Their discourse gets coverage in its own right (see, e.g., Hulteng & Nelson, 1971; Gormley, 1975; Lang & Engel-Lang, 1982). It is this processing of the multitude of input text and talk which lies at the heart of news discourse production.

News Gathering Encounters and Their Interpretation

Having established this main thesis for this chapter, various more specific questions may be formulated for further analysis. What is the nature of these various input texts or source texts? How do journalists hear and read them, and how are they understood and cognitively represented? What information from such source texts is focused upon, selected, summarized or otherwise processed for possible use in the production processes of a news text? How does this occur? Who are involved in the many verbal interaction types in which such source texts become available: interviews, phone calls, press conferences, or similar events in which journalists engage in encounters with possible news sources and news actors? What are the various rules and constraints of such encounters, and in which situations do they take place? Only a few of these questions have been asked, and still fewer answered, in microsociological studies of newsmaking. Needed is a perspective that allows us to analyze the discourse processing dimensions of this central aspect of newsmaking.

Even while detailed comparisons between source texts and news texts is certainly an important and necessary component of such an approach, however, even this approach is incomplete. It would still be too structuralistic, too static. We would not yet know *how* a set of source texts gets transformed into several versions of the final news text. Similarly, we may try to describe the detailed characteristics of various newsgathering encounters, such as interviews or press conferences. But again, this would only yield important insights into the interaction and situation structures of interviewing and press conferences. How such activities are planned, executed, controlled, and especially how they are understood and recalled by the participant reporter(s) cannot be made fully explicit in such a more structural approach to verbal news encounters. A crucial component is still lacking, namely, the cognitive account of the interaction and production processes. This is true both for the cognitive analysis of activities and social encounters of journalists and news purveyors and for the understanding of the actual processes of newswriting and journalistic decision making. Only in such a cognitive perspective are we able to make explicit how exactly a journalist makes sense of newsgathering encounters and newsmaking activities within the newsroom. Only a cognitive analysis shows exactly how the processes of source text understanding, representation, and summarization take place and how this information is used in the processes of news text production.

This analysis has two major objectives: an account of the transformation of source text and talk into news discourse and a formulation of these processes in terms of a cognitive theory. For many social scientists and scholars of mass communication, such an approach may seem very local, micro, or psychological and may be thought rather irrelevant with respect to the big issues in mass communication, such as the institutional controls, the organization of professional activities, or the social codes and ideologies at work in news production. Such an objection, however, would be short-sighted and would betray a narrow monodisciplinary bias. We have emphatically stressed that macrosociological and economic dimensions are crucial and inherent factors in news and newspaper production. We are also fully aware that microphenomena cannot be fully understood without their over-all macroembeddings. Yet, we hold that the reverse is equally true. It is not possible to show exactly how institutional control, economic power, professional organization, or journalistic routines and values work without a detailed analysis of their actual social enactment in the many activities of news production. Research in sociology since the 1960s has amply shown the relevance of such a microapproach of social phenomena (Schwartz & Jacobs, 1979). It has also focused on the discourse and cognitive features of social interaction, for instance in the analysis of everyday talk or other verbal encounters (Sudnow, 1972; Schenkein, 1978). It has been stressed repeatedly that not so much social structures per se but rather the rules and representations of social members—their cognitive methods of social analysis— provide the basic insight into the ways people understand, plan, and execute social action and interaction. Part of such an approach, advocated for instance in ethnomethodology, has been applied to newsmaking by Tuchman (1978a) and others (Molotch & Lester, 1974; Lester, 1980). Yet, two basic dimensions must be further explored, namely the discourse features of newsmaking and the cognitive processes of text understanding and production by journalists within newsgathering encounters. In other words, a consequent microsociology should include discourse analytical and psychological extensions. An intuitive characterization of news texts, news values, ideologies, and news interaction is not enough. We should go below the surface and investigate what is actually going on during such journalistic interpretations.

For a linguist or psychologist, such reminders may seem obvious, even if they would question each other's approach. The linguist would focus on the grammatical or textual structures of the news discourse itself, thereby claiming to study the most central and most concrete manifestation of news, namely the news text. The psychologist, on the other hand, would question the relevance of context-free structures and would emphasize the fact that production and understanding of news are processes that are fully determined by cognitive representations. The meaning of a news article is not objectively there in the text but rather arises from a reconstruction by the reader, to be made explicit in terms of memory processes and representations. Obviously, our approach integrates both directions of research, and a full-fledged account of news cannot be given without both discourse-structural and cognitive analyses.

Finally, both the linguist and the psychologist should recognize even further extensions of their inquiry into the nature of newsmaking. Obviously, news is not produced by isolated individuals, and this also holds for the understanding and especially the uses of news and the media. Hence, the fundamental relevance of the social embedding of the processes previously outlined. Journalistic activities and interactions, as well as the actual writing and rewriting of news texts, are also inherently social. Consequently, the analysis of source text transformations into news texts must be explained in terms of social cognitions within social contexts. Journalists participate in news encounters and write news articles as social members. This fact also affects their knowledge, beliefs, attitudes, goals, plans, or ideologies, all of which are also partly shared by a professional or wider social group. We have shown earlier that each stage of discourse understanding and production involves text features that may directly signal the social position of the speaker or the nature and context of the verbal interaction process. The formal nature of news style, or the persuasive and attitudinal implications of specific stylistic options, cannot be accounted for only in terms of grammar or a cognitive memory model of individual understanding and representation. Similar remarks hold for processes of understanding, influence, or other effects of news discourse on readers and publics, which will be address in the next chapter.

This plea for a truly interdisciplinary approach to the analysis of newsmaking implies that the cognitive account must involve social cognitions. Only in this way are we able to relate cognitive processes with their social context, that is, with social practices of social members, groups and institutions, and with class, power, and ideology. Only through such social cognitions can textual structures be connected with these features of the social context. In other words, there are no direct links between news discourse structures, on the one hand, and their many microsociological or macrosociological dimensions on the other hand. All processes of understanding and of social effects and functions are controlled by social cognitions of individual group members and of entire groups. It follows that our account is neither individualistic nor collective. On the contrary, it is meant as an integration, as a bridge between the verbal and the cognitive, between the cognitive and the social, and between the microaccounts and the macroaccounts of newsmaking.

Plan of This Chapter

After the cognitive model is introduced briefly it is explained in terms of its important social dimension. The results of such a combined theory of the social cognition of discourse processing are then applied in a theoretical framework of newsmaking. Finally, we report results from an empirical study into news production processes, carried out at the University of Amsterdam. Since the sociocognitive model of news processing is in part relevant both for production and comprehension of news, we need not repeat the introductory sections about cognitive processing in the next chapter. Large parts of this chapter, therefore, are presupposed in the framework provided in the next chapter. It should be added though that whereas there is some theoretical and empirical work about cognitive processes of news understanding, very little information exists regarding the cognitive study of news production. This is also true for discourse production (writing) in general. Our proposals are intended merely as a tentative framework, which needs further theoretical elaboration and empirical testing.

COGNITIVE PROCESSING OF DISCOURSE

The Development of Cognitive Text Processing Models

Many of the fundamental features of news production are shared with discourse production, speaking, and writing, in general. The same is true for the basic characteristics of production and understanding of discourse. That is, the cognitive processes involved in these various ways of dealing with discourse are to a large extent the same or similar. Therefore, this section presents some of the fundamental notions that have been proposed in recent work on discourse processing in cognitive psychology and Artificial Intelligence (AI). Then, some characteristics that distinguish production from understanding are identified and subsequently used in the account of news production processes.

The theoretical framework is essentially based on our work with Walter Kintsch (Kintsch & van Dijk, 1978; van Dijk & Kintsch, 1978, 1983). In comparison to our own earlier work and to much other work on discourse processing in psychology, our actual model is essentially a dynamic, process oriented theory (van Dijk & Kintsch, 1983). It does not merely focus on the structures of texts and their representations in memory but rather emphasizes the strategic nature of discourse production and understanding. This strategic approach allows a more flexible account of rules and representations and assumes that text production and understanding is basically geared towards an effective, context-dependent processing of textual and situational information.

Psychological models of discourse go back to the pioneering work of Bartlett (1932) about the understanding and reproduction of stories. Within an essentially Gestaltist perspective, he proposed that text understanding is not merely a passive registration of information but an active, reconstructive process. His fundamental notion of a schema, in which previous experiences and knowledge about texts are organized has had decisive influence on later work, as we shall see shortly. Unfortunately, his ideas about the social-psychological dimensions of text reproduction have received much less attention in current cognitive models, although they have found applications in the study of rumor (Allport and Postman, 1947).

We had to wait forty years before Bartlett's ideas and experiments received the recognition and further elaboration they deserved. Dominated by behavioristic approaches to verbal learning, both psychology and linguistics in the late 1960s saw a paradigm shift from verbal behavior studies to a recognition of the cognitive programming of grammatical rules. This shift was also the result of Chomsky's generative transformational grammar. Yet, this change was very much context-free, nearly completely neglecting the social dimensions of language use. Further, it gave no attention to discourse, as shown in Chapter 1. Around 1972, and parallel to developments in text linguistics, sociolinguistics, and anthropology, psychology finally became interested in the processing of discourse materials. Together with the new discipline of Artificial Intelligence, it contributed to this empirical study of discourse especially in the field of knowledge use and acquisition (Freedle & Carroll, 1972; Charniak, 1972). Attention was paid to meanings of sentences and sentence relationships, such as connection, topic and comment, presupposition, and similar phenomena that require a discourse framework (Bower, 1974; Kintsch, 1974; Clark & Clark, 1977). We proposed that besides such linear or local comprehension processes, macrostructures should also be considered to explain overall coherence understanding and the assignment of topics (van Dijk, 1972, 1977, 1980a; Kintsch, 1974; Bower, 1974; Kintsch & van Dijk, 1978).

The interest for discourse in AI focused on the fundamental problem of knowledge representation. In his dissertation about the comprehension of children stories, Charniak (1972) showed that the understanding of a simple sentence from a children story presupposes vast amounts of shared knowledge. Without an explication of such knowledge structures, it is not possible to account for the cognitive processes at work during understanding in general, and of text understanding in particular. It was recognized that such knowledge about the world should be effectively stored, organized, and accessed during understanding. This means that knowledge is at least partly organized in prepackaged forms, so-called frames or scripts, which we have already discussed in Chapter 2. (Norman & Rumelhart, 1975; Schank & Abelson, 1977; Schank, 1982). These frames or scripts are the more sophisticated offshoots of the schemata already proposed by Bartlett half a century earlier. They represent the stereotypical and consensual knowledge people have about actions, events, and episodes in social life, such as going to the movies or having a birthday party. Much of the information in texts about such episodes usually remains implicit because the speaker assumes that the listener knows it. It is also assumed that during understanding the reader or listener activates, applies, and perhaps adapts or changes such script information. The role of scripts or similar forms of knowledge and belief organization is crucial in the account of how people understand information by default, how they answer questions, or provide summaries for texts. They explain how readers can construct a meaningful representation even when the text itself is only fragmentary.

Whereas much of this work in AI remains at a rather abstract and formal level, and has been shown to be crucial in the computer simulation of text understanding, it was soon recognized in psychology that scripts must be a central component in a cognitive theory (Bower, Black, & Turner 1979). Nevertheless, even with an accurate model of the representation of knowledge in memory, an adequate cognitive model should also primarily specify the processes of the *use* of such knowledge clusters during understanding. In this respect, computer simulation may not capture what is really going on. For instance, it is highly unlikely that language users activate their complete knowledge script about an episode when they read a story about such an episode. They may only need part of it for effective understanding. It has been proposed, therefore, that language users apply handy strategies in the activation and application of script or other knowledge (van Dijk & Kintsch, 1983).

In the last ten years, an impressive number of books and articles have appeared in psychology and AI. Experiments have been conducted with many types of discourse and textual structures, for different language users, and with different goals investigate the details of understanding, memory representation, and retrieval. Details of this work cannot be mentioned here. For recent work and further references, see Graesser, 1981; Just & Carpenter, 1977; Mandl, Stein, & Trabasso, 1984; Le Ny & Kintsch, 1982; Flammer & Kintsch, 1982; Sanford & Garrod, 1981; Otto & White, 1982; van Dijk, 1982c.

A Framework for Processing News Discourse

Instead of reviewing all extant work in the field, we summarize some of the major insights into the processes of discourse comprehension as they also apply to news discourse (for detail, see van Dijk & Kintsch, 1983, which is the theoretical framework on which this chapter is based)

Decoding. Texts, like other information types (action, objects, persons, situations), are perceived and subjected to initial decoding in short-term memory (STM). This decoding involves categorization of forms and structures. For instance, words of English are recognized and isolated from graph or sound continua. Henceforth, we shall ignore these surface aspects of news text processing, although they are of course an important, final phase in news formulation and expression (Clark & Clark, 1977).

Interpretation. Simultaneously, interpretation processes start operating on such partly decoded strings and sustain the decoding process: Word meanings are assigned to words or word fragments (morphemes), and the structure of clause and sentence meanings is constructed in relation to surface structure phenomena like word order and syntactic categories. Similar processes are at work in the interpretation of action, interaction, and hence of speech acts and communication. Both decoding and interpretation have a strategic nature. Although for natural language these processes are basically rule-governed, language users apply effective strategies in decoding words and understanding word and clause meanings. They may use both syntactic and semantic information at the same time, or they may activate knowledge and context information to arrive at fast and plausible analyses and interpretations of input discourse. Interpretation not only involves the assignment of meanings to texts but also to the assignment of pragmatic functions (speech acts) or other context functions to surface forms, e.g., in the interpretation of stylistic markers signaling context type, social relationships, gender, or group membership.

Structuring. Next, still in STM, further structuring of the interpretations assigned takes place. Word meanings are organized in clause and sentence meanings, namely in terms of propositions (see Chapter 2, for detail). Next, propositions are connected into coherence pairs and sequences. Strategies are again at work here to link parts of sentence or propositions with previous ones. Thus, even the very first word or phrase of a sentence may be linked provisionally with previous information, e.g., sentence initial connectives such as "But" or "Moreover" or pronouns and noun phrases such as "She" or "The woman."

Cyclical Processing. In contrast to a structural-textual approach, a cognitive theory holds that STM has limited storage and processing capacity. Not all words and clauses, and hence not all propositions of long sentences or sequences of sentences, can be stored in the STM buffer. Space must be freed to receive new information. Therefore, a language user must strategically select information that is no longer necessary for immediate local understanding. This information is stored in long-term memory (LTM), that is, in the episodic memory (EM) part of LTM that records all incoming, interpreted information.

Macrostructure Formation. These major steps of local comprehension only account for half of the processing occurring in STM. At the same time, language users infer topics (macropropositions) from sequences of propositions, which define a text or text fragment globally. Macrostructure formation, like the other processes of comprehension is both top down and bottom up: Strategic macrooperations apply both to information from text and context, but as we have discussed earlier, these operations also need information from activated frames or scripts. The current macroproposition(s) control at a global level the processing taking place at the local level, while at the same time defining the overall coherence of the text. Together with other high level text and context information, it is assumed that macrostructures are located in a special control system, regulating the processing in STM and the information flow between STM and LTM.

Superstructure Formation. Similarly, global structures, e.g.. special form schemata (superstructures), such as those of narratives or news, may be assigned in STM to texts or parts of texts. This process is also top down and bottom up: Since schemata are often conventional, they may be activated and applied already in an early stage of processing, thus controlling the formation of macrostructures and, hence, the operations at the local level.

Representation in Episodic Memory. The result of the various operations described above is a hierarchical representation of the text in episodic memory. This text representation (TR) allows the language user to relate new information in the text to old information (by reinstatement procedures), to recall fragments of surface structure ("how things were said or written") and especially part of the meaning of the text, or to answer questions about the information in the text. In general, the high-level macrostructures (topics) are recalled best and basically form the information used to summarize a text. Under special circumstances, detailed microinformation may also be recalled on later occasions, e.g., when it has special personal or contextual functions or specific relationships with other cognitive or affective representations.

Situation Models. Yet, the ultimate goal of discourse understanding and production, is not the formation of a textual representation in memory. Rather, language users want to convey information about real or imaginary events in some situation. This information in cognitively represented in so-called situation *models* (Johnson-Laird, 1983; van Dijk, 1985d, 1987c). Models are stored in episodic memory and may be seen as the overall referent of a text: They are what the language user thinks the text is about. Existing situation models (SMs) embody our accumulated experiences of earlier events, including interactions and discourse. Extant models representing more or less the same situation may be activated and updated during the interpretation of a text (Schank, 1982). We have shown earlier that in news interpretation, readers often use and update a given situation model about an issue or series of events when interpreting a news article about the same situation. Much like frames or scripts, models play a crucial role in understanding. They provide the concrete missing information that must be supplied by the language user during the interpretation of events, actions, or discourse. They represent what we imagine to be the case when we read or write a text. Structurally, models are organized by a schema, consisting of fixed categories, such as Setting (Time and Location), Circumstances, Participants, and Action, each with a possible Modifier. Not surprisingly, these basic categories also appear in the semantics of sentences and stories; they are used to describe situations.

Learning: Knowledge and Belief Formation. Models have an episodic and personal nature. Yet, in order for information from text to be socially relevant, more general inferences may be drawn from text representations and models in EM. They may be abstracted from or decontextualized and generalized towards frames, scripts, or similar conventional (and hence social, shared) knowledge in LTM. This general information is located in what is usually called "semantic memory", although "social memory" might be a better term because much information in this store is not merely semantic: We also have general information of a more formal kind, such as general knowledge about the structures of stories, news reports, action, photographs, or natural scenes.

Subjectivity. Although the processes just described have a fairly general nature and although relevant parts of text interpretations may be shared by others, it should be stressed that the interpretation and representation processes also have a subjective dimension. Strategies may be applied in different ways, depending on various personal characteristics of the language user. Personal models may be different, due to different biographies, and, therefore, may control processing in different ways. Due to different knowledge and beliefs about a situation, different language users may notice different information types in a text and assign variable local and especially global meanings. The next section shows that groups of language users, as social members, also may have different opinions, attitudes and ideologies; and these also influence the interpretation process and the structures of text representations and models in episodic memory. In other words, discourse understanding is essentially relative to personal models and goals, on the one hand, and socially shared goals, frames, scripts, attitudes, or ideologies, on the other hand.

These are the major steps or phases in the processing of discourse. Many details and technicalities have been omitted. At this point we only want to introduce the central theoretical notions of a cognitive framework. In principle, the framework holds both for comprehension (on which we focused in the presentation) and for production.

Discourse Production

Production processes need not start with information input but may find their origin in situation models: People know (or want) a specific event to be the case and, within a communicative framework, they form intentions to perform a speech act, e.g., an assertion or a request, in which their model of the events is to be conveyed to the listener. Relevant macrostructures are derived from the model that control production processes at the local level. Next, meanings are specified that correspond to aspects of the model, e.g., successive actions of participants in a story. And finally, these meanings are formulated in syntactic forms and expressed in the appropriate word expressions and sentence intonation. Just as in interpretation, the various processes of production are strategic. That is, the order of production steps may vary. Information may be used from different levels or sources at the same time, and the whole process is geared towards the effective formulation of meanings and models that the speaker wants to convey to the listener. In spontaneous speech, planning in the form of macrostructure and superstructure formation may be at closer range and more ad hoc than in many forms of written communication of course. Here, we may first form a general outline (complete macrostructure) of a text, and only then fill it in with local meaning details. In reality, this process is more flexible, however. Local constraints of the communicative situation or memory restrictions of the writer may well cause a less-ordered process of production.

The principles outlined here also apply to the understanding and production of news discourse. Yet, because news discourse has its own characteristic structures, as well as specific communicative and social contexts, it also requires more specific analysis of its cognitive processes. Writing a news article involves other knowledge and procedures and presupposes different frames, scripts, or attitudes than the writing of a love letter, manual, or formal lecture. There is unfortunately little theoretical and experimental evidence, however, about such genre differences in discourse production. Most of the work concerns writing processes in educational settings (de Beaugrande, 1984).

DISCOURSE PROCESSING AND SOCIAL COGNITION

The account of discourse processing given in the previous section offers a more-or-less adequate picture about the understanding and production of discourse by individuals. It fails to consider, however, the important social dimension of language use. This social dimension has been implicit only in a few assumptions:

1. The cognitive principles involved have a general nature. Hence, they are shared by all language users. This guarantees that one important condition of social interaction, namely, the ability of mutual understanding, is guaranteed at some elementary level.

2. In perception and interaction, actors or observers may have similar experiences and hence at least partly similar models. This allows similar recall and communication about such experiences and the use of models in future action and interaction.

3. This shared partial understanding may be obtained especially for public discourse forms, such as those of the mass media. This allows large groups of people to have similar models of the same situations. These models may be used again as input for the communication about new events.

4. Most discourse is interpreted in social contexts. This means that it is interpreted together with a similar interpretation of this social context. Models are formed not only of the text situation but also about the communicative situation itself. Again, such interpretations may be shared by social members or groups that participate in such communicative events.

5. Learning involves the decontextualization and abstraction of models and the formation of conventional or stereotypical knowledge and beliefs organized in frames or clusters. This process is especially geared towards the preparation of information for more general, social use.

6. Memory, therefore, is cognitively designed to serve social needs. It involves information but also social communication. The acquisition of knowledge and beliefs through discourse in the lives of people has continually taken place in contexts of socialization, interpersonal and intergroup perception, and interaction. We may conclude, therefore, that, apart from a few universal principles of human information processing, cognition is essentially social.

These assumptions do not go far enough. To stress the social nature of language use and communication and the derived social nature of interpretation rules and knowledge representations is much too superficial. We have specified this claim by indicating where and how exactly the social dimension is relevant in discourse processing, but apart from the shared nature of such processes and representations, there is little social in such an account. Social members are present only as communicating individuals. No action and interaction goals, no special social relationships such as those of friendship or power, no social groups and their properties, no institutional constraints have been explicitly spelled out, even when they have been presupposed at each step of discourse production and understanding.

A first important addition, therefore, is the introduction of special forms of social cognition such as opinions, attitudes, and ideologies. These presuppose not only knowledge or beliefs but also norms and values, which define and are characteristically shared by social groups or cultures. It is assumed, therefore, that in discourse understanding, people do more than understand the meaning of a text and construct a model of a situation. They also form specific opinions about the text, speaker, or situation. These opinions may simply be defined as evaluative propositions: "It is good (bad, delicious, dangerous, etc.) that p", or simply "X is good (bad, etc.)." Opinions may be concrete and personal and, therefore, be part of ad hoc situation models in memory: They are part of our experiences. Yet, just as with knowledge and beliefs, they may also be instantiations of more general opinions, such as "Nuclear plants are dangerous" or "The press should be free." And just like knowledge, such general opinions may be organized in complex attitude structures or schemata, for instance those about nuclear energy, abortion, ethnic integration, or American foreign policy (Abelson, 1976; Carbonell, 1979; van Dijk, 1982c; 1987a).

General opinions and the attitudes they form are essentially social. That is, they are not personal, but shared, and define the goals, interests, values, and norms of a group, relative to socially relevant issues. Such cognitions are not distributed arbitrarily over groups of individuals but define socially structured organizations of social members. Social functions or roles, positions, class, gender, age, or ethnic group membership define such groups and, hence, the social cognitions of the group members. This also applies to the use of attitudes in discourse defined as social practice. The meanings of a text derive from a model, and if such models include instances of social opinions from shared attitudes, this will also show in the meanings and models conveyed in communication. This is in fact the channel through which group models and attitudes become formed, shared and confirmed in the first place, both through the media and through informal communication with other social members. Among other social practices, intragroup and intergroup communication through discourse is a central means for the formulation, reproduction, and confirmation of group definition, cohesion, common goals and interests, or other important features that define social groups.

Social psychology has increasingly recognized this social nature of cognition. The classical topics of that discipline such as person perception, group perception, attitude formation, communication, and interaction have been reformulated in more explicitly cognitive terms under the general concept of "social cognition" (Wyer & Carlston, 1979; Higgins, Herman, & Zanna, 1981; Forgas, 1981; see Fiske & Taylor, 1984 for a good introduction and survey). Notions like schema, problem solving, heuristics, or various other memory processes and organization features have been borrowed from cognitive psychology to represent the processes involved in the various social interaction types previously mentioned. Instead of rather arbitrarily defined personality traits, it has been proposed to elaborate the notion of person schema (Markus, 1977). Such person schemata are used in the perception, interpretation, and evaluation of other people and may supply information that allow inferences about others that are not actually based on immediate observation. The same holds for group schemata. Group members have a self-schema about one's own group and schemata about other social or ethnic groups. This is also the way group stereotypes and prejudices can be represented. Such schemata may be thought of as general information about the basic distinctive features of the group (appearance, social position, etc.), as well as about their shared norms, values, goals, and interests. Person and group schemata also explain how social members perceive and interpret the actions of other social members and how such information is stored. Various types of biases can thus be explained (for details, references and various recent directions of research in this area, see Hamilton, 1981).

These various approaches provide a richer and more social picture of cognition. It should be emphasized, however, that in much of contemporary social psychology this cognitive orientation has neglected the proper sociological embeddings of the discipline. Although many of the typical group-based processes, such as the formation and representation of stereotypes and prejudices, can be accommodated, it is obvious that important social factors are still missing. Women and Blacks are not just subject to prejudices because they form a discernible group for other groups (males, whites). These social cognitions are in turn embedded in cognitive representations of the conditions of domination, social and economic interests and privileges, power and exploitation, or institutional formulation and enactments. In this way, and through social practices, social cognitions as previously described may be linked to such relationships, structures, and formations of society. To make this link more explicit, the first obvious step is to introduce specific cognitions about these societal conditions, that is, about the interests, goals, and institutions involved. Next, within such integrated social representa-

110 NEWS PRODUCTION PROCESSES

tions, social interactions and contexts should be characterized. Action should be analyzed in terms of the social beliefs, attitudes, ideology, goals, interests, and the contextual and institutional constraints of group members.

Acts of discrimination, for instance, require specification in terms of underlying prejudices (ethnic group schemata and the strategies of their use in action planning), shared norms and values of an ingroup, general goals and interests, actual personal goals and interests, and a full analysis of the situation. This explains why such acts are not merely individual (and hence incidental) but are structurally tied to the cognitively represented and processed properties of the group. The reverse is also true: Social acts and their interests may contribute again to the formation and change of underlying conditions; prejudice is essentially formed because it is relevant and useful in the enactment of social domination. If we want to prevent ethnic minorities from sharing our work, housing, or social services, it is both cognitively and socially effective to first form an ethnic prejudice schema involving opinions about our own priorities and privileges, about their abuses of such commodities, or about other negative characteristics that might preclude them from such forms of equal participation in society. In this way, social cognitions—both representations (schemata) and actual strategies in their application—may be finely tuned to social needs, norms, goals, and interests of a group.

This discussion about social cognition is a crucial introduction into the study of discourse and communication and, hence, to public discourse like news. Thus, discourse production is not just the expression and communication of models or individual opinions. Rather, each speaker is engaged in social action and, therefore, speaks as a group member. To form a sociocognitive theory of (news) production, however, we must understand the consequences of this general statement. Obviously, the inherently social nature of discourse production shows the social knowledge and attitude schemata that are presupposed by the speaker as a group member. Similarly, the speaker enacts the norms and values, the interests, power relations, or ideologies of his or her own group. By their communication they are reproduced, confirmed, and diffused throughout the ingroup. We now have the outlines of a theoretical model of the cognitive and interactional processes on which such crucial social processes are based.

NEWS PRODUCTION PROCESSES

The theoretical groundwork for an analysis of news production processes has now been done. The general principles already outlined also apply to news processing. We now address the interesting specific questions: What special belief and attitude schemata, what models, and what strategies are involved in news production? How do newsmakers represent and reproduce the social context of news production? And how is news production as a cognitive process embedded in the enactment of this social context by its communicative interaction forms? Let us discuss the various production dimensions involved in terms of some elementary stages of news production.

The Interpretation of Events as News Events

It has been argued that most news is based on other discourse such as source text and talk, which may sometimes be news events in their own right. However, let us first imagine situations in which a more direct perception of events takes place, as in the case of the squatter eviction and demonstrations in Amsterdam discussed in van Dijk (1987b). One central question that comes up in many discussions of news production is the initial perception and evaluation of events as news events. It is usually assumed that these processes are controlled by a system of news values of the journalist. If an event matches the criteria spelled out in the news values, then it attracts more attention and has a higher chance of being selected by the journalist as a potential news event. Although this assumption is basically correct, it is also very general and vague. We do not know exactly *how* this process takes place. Also, a more explicit analysis is needed of what is traditionally called the bias of the news and the relationships between news discourse and its reconstructive relations to reality must be examined (see, e.g., Park 1940; Guback, 1968; Williams, 1975; Hofstetter, 1976; Schoenbach, 1977; Lange, 1980).

This cognitive framework suggests how text or event information is analyzed, interpreted, and represented in memory. These processes also hold for the analysis of events as potential news events. An event thus analyzed is represented as a model in episodic memory. Such a model features the dominant actions or events, participants, time and location, circumstances, relevant objects, or instruments of action, organized in a hierarchical structure. Thus, our study of the press coverage of the eviction events in Amsterdam in the early 1980s (van Dijk, 1987b) showed that such events have a dominant action: demonstration or destruction; dominant participants such as squatters, the police, and the city authorities; a time and place characterization; and objects such as police cars and cranes, shop windows, and Molotov cocktails. Obviously, an observing journalist can only have a partial model of the situation. This means, first, that the model must have a perspective or point of view, depending on the position of the reporter. The reporter in the squad room at police headquarters has a different perspective from the one in the middle of a demonstration. Second, the model may be specified by personal opinions and emotions about squatters, the police, demonstrations, and evictions. These may influence the very construction of the model. More details may be represented about the actions of the squatters than about those of the police, for example. Different categorizations may be involved: Persons or groups may be seen as demonstrators or as hooligans, and for each category different group schemata must be activated and applied to model building. Experimental evidence shows that more attention is paid to the actions of persons or groups when such actions confirm or are consistent with the group schema (Rothbart, Evans, & Fulero, 1979; Taylor, 1981; van Dijk, 1987a). Hooligans are seen to "run to type" when smashing windows. Policemen who batter hooligans may not be seen as committing illegal actions but as engaging in legal and expected forms of crime control. From personal evaluations of actions or actors in situations, we thus find the socially based insertion of shared opinions in models of the situation. These concrete opinions are instantiated from general ones, such as "Smashing windows is not permitted."

The result of event perception and interpretation, then, is a subjective but socially-monitored model of the situation in the memory of an observing reporter. Obviously, this is not adequate for a theory of news production because this process is not very much different from the observation of the same events by other social members. News gathering contexts involve special goals, namely the representation of the event in view of its potential reproduction in news discourse. That is, a model is formed that in principle can be used as the basis of a discourse production process. Special conditions are operating because the event and its details may need to be retrieved and expressed on a later occasion. If the event is complex, external memory aids, such as notes, may be necessary to help later reproduction of the model. Notes may contain details that are difficult to retrieve, due to their microfunction in the overall event (names, numbers), or they may pertain to the overall macroactions that define the situation and which may be used to retrieve more detailed component actions. General model and schema knowledge may be used to fill in the stereotypical details of the situation. Errors of instantiation are possible in that case: Description and note taking conform to the overall pattern that defined the kind of model— a demonstration, a riot, or a house eviction.

Similarly, that the event may need to be described in a news article has further consequences for the structures and contents of the model as formed and represented. If news articles conventionally require precise names and numbers, these need special attention in the model (or in external memory models: notes), which they might not get otherwise. If only a few actors should occur in a news story, specific attention to and selection of information about model participants will be the result in the control system that monitors the observation process. The same is true for the specific selection of negative, dangerous, violent, spectacular, or otherwise interest-

ing actions. Implicit news value criteria underlying journalistic routine observation provide the basis for such attention, selection, and decision processes. For example, widespread looting gets more attention than smashing
a big bank window, which in turn is more newsworthy than a scratch on a
car. In the model, the former events are represented higher in the hierarchy, dominate more details, and give rise to more opinions. The consequence is that the first events are easier to retrieve and, therefore, have a
better chance of being used in news production. At the same time, their
high position in the model facilitates macrostructure formation by strategically reading off precisely those events during discourse production: Looting and smashing windows of banks become main themes in the news
report. In other words, the interpretation of events as potential news events
is determined by the potential news discourse such an interpretation
(model) may be used for, and conversely. News production seems circular:
Events and texts mutually influence each other. Strictly speaking it is of
course not the later text that influences the perception of earlier events;
rather, textual goals and plans monitor perception and representation.

This does not only apply to the perception and interpretation of various
aspects of a given event but also to the very attention for and selection of
events as possible news events in general. It is well known that most events
do not qualify as potential news events. This suggests that there must be an
effective observation filter. This filter or net (Tuchman, 1978a) selects big
demonstrations or police actions and disregards most personal, mundane,
routine, or small-scale events and actions. In other words, the cognitive
categories that define the news event filter must involve concepts such as
public, public interest, difference, nonroutine, size, negative consequences,
and similar notions. During newsgathering procedures, the journalist must
feed this filter or news event schema into his or her control system, and
current situations will be scanned under the top-down control of this schema. Other events may be actually seen but not as possible news events.

Although this account is basically correct, it disregards journalistic practices. Reporters do not simply go around in streets, in institutions, or other
locations to spot possible news events. It is well documented that effective
newsgathering must be organized and routinized to find the appropriate
number of relevant news events (Gans, 1979; Tuchman, 1974, 1978a; Fishman, 1980; Lester, 1980). Even the unexpected must be brought under
control. It follows that news events, in addition to the schematic filter
categories, are constrained as to their time, location, and actors. Time is
essential due to deadline constraints and the periodicity of dailies and,
therefore, tends to exclude all nonmomentaneous events, such as structures
and processes. Location requires accessibility, so that public places and
institutional settings are preferred. Actors are associated with a whole set of
special requirements, which we may call news actor schemata. Such person

schemata (Markus, 1977) include accessibility (and hence publicness), position and status, social or political power, knownness, visibility, or simply
participation in highly negative or spectacular events (criminals, victims).
Journalistic routines are organized in such a way to maximize the chances of
satisfying most of these criteria—hence, the special beats for the political
center, the police and the courts, or other large institutions. The organization of journalistic routines compensates for the inherent limitations on
participation, observation, and cognitive modeling by journalists. Thus, the
number of possible news situations is considerably reduced to manageable
proportions, as are the kind of news events, actions, actors, locations, and
time segments. Moreover, known situations act as important data for the
construction of new models, so that the interpretation of new events is
easier. In other words, new models are not so much formed on the basis of
new, arbitrary situations. Rather, situations are seen that instantiate known
general models so that only some new details need to be added. Such old
models with new details form the basis of much news production processes.

We see how cognitive and social constraints operate and cooperate in the
location, isolation, perception, interpretation, and memory representation
of events as news events. Besides the social routines described in much
other work about news production, we may now also add a number of
cognitive routines or strategies to cope with events that could be used as
information for models for news discourse. Part of these routines are news
event schemata, news actor schemata, news situation schemata, and the
previous models formed about actual events that are instantiations of such
schemata. A police action against squatters in Amsterdam is a new instance
that can be interpreted easily on the basis of models of previous evictions.
Squatters or demonstrators are easy to categorize according to person and
group schemata within such a model. And finally, the reporter can understand and intelligibly report the eviction or the demonstration on the basis
of stereotypical, shared scripts of such social events. Once selected, a potential news event is interpreted according to these models and schemata and
strategically adapted to the now current situation, as well as under the
constraints of the news discourse goals and plans of the reporter.

Processing Source Texts

Most news, however, is not based on the immediate observation of news
events. Most news derives its information from discourse. We should distinguish in this case between discourse that is itself a news event, such as
declarations of important politicians or the publication of an important
report or book, and discourse that is only used for its information content,

not for the news value of the communicative event in which it has been produced. Intermediary cases are possible, of course. Discourses as news events are processed much in the same way as we have described for news events in general. They are accessed, observed, interpreted, and memorized just like any other action. Yet, their discourse dimension has important consequences for processing. Unlike actions, they also have symbolic content, and this may draw more attention than the perhaps uninteresting communicative event, such as a press conference, itself. This means that the reporter uses preformulated information. The reporter not only must form a model of the situation but already gets a coded version of the model, which may include opinions, attitudes, perspective, and other information about the model of the speaker, as well as specific meanings, hierarchies (topics, schemata), and stylistic and rhetorical forms. Instead of reformulating the models conveyed, the reporter can in principle copy the very source discourse, as is the case in quotations. Yet, most reporters do not actually record and transcribe full discourses that are news events. Time limitations force them to record only fragments (make notes) or to provide summaries.

The same occurs with source texts that are not themselves news events. Portions may be selected, copied, quoted, or summarized. If more source texts are available, as is often the case for dispatches from the wire services, information from various texts may be used. In addition, information may be drawn from interviews, phone calls, the documentation department, sourcebooks, or other media messages. How exactly does this happen? What are the cognitive and social routines that allow reporters to write a news text on the basis of so much, and such diverse materials? Let us examine some major strategies.

Selection. The most effective strategy of complex source text processing is selection. Yet, selection is itself often the result of a number of other strategies. After all, the decision to use one source text or source text fragment rather than another presupposes criteria for decision making. And selection may apply to communicative events, such as press conferences or interviews or to already available source texts. A priori choices or choices based on reading and evaluation may be made from available source texts. A priori choices may be based on credibility or authority of the source. A reporter who has both a police report and a squatter's press release about an eviction or demonstration will more likely choose the first source on a priori grounds, based on source selection criteria. This selection process is also reflected in the position within the relevance structure and the amount of attention in the final news item. And finally, selection after reading and evaluation presupposes opinions about content characteristics of the source text.

Reproduction. Once a source text (fragment) has been selected as an information base for processing, literal reproduction is undoubtedly the easiest strategy. In our study of international news (van Dijk, 1984b, 1987b), we found for example that large parts of news agency dispatches are copied directly in the news item, with only occasional and slight changes of style. In our case study of news production, which is discussed in the section "A Field Study in News Production", we also found that especially in foreign news production, source texts from the agencies may be taken over literally. Major conditions for literal reproduction are lack of time, lack of other information, the news quality of the source text, and the general credibility of the source. Of course, reproduction may also be partial, for example, to meet size constraints, in which case usually irrelevant passages are deleted. At this point, selection and summarization are involved in reproduction.

Summarization. The next major strategy for the processing of large amounts of source text information is summarization. In our account of the psychology of discourse processing, we found that summarization involves the derivation of macrostructures. A summary is a partial expression of such a macrostructure and indicates what according to the reporter is most relevant or important of one or more source texts. The summarization strategies that have been analyzed theoretically and experimentally are deletion, generalization, and construction. Deletion applies to local information that is not further used, as a presupposition, for the interpretation of the rest of the text. Generalization occurs when similar properties are relevant for different actors or situations or when a given property can be applied to different members of a set, as in "The rioters looted many stores." Construction requires the combination of several partial acts or events into an overall, macroact or macroevent: A series of different acts (fighting with the police, destruction of property, etc.) may be subsumed under the general action category of rioting. Obviously, summarization is necessarily subjective. It presupposes personal and professional decisions about what information is most relevant or important and which overall categories, which need not be expressed in source texts themselves, are chosen.

Summarization takes place in every stage of source text and news text processing. The account of a press conference, of an interview, a court trial, or a long report usually involves summarization. The important role of summarization in news production becomes obvious when we realize that this allows the reporter to (1) reduce large texts to shorter texts; (2) to understand local details of source text information relative to its macrostructures; (3) to define the most important or relevant information of source texts; (4) to compare different source texts regarding their common topics and relevancies; (5) to use the summary as a ready-made lead, and hence as a basic semantic control instance in the writing of the news text, and to derive headlines from such a summary; and (6) to use the summary as a plan or design for a news text and for discussion with colleagues and editors. In the multitude of possible source texts and the complexity of their information, summarization is the central process of effective news production and control, once primary selection has taken place. It is the main strategy for the reduction of information complexity.

Local Transformations. Whereas summarization involves the transformation of microstructures into macrostructures, news production also may require local transformations of various sorts. *Deletion* also operates here as a first and strategically efficient move. Its conditions may be internal and external. Internal criteria involve decisions about the relative irrelevance of details or details that are not consistent with the models, scripts, or attitudes of journalists or those (assumed by the journalist) of the readers. External conditions are space limitations or the impossibility to verify an important but controversial detail on the basis of other sources. *Addition*, on the other hand, requires the insertion of relevant details from other source texts or from previous models and general knowledge of the reporter. Often, additions are used to provide further information about previous events, context, or historical background and then have the function of explanation and embedding. Expanding addition is the insertion of relevant new information from other source texts, for instance precise numbers, quotations, or similar details that belong to the general criteria for adequate news discourse. *Permutations* are frequent in news production when the source text does not have news schema structure. Basically determined by relevance criteria, important information may be moved forward (up), or unimportant information may be moved backward (down). Also, the canonical news schema structure should be respected, so that Main Events come before Context, Background, Verbal Reaction, and Comments. And for each category, the higher level information (as specified by the macrostructure expressed in the summary) must occur first. These news text constraints may require many permutations of input source text data. Finally, *substitution,* much like addition, requires that an alternative account of the same facts is available in other source texts. Clauses, sentences, or whole paragraphs of a given source text may thus be replaced by comparable fragments of another source text.

Stylistic and Rhetorical (Re-)Formulation. The operations just discussed are mainly semantic. Many transformations of source text are also stylistic or rhetorical. The word "demonstrator" in agency dispatches may be substituted by "rioter", much in the same way as "guerrilla" may be changed to "freedom fighter" (for details, see van Dijk, 1984b, 1987b). Apart from selection and relevance changes of original texts, style changes are the most effective means to inject personal or institutional opinions into the news text while writing about the same events. And rhetorical reformulation allows the reporter to make a story more effective by the use of understatements or exaggerations, comparisons, and suggestive metaphors. At this point, there is no longer a direct transformation of source texts but, in fact, the production of another text.

The various operations mentioned here require an extensive cognitive framework. Texts are not simply compared or copied directly. Any process of selection, reproduction, summarization, or other transformations of such source texts presupposes comprehension of source texts. Hence, the reporter must at least have partial textual representations of such source texts in memory. Similarly, if comprehension is based on situation model activation and updating, so are comparison, summarization, and other transformations. Indeed, the very decision that texts are about the same event is based on an analysis of the model conveyed by these texts. Decisions to delete information are based on the evaluation that a detail may not be relevant in the understanding of the news text, that is, in the construction by the reader of the underlying model. In other words, all text transformations taking place in news production are essentially model based. And because such models were assumed to contain personal experiences and opinions, as well as instantiated general opinions or attitudes, it becomes clear how and why any transformation of source texts into news texts must involve subjective or group-based (professional as well as ideological) norms and values.

Transformations of source texts are not only model based but also monitored by plans and goals. Many of the decisions that underlie selection and change are determined by external constraints on the routines of news production (deadlines, size, agenda, etc.), as well as by the internal constraints of content and structure. The decision that some source text or its information is less important or less relevant is not made in isolation but relative to the production process of the news text: It is irrelevant for the news text (according to the reporter or the supervising editor). Similarly, summarization not only reduces information so that short news texts can be written about complex events; but this operation also yields leads, headlines, and a general control plan for production of a news text. In other words, the properties of the intended news text seem to have feedback on the transformation processes in production. Source text processing is a cognitive operation that is controlled by overall text plans: The source texts are heard or read with a possible idea or even details of a news article in mind.

The various operations for the transformation of source texts into news texts are more-or-less similar to those at work in the processing of the news text itself until its final version. In that case, there is but one source text, and authors may be identical (if the reporter rewrites his/her own text). Selection may take place even here: A story may eventually not be published. Of the transformations, deletion seems to be most effective, mostly because of size constraints. The overall structure of a news article allows the deletion of the tail of the item, which by definition only contains the least important details. Style changes may be necessary to enhance readability, to avoid unwanted opinion inferences, or to take care that allegations are vague enough to avoid libel. More than with the processing of source texts, final editing requires the influence of assumed reader models: Comprehensibility, previous knowledge, and assumed opinions of the readers play a role in judgements about the appropriateness of earlier versions of a news item.

Within the routines and constraints of news gathering we have emphasized the importance of source text processing. It was shown that a few basic operations are applied in news production based on such source texts. It appeared that selection, summarization, local semantic, and stylistic transformations are the central operations involved. They are cognitively controlled by five major factors: (1) the subjective model of the situation; that is the interpretation of the events of the input texts; (2) the model of the reporter about source characteristics (credibility, authority); (3) the goals and plans of news text production, involving news schema and macrostructures; (4) models of the readers, and finally; and (5) the model of the production context, including general and particular knowledge about newsgathering routines, deadlines, and interaction constraints. Theoretically, factors (2) and (3), involving beliefs about the source and plans of text production, are part of this overall context model of news text writers. We now have some general principles of news text production strategies. Details and examples can only be given in a more concrete case study of the processes involved, which we address in "A Field Study in News Production."

NEWS VALUES REVISITED

In this and in many other studies of news production, the notion of news value has often been used to explain the selection of news items, their chances of being published, or the actual formulation of news (Breed, 1955, 1956; Galtung and Ruge, 1965; Gans, 1979; Tuchman, 1978a; Golding & Elliott, 1979). These news values need not be repeated in detail here, but some of them require a more systematic and explicit cognitive definition. The very use of the notion of value suggests the location of news values in social cognition. They are values about the newsworthiness of events or discourse, shared by professionals (Lester, 1980), and indirectly by the public of the news media (Atwood, 1970). They provide the cognitive basis for decisions about selection, attention, understanding, representation, recall, and the uses of news information in general.

In general, different types of news values may be distinguished. First, are those news values formulated in the economic terms of news production in different market systems and within profit-oriented organizations. Constraints such as sales and subscriptions, budgets for newsgathering, or the amount of advertising, to name only a few factors, determine the general limitations on the amount of editorial space. Assumed beliefs and opinions of both powerful news actors (sources) and the public determine agendas for topics and issues and the ideological orientation of the opinions formulated or implied by selection and treatment of stories. The amount of domestic and especially foreign news depends on the budget for foreign correspondents, agency subscriptions, and the number of reporters and the beats they can cover. Although strictly speaking the constraints derived from economic conditions are not values but material factors, they are important in the formation and confirmation of values. Social and political ideologies, for example, are simply not free for profit-run newspapers that depend on advertising, sales, and subscriptions. Decisions of importance and relevance are similarly constrained by limitations of space and budget.

The second category of news values is more closely tied to the social routines of newsgathering and organizational production, which in turn are partly linked with the economic constraints (such as those of competition, leading to the professional aim to bring news as quickly and as reliably as possible, or to beat other media with a scoop). The periodicity of newspapers, marked by daily deadlines for instance, determines the overall preference for momentaneous spot news: instants of events, with clear beginnings and ends. Similarly, the organization of newsgathering in different sections or beats gives preference to stories about events produced and defined by corresponding sectors and actors of social and political life. Accessibility of sources favors stories and news actors that have organized relationships with the press, such as spokespersons, press releases or press conferences. The routines of news production thus reproduce social structure by their special selection of and attention for the organizations, institutions, and persons that meet these requirements. This explains part of the special interest for political and social elites, elite countries, or elite organizations. Social prominence and power of elite actors and their events are reproduced and confirmed by the press. These social constraints have cognitive antecedents and consequences. This special and repeated attention for elite persons, groups, and countries also leads the journalist to models and frames in which such elites are dominant actors. That is, journalists internalize the social picture that results from the social and professional constraints on newswriting (Atwood & Grotta, 1973). And this model or schema in turn favors the selection and production of news stories about the same elites. It has proved to be very difficult to break this vicious cycle.

Hence, news values reflect economic, social, and ideological values in the discourse reproduction of society through the media. We assume that such constraints have a cognitive representation. However, apart from such dominant pictures of society, as they are shared by journalists, there are a number of more specific cognitive constraints that define news values:

Novelty. The requirement that news should in principle be about new events is fundamental. Readers should not get information they already know, which is a general requirement of any speech act of assertion. Cognitively, this means that the model conveyed by a story must contain information not yet present in the current models of the reader. The result is possible updating of present models.

Recency. Not any new information is possible news. For news in the press, a further requirement is that the events described be new themselves, that is, recent, within a margin of between one and several days. Since models are representations of situations and events, recency is an important updating and retrieval cue of models, viz., by their time dimensions (things that have just happened). Also, recency is a major factor in attention, interest, and recall, both for events and for texts.

Presupposition. The evaluation of novelty and recency presupposes extant knowledge and beliefs. We have shown in detail why and how events and discourse can only be understood on the basis of vast amounts of old information. Hence, updating presupposes previous models about a situation. Understanding also requires the activation and application of frames and scripts. Much of this information in news may be left implicit. Yet, part of it must be expressed as a signal for what is presupposed. Journalists must assume that readers may not have read, or may have forgotten, previous information. Hence, presupposed information of a particular kind, that is, previous models, may need partial expression or summarization as background or context for actual events. We have seen that news schemata have special categories for such already known information. In other words, novelty in the news is limited. It is the tip of an iceberg of presuppositions and hence of previously acquired information. Also, complete novelty is by definition incomprehensible: Without previous models and schemata, we cannot understand what a news text is about.

Consonance. News should be consonant with socially-shared norms, values, and attitudes. This is a special case of the presupposition value. Instead of previous knowledge and beliefs, existing opinions and attitudes are involved. It is easier to understand and certainly easier to accept and, hence, to integrate news that is consonant with the attitudes of journalists and readers, that is, with the ideological consensus in a given society or culture. This condition needs qualification, however. News is also about persons, countries, or actions that are dissonant with our dominant attitudes, but (1) such news has less chance to be covered unless (2) it confirms our negative schemata about such persons or countries, and (3) the perspective of description is consonant with these schemata. Even then, the cognitive intricacies are far from straightforward for this news value. Although it is generally true that news stories are selected, which are consonant with the ideological consensus, this does not mean that dissonant stories are less newsworthy per se: They may be more interesting and memorable precisely because of their deviance from the consensus (see Deviance and negativity). Therefore, we should distinguish carefully between news values that pertain to news events and those that pertain to stories about such events. News may well be about ideological villains, if only their actions are shown to be consistent with this schematic role. We have given ample demonstration of this principle in our study of ethnic minorities and squatters (van Dijk, 1983a, 1987b). The same holds for the coverage in the Western press of the communist countries, to which we briefly return in the next section.

Relevance. In general, information is preferred about events or actions that are relevant for the reader. This information provides models that may be used for the interpretation of other discourse or for the planning and execution of social action and interaction. Interest for large groups of readers, thus, is both a cognitive and a social constraint on news selection. Apart from the many other criteria that select social and political news, relevance criteria show how events and decisions may affect our lives. News about unemployment or social services, laws, and regulations are examples of information that meets this condition. As with the other values mentioned here, the relevance criteria also have a counterpoint: News most certainly is not selected primarily according to its relevance, let alone its usefulness, for the reading public. For one, there may be many different groups of readers, with different interests and expectations. Hence relevance must be defined in terms of large or powerful groups. Minority relevance is much less emphasized. Second, relevance is also determined by the interests of those in control of the social system. There are large domains of information that would be highly relevant even for the public at large, but which are not or little covered by the press. Structural problems, for instance, do not meet many of the other criteria and, therefore, tend to be under-covered. Other relevant information may be threatening to the interests of those in power and, therefore, will not be released by precisely those sources from which the press appeared to get most information: the authorities. A recent example is the lack of information about radioactive fall-out in France after the nuclear disaster at Tchernobyl in May 1986: Since France has a large number of nuclear energy plants, it was clearly not in the interest of the authorities to risk increasing opposition against nuclear energy by giving out possibly disquieting warnings.

Deviance and Negativity. Best known perhaps is the general value of negativity of the news. That is, generally, much news discourse is about negative events such as problems, scandals, conflict, crime, war, or disasters. Why? Although intuitively, it seems a widespread, if not universal, phenomenon that people are interested in such news this does not explain why. Explanations may be given in sociological, psychoanalytical, or cognitive terms. Psychoanalytically, these various forms of negativity in the news might be seen as expressions of our own fears, and their incumbance to others both provides relief and tension by proxy participation. Models of such negative events, then, are directly meshed with the emotional system of self-defense, in which fascination with all that can go wrong is an effective preparation for evasion or protective action. In more cognitive terms, we might say that information processing about such events is like a general simulation of the possible incidents that may disrupt our own everyday lives. At the same time, such information is a test of general norms and values. Especially when deviance of various types is involved, it provides ingroup members with information about outgroups or outcasts and the application of a consensus of social norms and values that helps define and confirm the own group. This is a combination of a cognitive and sociological approach to the explanation of the role of negativity in the news. And finally, most models are about everyday routine situations and actions. Information about deviant and negative situations provides deviant models, which can be better retrieved and recalled due to their distinctiveness (Howard & Rothbart, 1980). This allows storytelling among readers about such news events because everyday stories also have a central complication category.

In other words, several independent factors favor negative news. Each of these factors requires extensive theoretical specification. But whatever the kind of explanation given, we find that the model representation of deviant or negative events plays a central role in cognitive, emotional, and social information processing of readers. Yet, this condition is not absolute. Whereas novelty requires previous knowledge, deviance, and negativity require conformity and positivity. Stories about problems, conflicts, or disasters also require happy ends. That is, in the simulation of possible problems, we also need models of problem solving, and the reestablishment of the goals, norms, and values shared in the group or culture. Hence, the special attention in crime news for the role of the police. And in disaster stories, we expect prominent attention to rescue operations and to heroes that solve the problem (as was the case for instance in the coverage of the Ethiopian famine in 1985). Negative news without positive elements of some kind is probably hard to digest. As for the other news values discussed, we need experimental research to test such hypotheses. Our cognitive framework provides a theoretical basis for the detailed specification of the predictions of such hypotheses in terms of journalistic and readers' selection, attention, comprehension, retrieval, recall, and reproduction of news information that meets these values.

Proximity. The value of local and ideological proximity of news events can be inferred from the various criteria we have discussed. Ideological proximity derives from general consonance criteria. Local proximity includes knowledge presupposition and relevance: We know most about our own village, town, country or continent, partly through direct experience and through informal communications about the experiences of others we know. Hence, media messages about close events are better understood because they are based on models that are more complete and more available (Kahneman & Tversky, 1973). Second, such news may be more relevant because it may provide information needed for direct interaction or other cognitive and social activities. Close events also yield better topics for story-telling in everyday conversation. The general necessity of information reduction not only leads to ready-made frames and scripts or to stereotypical attitudes but it also requires that our models of the world be kept within the boundaries of retrievability and updatability. If a general selection procedure is needed, therefore, the most relevant models,—those about close events—also have priority because they are formed and updated by other information: We know the locations, the circumstances, and many of the actors of such models.

This brief discussion of some of the news values that underlie the production of news in the press has shown that most values should be defined in interdisciplinary terms. They involve economic, macrosociological, microsociological, and psychological criteria of newsworthiness. We have shown, however, that in all cases a detailed cognitive reformulation is necessary to explain these various criteria. Only when we assume how news discourse and information is read, understood, represented, and used by journalists and readers can we show how social and economic interests and goals can be translated into the terms that define actual news production. Cognitive models and their underlying social schemata, attitudes, and ideologies appear to play a crucial role in the application of these values to the production and uses of news discourse.

A FIELD STUDY IN NEWS PRODUCTION

Set-Up of the Study

In the spring of 1984, a field study was carried out at the University of Amsterdam to explore and specify further some of the assumptions formulated in the previous sections. As part of their course requirements, a group of students was instructed to contact reporters of several newspapers in the Netherlands, with the request to follow them during their daily work for one or more days. The aim was to gather all possible source texts, different news article versions, as well as the final versions of published news articles. Source texts might include agency dispatches, other media texts, reports, official statements of politicians or other news actors, press releases, press conferences, phone calls, letters, interviews, or any other materials used by the reporter. Data also included scrap notes of reporters. Conversations, including interviews and phone conversations, were tape-recorded and partly transcribed.

Both national and regional newspapers and the national press agency ANP were asked to participate. Permission was asked first from the chief editor of the newspapers. There were considerable difficulties getting these permissions. Sometimes the editors simply refused or did not answer requests. Others were concerned about the extra work this might give their reporters. Often a feeling of suspicion was expressed regarding the aims of the research and about what might happen with data and results. One chief editor denied access to "his" newspaper (*De Volkskrant*) because of the earlier critical stance about race reporting in that newspaper by the researcher (van Dijk, 1983a). Whereas chief editors often displayed caution, reporters themselves were mostly very helpful. Although we finally obtained permission from a sufficient number of newspapers editors and reporters, it should be noted that access to news production processes by mass communication researchers is not always easy. It is very difficult, for example, to obtain natural and direct data about internal meetings or editorial conferences. Only when researchers already know a reporter or editor personally are such data easy to obtain. When a critical analysis of data is assumed, one might find all doors closed. Although such an attitude is understandable up to a point, it also sheds a different light on the widely claimed freedom of the press. Reporters must be able to access important news actors and institutions, even when their reporting may result to be critical. Apparently, for many newspaper editors this freedom does not extend to a comparable freedom of research. We have observed earlier during our various studies of the press that few institutions are more allergic to critical inquiry than the press itself. Unlike most other public institutions, they are not used to published criticism because the press seldom publishes critical analyses about itself.

Materials were collected from six national newspapers (*De Telegraaf, De Volkskrant, NRC-Handelsblad, Trouw, Het Vrije Volk,* and *De Waarheid*), and two regional newspapers (*Utrechts Nieuwsblad* and *De Gelderlander*), as well as from the national news agency ANP. Reporters from several newspapers were followed on their beat and during various news production stages. The amount of material collected was impressive, and its full analysis would require a separate monograph.

The various source texts were categorized, and, for those source texts that resulted in a final news item, a detailed analysis was made of the textual transformations defining the production process. This is relatively easy if written or printed source texts are available and have been used as a single source. This is usually the case for agency dispatches or when a written version of an important political statement is available. Much more difficult is the registration and analysis of all phone calls, talks with authorities, press conferences, and other spoken source data, and when multiple source texts are being used.

Types of Source Texts

The following types of source texts were immediately available to, and/or used by, the reporters (we ignore contents or specific names here; only source type and categories or functions of source actors are given):

1. Dispatches of international news agencies (AP, UPI, Reuter, AFP, TASS).
2. Dispatches of the national news agency ANP.
3. Dispatches of regional news services (GPD).
4. Letter from a school of social work to a parliamentary committee.
5. An agenda of the public relations office of the city of Amsterdam.
6. Press release of the city of Amsterdam.
7. A report of the Ministry of Internal Affairs.
8. A report about statements of the Minister of Internal Affairs.
9. Press releases of the National Public Relations Office.
10. Press release of the Ministry of Foreign Affairs.
11. Press release of large industrial firms.
12. Press documentation (previous articles) of the newspaper itself.
13. Notes of phone calls with various persons and organizations.

14. Daily press conference of a police spokesperson.
15. Notes made during a press conference.
16. Agenda and materials of meeting of provincial government.
17. Interview with press agent of province.
18. Agenda and materials of meeting of regional council for employment.
19. Agenda of the appeal court in the Hague.
20. Press release of school of medical assistants.
21. Letter of public relations office of province.
22. Press materials from a hotel in Scheveningen.
23. Article in another newspaper about hotel in Scheveningen.
24. Agenda and materials for a meeting of the personnel committee of the city council of the Hague.
25. Announcement of a press conference of the city alderman for economic affairs of the city of the Hague.
26. The daily agenda of Parliament.
27. Printed versions of planned interventions of various members of Parliament during a debate.
28. Notes of an interview with a representative of an organization for ethnic minorities.
29. Announcement of a theatrical play.
30. Press letter and copy of letter of minority organization to the Minister of Justice.
31. Letter of directors of state organizations for social work.
32. Phone call with the Ministry of Social Affairs.
33. Law on social welfare.
34. Agenda and materials of the meeting of the National Council for Social and Economic Affairs.
35. Information about a dog auction.
36. Notes of interview with organizers of dog auction.
37. Press release of organizers of a "freak festival."
38. Notes of interview with organizers of "freak festival."
39. Interview with police officials about a murder case.
40. Agenda of parliamentary/social economic desk of newspaper.
41. Text of media debate in Parliament.

Except from many other small routine phone calls and notes for colleagues, this is an approximate list of the various kinds of source texts used by reporters to write a dozen news reports. Although all this material was available on the desk of the reporters when they decided not to write an article about a given topic or when they actually wrote an article, a large part of the source texts was not used at all; those that did become sources were used only as fragments.

The variety of the list of source text types requires further categorization. For fairly routine days, such as those studied, reporters make use of the following kinds of information:

1. Dispatches of national and international news agencies.
2. Press releases of institutions, organizations, firms, etc.
3. Press conferences, including invitations for them.
4. Agendas and materials of a large number of legislative bodies, committees, and organizations.
5. Reports from various organizations.
6. Interviews with representatives of organizations.
7. Phone calls with representatives of organizations.
8. Notes of interviews, phone calls, press conferences, etc.
9. Official letters of organizations (often to other organizations), sometimes accompanied by documentation.
10. Articles in a variety of foreign and domestic newspapers.
11. Documentation, including of own newspaper (clippings).
12. Printed versions of speeches, interventions in meetings, and debates.

From this further categorization and reduction of the data, we may first conclude that source texts from state or city institutions dominate. These source texts themselves may be routinely preorganized: there are standard ways to distribute them, to put them on the agenda, or to prepare them; newspapers and reporters regularly receive such announcements (of meetings, press conferences, reports). Secondly, agencies and other news media play an important role in the preparation of news articles, and this preparation may include rereading clippings of previous articles in the same paper. Third, many news articles are based on several source texts and may include the typical combination of a preorganizer (e.g., an agenda, announcement, or invitation), source data about a main event (meeting, press conference, exhibition, etc), inclusion of notes of the reporter or documentation, and finally further talk, such as an interview or brief phone call with one of the news actors involved. Thus, standard domestic news production is characterized by order in the reception, acquisition, and uses of source texts. This order is defined by three major categories: preparation (invitations, announcements, agendas), main event text data (documentation, press conferences and notes about them, recordings, etc.), and follow-up or background text data (interviews or phone calls with news actors or representatives of organizations, documentation, etc.). A possible fourth category, control text data, including additional phone calls, double checking, talks with colleagues, etc., may also be considered.

From this brief analysis of source text types, it may be concluded again that the processing of source texts is a rather close image of the organization of news gathering routines themselves. Indeed, to a large extent, news gathering appears to be an effective set of procedures for the reception, acquisition, selection, reading, and further processing of source text data. News actors are selected for coverage depending on their capacity to produce source text data that meet both the professional requirements and the ideological values. At the same time much more information and texts reach the newspaper or its reporters than can possibly be followed, investigated, or written about. That is, much in the same way journalists organize their news production in a sequence of routines, the many other private or public organizations follow such routines, including sending statements or other texts to the media. These two systems interlock in complex and mutually dependent ways. This shows in somewhat more detail how and why the press produces and reproduces part of the political, social, and economic status quo. The organization of news gathering and source text management means that, to a certain extent, the press will be a mouthpiece of the organizations that provide the necessary input texts. The assumed freedom of the press consists in the possibility to voice interests of conflicting organizations, to make rigorous selections in the mass of offered text data on the basis of the news value criteria mentioned above, to pay limited or biased interest to noninstitutional events (e.g., protest demonstrations, squatters, strikes), and to transform the input data. Yet, when one examines empirical data about the total input of materials and their transformations, one also finds that this freedom is highly constrained. Even if actively solicited, alternative sources and source texts are not always available, and there may be no time for independent transformations of source texts. Moreover, noninstitutional sources or events may not pass the tests of credibility, newsworthiness or authority. In other words, our news, news production and newspapers are caught in the very web they have spun themselves to routinely and effectively gather their daily news.

Source Text Transformations

A selection was made of source texts and final news articles for further analysis and comparison. News agency dispatches, interviews, press releases, notes, and telephone conversations were analyzed into propositions and compared with the first and final versions of the news reports. Because of space limitations, we only summarize the general results.

1. In an analysis of dispatches of the national and regional news agencies and their processing by an editor of a regional newspaper, it was found that most agency material was copied without any changes in the six articles that resulted from the dispatches. Apart from a few minor stylistic changes, the only substantial changes appeared to be an addition about the historical background of new developments in the current political discussion about a third TV channel (the position of one of the parties involved) and an addition about the expected debate about the issue in Parliament. The latter information must have been drawn from the parliamentary agenda.

2. In an analysis of one item in a regional newspaper about a theater project, it was observed that the information was based upon three sources: (1) a press release of the organizers of the project, (2) an interview of the reporter with the organizer, and (3) a few notes made during the interview. It appeared that most information in the news report was drawn from the interview, with additional practical information from the press release. Instead of literal reproduction, the news item featured summaries of the statements made during the interview. Notes of the reporter are very brief and contain only a few brief key terms from the interview. Information based on these notes mostly appears in the news report. That is, notes seem to function as effective summarizers and retrieval cues. Quotes of statements made by the interviewed person are seldom literal but rather express the gist of what was said. The first and last paragraph of the news item are an introduction and a closure with practical information about the theater production.

3. Other media often serve as sources for news reports. The evening paper may use information from the morning paper, and vice versa. Thus, for an item about the imminent expulsion of a young Moroccan boy some information was used from the morning paper, but an interview was also held with an organization of migrant workers. Although notes were taken of this interview, except for a few words, no literal quotations were used. The reporter adds information from her general knowledge about earlier cases. Interestingly, the rather impersonal headline used in the first version of the news text, "ANOTHER EXPULSION OF YOUNG MIGRANT," is changed to the more personal headline YOUSEF (12) THREATENED WITH EXPULSION. This use of a proper name is important in the light of the current practice in which protests against actions of the immigration authorities in the Netherlands are often given a human touch by using the (first) name of the victim (for details of the media coverage of immigration, see van Dijk, 1987b).

4. An item about the increasing interest for business investments in the Amsterdam red-light district appears to be based on a meeting of a city council commission and its coverage by the national news agency ANP. Again, at crucial points, the reporter adds personal previous knowledge, which may provide explanatory background to the current events. Surprise from city officials about this is framed by the reporter's sentence "This street was run down in recent years because of the heroin traffic." Other items in the same newspaper were completely based on information from phone calls made with an organization of ethnic groups, with a city official, and a member of Parliament (of the same political persuasion as the newspaper). Information from these interviews was heavily summarized. Again, we find the reporter's own information when new information is added about the planned activities of the minority organization. In an article based on the information from the national news agency, the newspaper editor simply omitted the second part of the item. This confirms assumptions about a well-known practice during newsmaking, as well as the necessity of relevance ordering in news discourse: the most important information should be placed first.

5. In a comparison of another news item covering the parliamentary debate about a third TV channel, based on the declarations of the Minister of Culture and Welfare and various spokespersons of the major parties, it was first observed that the printed version of the item was identical to the first version of the parliamentary reporter in The Hague (except for the proposed headline). The rather formal and devious style of the Minister is transformed to a more direct and colloquial style in the news item (we translate literally):

> *Minister:* "If an increase of broadcasting time is discussed in the form of a third channel, the coherence should be extended such that the increase of broadcasting time during the day as it is being actually planned, also will be discussed in principle.

> *Newspaper:* "THIRD CHANNEL? NO EXTRA AIRTIME. If a third TV channel is coming, the planned airtime increase on Netherlands 1 and 2 will be off, as far as the cabinet is concerned."

6. When a final news report about the announced layoffs with a food company is compared to an earlier version of the article, a press release of the company, and a dispatch of the national press agency, we find that basically only the declarations of the company are printed in the final version. Declarations from union leaders, which were partly mentioned in the ANP wire, and which were also detailed at the end of the first version, are deleted in the printed version of the news item. Their low-level appearance

in the first version, which already suggests the relevance assigned to declarations of the unions may lead to complete deletion in the final stage of editing.

7. Another news report is based on a formal note of a minority organization, addressed to the Minister of Justice, about the legalization of "illegal Surinamese" in the Netherlands. This note is accompanied by a press release of the organization. Both serve as rather direct sources for the final news report: Large parts of the note are quoted literally.

8. Finally, several news items about social affairs were examined. They were based on ANP wires, which were followed sentence by sentence. The ANP items themselves, however, which were also traced to their sources during the field work, were based on rather long and technical minutes of a meeting of the Social Security Council, a letter to the Minister of Social Affairs, and an interview of the ANP reporter with a representative of the National Organization of Women on Welfare. Long passages from the minutes, the letter, and the interview are summarized in a few sentences. Only the decision of the council to investigate cases of discrimination against women is mentioned in the press accounts of two newspapers, whereas the detailed allegations of women's organizations (about how women are treated by doctors), are merely summarized by the vague and general statement that women's organizations "claim that there are many cases of discrimination."

From these examples, the following conclusions may be drawn:

1. News agency dispatches, when used, tend to be followed rather closely, if not literally, especially when no other information is available.

2. Press releases may be quoted literally, though only partially, whereas interviews give rise to summarizing and quasi-quotation. That is, the news item often suggests that a statement is made by a news actor as represented in the literal quotation marks, but such a statement is often a summarization by the reporter of the words of the news actor.

3. Complex source texts such as meetings, reports, formal letters, and quotes are heavily summarized and translated into a less formal style.

4. Statements or press releases of state or city officials, agencies, or of national institutions tend to be given more, and more prominent, attention than the reports or statements of groups or organizations of ordinary people involved in the official discussions or decisions (as is the case for women on welfare when they accuse a powerful male group, viz., company doctors). Similarly, the press release of a big firm about layoffs is printed, whereas the

critical remarks of union officials is completely deleted from the news report.

These few points suggest that the news production process is largely organized by effective routines of source text processing (selection, summarization, deletion, etc. of available printed materials and interviews). On the other hand, these routines are not just professional ways of handling large masses of source text information. Choices and transformations appear to have an ideological basis, as for instance when less powerful groups are given less or less prominent coverage.

Special Topics

A few special studies were made of the news production processes involved in the transformation of our source text data into final news articles. Results of these studies, which were carried out by students, are reported here only in succinct form.

Summarization. De Bie (1984a) studied in detail the role of summarization in the processing of press releases and agency dispatches. It was first found that the macrorules, discussed in earlier chapters in this book, appear to apply also to the summarization processes in news production. Second, it was found that several source texts and micropropositions of such source texts may be used in the construction of lead paragraphs, in which summarization is crucial. As soon as the news becomes more detailed, this construction rule makes a place for more direct selection, and hence reproduction, of source text details. When source texts are used, a considerable part of them is reproduced literally. Deletion is essentially governed by rule: Irrelevant details are omitted. Also, details may be omitted because they would make the final story too complicated. This could be called an instance of a simplification strategy. Notes made during interviews are much less integrated into news copy but serve as external memory aids for retrieval of information provided. Interviewing itself also prepares macroprocessing in that most questions of reporters are about rather general facts. Spoken source materials tend to be subjected more to reconstructive macroprocessing than written source texts, wich tend to be reproduced more directly after selection. In general, it may be concluded that apart from lead information, news articles are produced under the combined selection/deletion macrorules, especially when written/printed source texts are used.

Superstructures. In a study about the way schematic superstructures of agency dispatches are handled in news production, Coerts & Vermeulen (1984) compared eight news articles with 11 source dispatches from international and national agencies. An earlier version of the superstructure schema proposed in Chapter 2 of this book was applied, and it was first found that this schema is adequate for the description of arbitrarily chosen news articles. After the Summary category of Headlines and Lead, Main Events are the dominant category of the news episode, although the lead may already provide a first installment of the main event. Context and Background, Consequences, Verbal Reactions, and Comments follow more or less according to schema. Top-down realization appears in the installment delivery of the most important information (macropropositions) of each category in the episode. A quantitative analysis of the size of each category revealed that Context may occupy up to 30% of the space of news articles, followed by Main Events and Verbal Reactions (each about 15%). The other categories have much smaller percentages. Comparison with agency dispatches first shows that even when several agency source texts are used, only one agency may actually be mentioned. Also our other studies reveal that newspapers tend to be rather sloppy when mentioning their sources. Agency dispatches also exhibit the general news schema, except from Headlines, Lead, Previous Information, and Comments. Apparently, these are the kind of categories typical for news articles in the press: Headlines and Lead are omitted from dispatches for obvious reasons, and Comments are absent because of the intentionally factual nature of agency news, which must be used by many newspapers in the world. Although dispatches have no separately marked lead, their first paragraph(s) do seem to have lead functions: They summarize and introduce the events and name the major participants of the story. In agency news, too, Main Events come first before Context and Consequences. More than 40% of agency news was categorized as Context, more than 20% are Verbal Reactions, and only about 13% is Main Event news. In other words, both newspaper and agency news seem to have more Context than Main Event information, and both represent significantly the Verbal Reaction category. This tendency is even stronger for the agency material; much Context and Verbal Reactions is deleted in the final news article. The major semantic transformation of agency source texts is deletion: Fragments of Background and especially of Context and Verbal Reactions are omitted. Apart from small, though sometimes significant changes of style, it was also found that in news about food rationing in Poland, the newspapers tended to pay more attention to the negative aspects of the situation. In a comparison of a domestic news article about the media (a third TV channel) with the dispatch from the national news agency, it was found that the reporter inserted many personal evaluations and expectations about the political controversies surrounding this issue.

3. NEWS PRODUCTION   135

Agency and Newspaper Reporting of Eastern Europe. Rood (1984)
made a comparative analysis of all international agency dispatches available
to the Eastern European editor of a national newspaper and the actual news
published. In particular, Rood examined the general assumption that a
negative image is constructed in the Western press about the communist
societies in Eastern Europe. Most studies focus on the inverse portrayal:
How the West is described in the communist press (Lendvai, 1981; Merrill,
1983; Martin & Chaudhary, 1983). This schema contains propositions about
lack of civil rights, bad economic planning, oppression, international aggression, unpleasant daily circumstances of ordinary people (food or other short-
ages), etc. It appeared that of 19 different stories, only three were used.
These three stories all had a negative implication and confirmed the prevailing image about Eastern Europe: food rationing in Poland, tourists evicted
by the Russians, and complaints about the tensions between church and
state in Poland formulated by Cardinal Glemp. Not selected are stories
about political activities of Eastern European leaders, an earthquake in the
USSR, accidents, critique by media, and the arrest of people coming from
the West with propaganda materials. Of the three stories that were treated,
the agencies' neutral information was replaced in the newspaper by a more
negative presentation: Food rationing was abolished in Poland, but the
newspaper emphasized that still few articles were excepted. The article
about Glemp covered his visit to Argentina, and only a small part of it was
about Polish home politics. The tourists evicted from the Soviet Union
appeared to have distributed anti-Russian propaganda. Although source
texts are reproduced fairly literally, except for deletions, sometimes a more
negative style is used in the newspaper reports (e.g., uses of "sharp in-
crease", "by many", or "drastic" are words that do not occur in the agency
text). These data suggest that selection and use of agency material about
Eastern Europe by a national newspaper may contribute to the negative
enemy-image that most readers of Western newspapers, also in the Netherlands (though much less than in the United States) have about these countries. Events that would have been covered had they occurred in a Western
European country (e.g., a small earthquake) were not reported, and special
attention was paid to issues that confirm the oppressive nature of communist societies. This may also happen through the use of subtle stylistic
details, which contribute to the dramatization of the circumstances in Eastern Europe. For our study of news production, this means that newspapers
may further enhance tendencies in the coverage of the international agencies by specific (negative) selection and specific (negative) transformations
of source texts.

Quotation. In an analysis of the newspaper coverage of a speech delivered
by the President of the National Bank of the Netherlands who dictates

monetary policy and has much influence on government decisions, Pols (1984) examined how the words of the bank president were presented in the press. News articles about this speech from 14 national and regional newspapers were collected and subjected to analysis, and the results were compared with the contents of the printed speech. Of 200 newspaper sentences, 139 were selected for comparison with sentences in the speech. Some newspapers appear to have used the dispatch about the speech by the national press agency ANP. A study of quotation patterns first revealed that most sentences in the press (65) were indirect quotes, whereas the rest of the sentences were either direct quotes, marked or not marked as such. The most important finding is that for such speeches the press tends to faithfully reproduce the original (printed handout) of a speech, though often applying deletions and using much more literal quotes than suggested by the news article. Those passages with a clearly evaluative and stylistic implication are especially marked by explicit quotes. Apart from precision, vividness, or dramatic effectiveness, it may be concluded that quotation is often used to establish a distance between the newspaper and the person or opinions quoted. The use of communicative verbs in clauses that dominate embedded content clauses used in indirect discourse, sometimes express the evaluation of the reporter about the content of the speaker: "He criticized X by saying that . .", or "The Unions advocate . . . ."

Conclusions

The results of our case study seem to confirm extant hypotheses and observations about the routinized nature of source use and source text processing. Powerful and credible sources are used and quoted most, especially leading politicians, state and city agencies, and representatives of large organizations. The reporters appeared to receive massive daily information about the actions and decisions of such elite sources. They are most often covered and quoted in the continuous dispatches of the national and international news agencies. In addition, reporters receive many types of press releases, official notes, agendas, formal letters, invitations, etc. for public or press meetings in which the officials can communicate their opinions and actions. Press agency materials are widely used, whether of international, national or regional services and often copied rather closely when selected. Selection of dispatches takes place according to both the news value criteria in general and according to the particular ideology of the journalist or newspaper. Thus, Eastern European dispatches have a higher probability of being selected when they convey negative news. Less powerful groups or opposition voices receive less attention, lower relevance, and have the highest probability of being deleted. These findings generally confirm the results of the qualitative case studies we have reported in van Dijk (1987b) and further confirm and detail existing theories of news values in news production.

Structurally, news production is a function of the constraints previously formulated. That is, the various structural transformations of source texts to final news discourse depends on the (1) format of the news discourse; (2) the relevance of a given topic or issue; and (3) the various news values discussed earlier. Superstructures (schemata) of agency dispatches are similar to those of the final news discourse and largely specify Context and Backgrounds for central main events. But a Comments category is more typical for news discourse in the press. Most transformations of source texts can be adequately characterized in terms of macrooperations. For long and complex materials, deletion and constructive summarization is most common. Quotations are often constructed and seldom literal. Important news actors or source texts have higher chances to be quoted literally. Interviews and phone calls have various functions but tend to lead to summaries rather than to literal reproduction, except for opinions and comments, which may be quoted more-or-less literally in the Comment category of current events. Notes function as marginal external memory aids. Information retrieved through such note cues has a higher probability of inclusion in the final news discourse.

These general conclusions are tentative. Much more empirical work is necessary about the discourse processing of source texts and their transformation into final news discourse. It seems clear, however, that these transformations are not simply effective cognitive operations for fast news text processing or even processes that depend on the various interaction constraints of routinized newsgathering. Rather they are directly linked to the criteria derived from news values and other social ideologies of newsmaking.

4

NEWS
COMPREHENSION

INTRODUCTION

A psychological theory of news comprehension is a crucial component in an interdisciplinary theory of news. An analysis of news production and news discourse structures ultimately derives its relevance from our insights into the consequences, effects, or functions for readers in a social context. This chapter, therefore, focuses on processes of news understanding by the reader of news in the press. The cognitive framework sketched in the previous chapter will serve as our orientation. After a theoretical introduction and a survey of current research on news comprehension, we report first results of field and laboratory experiments about recall for news in the press.

Whereas the study of mass communication has generally paid much attention to the central issue of effects, comparatively little work has been conducted on the major conditions for such effects, namely the processes of reading, representation in memory, and the strategies of news information retrieval. Our understanding of effects on opinions or attitudes, and *a fortiori* those on action, presuppose such elementary insights. The cognitive interface between mass media messages on the one hand and behavior of the public on the other hand has been neglected within the traditionally behavioristic, stimulus-response paradigm of the study of media effects. It is not surprising, therefore, that no full-fledged, coherent theory of media effects could be formulated in earlier decades and that predictions of earlier theories were often conflicting. Sociological theories, as well as traditional social psychological models of the effects and uses of media messages, were ill-equipped to account for the detailed processes of comprehension and representation. We hope to show that a new and adequate cognitive framework can potentially remedy at least some of the shortcomings of effect studies. It is emphasized that an analysis of effects in terms of behavior is irrelevant or at most premature as long as other questions are not first answered. The reason for this claim is simple. Practically no social action is based on information derived uniquely from the media; therefore, it requires an independent social psychological and sociological account. More relevant is a study of how people use the media; from our perspective this means an analysis of the processes that are involved in the acquisition and modification of information due to the understanding of media discourse such as news.

We have stressed earlier that processing media information is not a purely cognitive affair, however. Understanding and representing news is at the same time a social accomplishment, if only because of the participation of the reader(s) in processes of public communication and because of the vast social knowledge and beliefs that are presupposed in these processes. Moreover, news is read and understood in social situations, featuring norms, values, goals, and interests that are socially shared. People usually do not read news just to update their personal models of the world but also because such models may be relevant for further social interaction, if only for daily talk about topics in the news. This means that, just as for a theory of news production, a psychological approach to news comprehension involves a theory of social cognition and a theory of the social contexts of news reading, representations, and use. This chapter, however, can only deliver an outline of half of such a research program, namely, its cognitive basis.

A THEORETICAL FRAMEWORK FOR NEWS COMPREHENSION

The cognitive framework sketched in the previous chapter is relevant not only for an account of news production but also because it forms the basis for a theory of news discourse comprehension. The general principles we have outlined apply not just to discourse comprehension in general but also for news understanding in particular. Interesting here, therefore, are the specifics of such a general theory as it applies to news in the press. Unfortunately, there is little empirical work that might serve as guidelines for the development of such a more specific theory. Although relevant, most work on news comprehension is about the comprehension of TV news. TV news discourse on the one hand is less complex than press news: Spoken news items are usually much shorter and in many ways have simpler organization. On the other hand, visual information such as news film, photographs, and stills of various forms plays only a secondary role in press news.

News comprehension involves several major steps: (1) perception and attention; (2) reading; (3) decoding and interpretation; (4) representation in episodic memory; (5) the formation, uses, and updating of situation models; and (6) the uses and changes of general, social knowledge and beliefs (frames, scripts, attitudes, ideologies). Strictly speaking, this is only part of a theory of news understanding. Also, the retrieval, application, and uses of news information should be added, if only as a necessary presupposition of the initial comprehension process: We can only understand news fully if we retrieve, apply, and use what we have learned from previous news reading experiences. The important concept of updating would be pointless without such an integration of previous experiences and, hence, without an account of what people do with news. Let us briefly comment upon each of the components mentioned above. Details are given in van Dijk & Kintsch (1983).

Perception and Attention. This obvious precondition for reading and understanding news discourse needs no special analysis here. Attention is constrained by communicative intentions, involving macroplans such as "I want to read the paper", "I want to read about X", etc., which are then located in the control system for further monitoring of the entire process. Adequate understanding requires nearly exclusive attention for a given news text, and attention given to any other information source in the communicative situation causes interference with textual processing. Perception processes of news text involve the identification of newspaper formats and news item layout and is matched with the visual information associated with our general knowledge about news articles in the press. Certain forms of advertising, stock market tables, or comics would not match the canonical schemata of news article form. Especially relevant for our discussion is the perception and primary categorization of headlines as salient factors in printing layout. Since most headlines are printed across the full width of a news article, they also figure in the strategies for the very perception and identification of news items. Third, news headlines are first and on top and for that reason are markers that monitor attention, perception, and the reading process: Readers first read headlines and only then the rest of news items. And finally, there are (for English and many other Western languages and newspapers) perception strategies that allocate and order attention to various parts of the newspaper page, e.g., from top to bottom, and from left to right, in the same order as general reading strategies. Note, though, that this is a general strategy. There may be many factors that influence such a strategy and, hence, also different perception patterns, such as the use of a big headline on another location of the page, the use of photographs, or the partial display of the page.

Reading. Reading is not an isolated process that can be separated from decoding and understanding (Laberge & Samuels, 1977; Spiro, Bruce, & Brewer, 1980; see also the references given in section 2 of Chapter 3). Reading involves all of these processes, including the distribution of attention and perception previously discussed. In a slightly narrower sense, then, reading means the specific voluntary act of decoding and interpreting a given text. That is, we can begin and stop reading such a text. We are concerned here with the overall reading strategies that control the various processes of decoding, interpretation, and representation. The first step in such a strategy would be, for instance, the reading of headlines. Interpretation of the headline may lead to a decision to continue or to stop reading the rest of a news report. This decision process involves matches with models and schemata, which feature previous knowledge and opinions about, or interests for, such special topics.

Skimming the newspaper is the effective strategy that consists of a series of such partial textual interpretations, which may be sufficient for global news processing; the output information from this process is fed to the decision process that may lead to further reading. The same process may reoccur during the reading of the rest of the article, however. That is, at any point a reader may decide that he or she is no longer interested or knows enough (has no more time, should allocate attention to other information in the situation, etc.) and stops further reading. This is not an execeptional strategy but probably the usual way of reading news in the press: It may be assumed that many news articles are read only partially. Moreover, reading time is often constrained, so that only a selection of articles is read.

These properties of news reading are crucial to the explanation of news discourse structure: The top-to-bottom, relevance hierarchy of news items both favors and is favored by such reading strategies. Even partial reading of the first part of the text provides most macropropositions and, hence, the most important information of the discourse. We see that time and attention allocation by readers in the context of newspaper reading is a partial explanation of news discourse structure and shows why news articles have such a specific form. Most other printed text types (novels, stories, manuals, textbooks, instructions, etc.) do not have this structure and do not have dominant strategies of partial reading. On the contrary, for several text types, such as crime stories, the last parts of the text may even be most important. The same may hold for the results or discussion sections of psychological articles. In other words, both structure and reading strategies of press news may be rather specific. The constraints, though, are social: Time, situation, and reading goals ultimately control the boundaries of variation in attention allocation.

Understanding. Since reading strategies first focus on the headlines of a news text, the first step in the understanding process is the decoding and interpretation of the headlines. According to our theoretical model, headlines and titles in general should express the most important or most relevant part of the macrostructure of the news article. Ideally, therefore, they are the expression of the top level of the macrostructure as it is expressed by the lead. The interpretation of the headline itself is the same as that of any other sentence: Surface structure decoding, syntactic analysis, and (at the same time) the semantic interpretation of words and phrases. This process presupposes the activation of relevant concepts, knowledge frames, or scripts, as well as of previous models about the same event, person, institution, or country. At the same time, new opinions are formed, or existing ones activated, about the event denoted by the headline. That is, as soon as the headline has been read and interpreted, the cognitive system is extensively prepared for (1) decisions to continue or stop reading and (2) the interpretation of the rest of the text.

The result of headline interpretation, then, is a propositional structure that is tentatively assigned macrostructural functions and that is, therefore, placed into the control system. The same holds for the activation, retrieval, and application of models, frames, and attitudes: Their macrostructures are also placed into the control system and facilitate further comprehension. That is, after reading and interpretation of the headlines of a news article, the control system should feature the following information:

1. Macrostructure of the context of communication (including type of context, identity of newspaper, goals of reading, opinions about the newspaper, news values).
2. Schematic (superstructure) of a news discourse, which allows the reader to recognize and evaluate the headlines as a Headline of a news schema in the first place.
3. A tentative semantic macrostructure fragment for the news article.
4. Macrostructural information about relevant situation models, scripts, or other schematic beliefs, such as opinions and attitudes about the denoted events and their components (types of action, participants, location, circumstances, etc.).
5. A partial reading plan, involving the decision to carry on reading, to read only a little bit, etc.

We see that even after reading a single headline, the control structure generated is already fairly complex. This allows much top-down processing, which facilitates reading and comprehension. It may be assumed, therefore, that reading headlines requires substantial resources and hence extra time. Once the control structure is established, sentences of the news text are easier to understand and represent in episodic memory: The overall topic, the relevant scripts, and the design for the actual model are ready.

In order to understand a headline, its grammatical structure must be analyzed. Articles and verb auxiliaries are often lacking, so that headline reading is impaired on a number of points. Compared to full sentences they may be more ambiguous, vague, or syntactically complex. This means that much processing is left over to semantic interpretation. Analysis is not so much syntactic as conceptual, much like in understanding telegrams. This means that strategic guesses about the model of the situation become very important: Many headlines can only be understood when we can guess the situation they describe. This guessing strategy is facilitated by the topical organization of news in the newspaper: Foreign or domestic news is often grouped together and, hence, provide preliminary interpretations about the news event category. Mention of a single name such as "Reagan", "Poland", or "Lebanon" is often sufficient to retrieve the appropriate schemata or models. And information in such schemata or models suggests what other information may be expected in the headline sentence. Lack of knowledge about local politics is often a major impediment to the full understanding of headlines in a foreign country, even if we fully master the foreign language. Hence, headline interpretation is not only a syntax problem but also a knowledge problem.

Once the headline is interpreted and the control structure established, the reader interprets the first words, phrases, and sentences of the news text. As stated earlier, this means that the reader processes a lead section, which may have the canonical function of a Lead category that, together with the Headline, has Summary function. In other words, apart from the local understanding of the lead sentence(s), its interpretation contributes to the further construction of a macrostructure for the text as a whole. This macrostructure is added to the control system and may even change the provisional main topic derived from the headline. After all, headlines may be incomplete or biased, by promoting lower-level macropropositions to a higher position in the thematic structure. Conversely, this biased topic may of course also influence the interpretation of lead sentences.

Lead sentence interpretation provides the more detailed specification of a provisional macrostructure of the news text. By definition, especially for news, this also means that the reader now knows the most important or relevant information of the news text to be specified in the rest of the article. The major time, location, participants, event or action, and circumstances are now known; and the outlines of the situation model can be created (or updated) in episodic memory. This special role of leads may be marked in many newspapers by special printing type or layout. Since the outline of the story is known after lead interpretation, the reading strategy may find a break-off point after the last words of the lead.

The interpretation of the rest of the text proceeds clause by clause and also by the formation of propositional structures, connected by conditional and functional relationships that define local coherence. This process takes place, both top down and bottom up, under the control of the information in the control system. This means that various specification relations are involved, as discussed in Chapter 2. Thus, for each macroproposition various details are assembled that specify the lower-level properties of events and actions and their participants. Locally, however, this process is not primarily linear but hierarchical: In each fragment of the thematic structure, the important propositions come first. The installment structure of news text ordering forces the reader to jump from one high-level topic to another and then again from an important detail of one topic to that of another. The additional control exercised here is that of the news schema categories: Each proposition is not only assigned to a topic but also to a schema category such as Main Event, Context, Background or Verbal Reactions. The comparatively difficult process of jumping between different topics is probably compensated by the canonical structure of the news schema. At the same time, the situation model highly facilitates the correct interpretation of a news text that has this kind of discontinuous structure. Experiments with jumbled stories have shown that adults are fairly good at interpreting incomplete or discontinuous texts (Mandler & Johnson, 1977). In general, it may safely be assumed that, as for discourse in general, the more we know about an event or topic, the better and easier we understand news discourse about it. If we already have a fairly complete model of a news event situation, new information can easily be accommodated into such a structure, even when the input discourse is rather difficult.

Representation. After processing in STM, textual structures are stored in episodic memory in the form of a textual representation. Although this representation is predominantly semantic and schematic, there are also traces of surface structure analysis: We may later remember on which page, where on a page, and under what kind of headline an article was displayed. Also, we may remember stylistic particularities. Yet, such surface structure memory usually has only secondary importance: It is the semantic information, the content, which is relevant for further processing. The text representation (TR) of a news discourse is hierarchical, with macropropositions on top and details below. Note that the discontinuous nature of thematic input need not be recorded as such. It is assumed that information from each topic is appropriately filed under its respective topical head. What is linearly ordered in installment style in the news discourse becomes reorganized to form a proper thematic structure. The actual TR is used to retrieve information as expressed in the news text itself. This is essential, especially during processing: The reader must know what information was given earlier in the text.

Yet, we have repeatedly claimed in this book, that the ultimate goal of information processing is the establishment of a situation model (SM) in episodic memory. This SM is a representation of the text situation and features general schematic categories such as Time, Location, Circumstances, Participants, Actions, and Events, each with their possible Modifier(s). For news discourse, understanding often means the retrieval and updating of existing models: When we read about Poland, Nicaragua, or Lebanon in the paper, we often already know the situation, and the actual text adds new information to such an SM. Since each situation, strictly speaking, is unique, their cognitive models are also unique, consisting of retrieved information from previous, possibly rather general SMs and the new information. This also allows the combination of several SMs. Thus, for our understanding of the news about the assassination of president-elect Bechir Gemayel of Lebanon in 1982 (see van Dijk, 1984b and 1987b), we construct a new SM from previous models about the situation in Lebanon (featuring various groups, the earlier civil war, etc.) but also use an instantiation of the assassination script. Photographs of the results of the bomb attack help construct such a particular, ad hoc model of the current situation. Later, when information must be processed about the election of a new president, this assassination model may again be partly relevant for understanding, for instance, when there is a brief reference to the previous event of the assassination.

Whereas the textual representation (TR) in episodic memory is organized by macrostructures and superstructures, which are both the input and the output of actual text processing, SMs have a general canonical form, consisting of the categories mentioned above. This allows the reader to strategically insert TR information at the appropriate places in the model. The terminal categories of the model may consist of information complexes that are themselves organized by macropropositions. For the many events in Lebanon stored in our Lebanon model, we need overall macropropositions that organize such events, for example propositions such as "There are armed conflicts between different Christian factions", or "The PLO left Beirut", which correspond to the higher level topics of, often, many previous stories about these events. Only under special conditions is it possible to retrieve details of these earlier events, for instance, when earlier particular models have not yet been integrated into more general models.

Recall that SMs are subjective. Unlike TRs, they also feature personal or group opinions about the events (van Dijk, 1982b). It is at this point that general attitudes and ideologies are brought to bear on the representation of actual events: Opinions are derived from new input information about the actual events and are formed under the control of activated general opinions (e.g., about assassinations) and attitudes (e.g., about the situation in the Middle East). Finally, ideologies organize the various attitudes into a more coherent whole. That is, our attitudes about the Middle East may be coherent with our attitudes about the East-West conflict and those about the role of the USSR and the United States in that conflict. This allows us to evaluate the role of the United States in the Middle East in general and Lebanon in particular. Even for quite diverse models and attitudes, the ideological framework assigns coherence to various general opinions, for example, about the PLO in the Middle East and squatters in Amsterdam. Ideologies, therefore, are the fundamental cognitive framework that organizes our frames, scripts, and attitudes. They represent our general views of society and involve overall themes, goals and interests, which again monitor our social practices. Unlike more personal models, such ideologies are group-, class-, or culture-specific.

Whereas these evaluative frameworks play an important role in processing and determine the subjective evaluation of news events by readers, they may also change due to the construction of new models. New information may lead readers to reevaluations, first of particular opinions, then of more general opinions if further information is consistent with this new opinion, and finally even of general attitudes. The latter changes are more complicated and hence more difficult, because they involve the restructuring of large amounts of beliefs and opinions. This is a fortiori the case for ideologies. Once established, the ideological framework serves such fundamental functions in all cognitive and social information processing, that changes in such a framework are usually slow, difficult and only partial.

This cognitive approach to the representation of news discourse in memory also provides the framework for a new and more explicit account of the famous effects of mass-mediated messages. We have suggested that such influences are never direct and that many steps, representations, schemata, models, and similar structures are involved. Particular opinions may be changed, but general opinions and attitudes take much more cognitive processing. And the latter are the real and more permanent changes that persuasion is all about (Roloff & Miller, 1980).

Finally, it should be stressed again that the processes previously described are essentially strategic. They do not operate according to fixed rules or at separate levels of analysis and understanding. Most of the processes take place simultaneously and mutually assist each other in the establishment of fast, effective interpretations. These are hypothetical until confirmed or denied. Syntactic analysis is assisted by semantic analysis and vice versa. Macrostructural interpretation is integrated with overall schematic analysis of news discourse; and all semantic processing is dependent on the activation and application of models, scripts, and attitudes. Such models and scripts are, of course, not applied as wholes but may be strategically applied only in part. Besides the vital role of previous beliefs and opinions during understanding of a text, there is also the concomitant interpretation of the communicative context and the social situation. These generate expectations about possible topics, schematic structures, and style. Indeed, when we start reading the newspaper, we already have good guesses about the possible news topics, formats of news discourse, or the (formal) style of news language we may find.

Understanding, then, is a complex integrated process of strategic selection, retrieval, and application of various information sources in the construction of textual representations and models. Once we have constructed an acceptable, i.e., relatively complete and coherent, model of the situation, we say that a newspaper item has been understood. This model may then be used for further generalization, abstraction, and decontextualization, that is for the formation of general models, scripts, and attitudes, on the one hand, and for the cognitive planning and execution of future action and talk, on the other hand.

A BRIEF REVIEW OF EXPERIMENTAL RESULTS ON NEWS COMPREHENSION

Whereas we lack systematic experimental evidence about the cognitive processes of news production, there is at least some psychological work on news comprehension. Within a tradition of mass media effect studies, on the one hand, and given the necessity of the news media to be understood by the public, on the other hand, such research can be expected. Unfortunately, most of this work is about understanding TV news (for recent surveys, see Woodall, Davis, & Sahin, 1983; Höijer & Findahl, 1984; Robinson & Levy, 1986).

Understanding Stories

Cognitive psychologists have dealt mostly with story understanding in general. Results of this work apply partly to the comprehension of news stories, although most work on stories involves very simple children's stories and seldom very long and complex storytelling. Since this psychological literature on story processing is vast, it cannot be reviewed in detail here. Two major directions of research in this area include the story grammar approach and the action theoretical approach prevalent in Artificial Intelligence work on story simulation.

Story grammarians believe that readers or listeners of stories make use of some kind of narrative grammar when understanding stories, much in the same way as they use a linguistic grammar when understanding sentences (Rumelhart, 1975; van Dijk & Kintsch, 1978; van Dijk, 1980a; Kintsch & van Dijk, 1975; Mandler & Johnson, 1977; Mandler, 1978). Narrative categories are used to analyze and order text segments of a story and help the representation of stories in memory. Such additional structuring of a discourse is also relevant during retrieval: Discourse segments that correspond to a narrative category (like setting, event, reaction, or similar general categories) can be retrieved better because language users can use the story grammar categories as a routine retrieval cue. If a story is presented in random order, readers are also able to reconstruct the original order due to the story schema (Mandler & Johnson, 1977). And finally, readers are able to judge whether a story is complete or well formed on the basis of such a schema.

AI researchers have maintained that story grammars are not real grammars and are not even necessary to account for the experimental results. They prefer to analyze stories in action theoretical terms, such as plans and goals (Schank & Abelson, 1977; Black & Wilensky, 1979; Wilensky, 1978, 1983; and the commentaries given about this 1983 article). That is, they not so much analyze stories as discourses but analyze the referents of the stories, namely action structures of human participants.

It has been stressed on several occasions (van Dijk, 1980c; van Dijk & Kintsch, 1983) that both orientations (1) are more similar than usually assumed; and (2) that both directions of research are relevant in an account of story comprehension. The action theoretical approach is necessary in an account of the knowledge presupposed during the understanding of stories: It provides the reader with scripts or models of what story topics can be, namely plans, goals, and actions of human participants. That is, an action theory provides the general semantic (referential) basis of story comprehension: It describes the structures of situation models for stories. The illustrations of this direction of research are often not stories in the strict sense but rather action descriptions, which also include the many routine actions we accomplish in daily life, such as taking a bus or eating in a restaurant.

Obviously, however, a story is more than an action discourse. First, it is about very specific actions, which involve problems, frustrated goals, and above all some level of interest. Such criteria might also be built in, and have been built in, by an action theoretical approach (Schank, 1979; Brewer, 1982). Even then, a story in the narrow sense may be organized in a different way than the actions it denotes. Permutations of events may occur; some information may be given only at the end of a story (as in crime stories); and much action information (e.g., about everyday routines) is presupposed, not expressed. Conversely, certain parts of stories are not represented in the action structure. For example, many stories begin with a summary, which is not part of the action structure. In addition, the initial description of a setting is not part of an action sequence. Finally, description may take place at several levels of specificity or generality: Interesting and important actions, events, or participants are described in detail, others only in macroterms. These are conventional properties of stories as a type of discourse and not characteristics of the action structures denoted by a story.

Thus, we must make a clear distinction between action discourse and action structure. The latter requires analysis in terms of models and scripts, the former in terms of textual rules and strategies or story schemata. Note, however, that for many story grammarians, the categories of a story grammar are also rather close to those of an action–theoretical approach, e.g., event, action, reaction, intention, or goal. We have already stressed that these categories belong to the base semantics or model theory of action discourse in general and not to the particular formal schema of story organization. Therefore, we prefer to work in a psychological framework with the kind of schematic categories we also have met for news discourse—Summary, Setting, Complication, Resolution, Evaluation, and Coda (Labov & Waletzky, 1967; Labov, 1972b, 1972c; van Dijk, 1972, 1976, 1980c). These story categories have a formal nature. They organize semantic macrostructure and are conventionally shared within a given culture. Kintsch & Greene (1978) showed for instance that Western readers have more difficulty understanding American Indian stories that do not have such a conventional, Western narrative schema. Although there is still much theoretical and empirical work to be done, we consider further debate about the relevance of story schemata or of action schemata rather fruitless. In a complete account of story understanding, we need both. The action theoretical approach is necessarily less specific: It accounts for action planning, execution, and understanding in general and, hence, for action and action discourse understanding in general. Specific genres such as stories need more specific schematic categories, and readers socialized in our culture use such categories and the strategies of their effective application in the understanding of stories.

Understanding and Memorizing News

We have briefly summarized this story work in psychology and AI because experimental work on news discourse has or will have similar questions to answer. For instance, do newspaper readers have and use an implicit news schema, learned by repeated reading and understanding of news discourse, or should we account for news structures simply in semantic or model–theoretic terms and terms relating to script? We propose that not only journalists but also readers have an elementary news schema. They know and recognize headlines and leads; they are able to identify the main, actual news event and its backgrounds and context; and they know that verbal reactions may be expected in a news story. These various categories are not ontologically or semantically necessary and cannot possibly be explained in terms of real, social, and political events or actions alone. The initial Summary (Headline and Lead) of news discourse is a specific, conventional news category. Let us see what evidence can be found for this and other properties of news understanding (see also Robinson & Levy, 1986, which appeared when this book went into press).

Thorndyke (1979) has been one of the few cognitive psychologists who explicitly tested hypotheses about the structural organization for newspaper stories. His earlier work (Thorndyke, 1977) assumed that stories have conventional schemata, which help understanding, representation, and retrieval. In the present experiment, a natural news story was read. In addition, a few other versions were read, which had narrative, outline, or topical form created by deleting or transposing irrelevant or redundant information from the original news item. Condensed versions of the news story led to better recall than the original news item. Yet, structural reorganization by itself did not lead to better recall when compared to versions of the news item that had news story structure but from which irrelevant information was deleted. In general, then, it was found that theme–relevant information in news stories is better processed and recalled than background and context or other extraneous information. The effectiveness of the structural organization also depends on the nature of the semantic content the perspective of the reader. That is, in a news story with historical developments and cause–consequence relationships, a narrative schema might be more effective for the comprehension and recall of information. For the description of actual events and their consequences, a news story organization may be more relevant. In other words, Thorndyke concludes that each genre, content, and perspective may require different schematic organization patterns.

Goal-based perspectives are an especially powerful factor in the understanding and representation and, hence, the recall of news stories (see also Anderson & Pichert, 1978). This perspective, we suggested, is primarily represented in the control system and monitors the understanding of a story. In other words, a presumably nonfeminist oil baron and a feminist follow the developments in present-day Iran with different presupposed interests and beliefs, which will create different perspectives on the same story about events in Iran. Finally, it should be noted that the notion of typical news story structure is not made explicit by Thorndyke in an explicit set of rules or a categorical schema.

Although Thorndyke's textual variations do not produce real alternative text genres, making the results of his experiment open to challenge, we concur with his conclusion that there are alternative organizational schemata. Thus, we have some confidence in the assumption that news schemata exist in the sense that they may be used for the processing of news text. We have found in our case studies (van Dijk, 1987b) that sometimes narrative organization forms may be used in the news, and that in these cases, they may be most effective for processing. Thorndyke also observed that news discourse contains numerous topic changes. These require much repetition and redundant information, so that readers can keep track of the main topics. Our assumption that macrostructures are generally recalled best, more-or-less independently of their linear organization, therefore, seems warranted. This is especially true when such macrostructures are specifically signaled, as is the case for the headline and lead in news discourse. However, it may be asked whether the conventional organization of the body of news items in discontinuous installments is the optimal form of news structure for comprehension (see also Green, 1979). The headline, lead, and highly repetitive structures apparently must compensate for much disorganization, which must be unscrambled by the reader. It is possible that a combination of relevance structuring (headlines and lead) together with a narrative organization of the news story might produce better understanding. Indeed, this is the writing strategy of much of the popular press.

It is also interesting to see that further details in a news story do not seem to contribute very much to the understanding and recall of the major topics. This finding confirms research done by Reder & Anderson (Reder & Anderson, 1980, Reder, 1982). Although these studies analyzed educational materials, the researchers found that whatever elaborations are given to a central topic, recall is not better for a long text with many details than for the summary or outline of such a text. On the contrary, sometimes elaborations may even make overall understanding and recall more difficult.

For news discourse, this would suggest that reading the headlines and the leads would produce the same recall effects as reading the whole news stories. In that case, people just skimming the paper would recall just as much. These findings agree with our earlier work which showed that, after some time, people are able to retrieve only the macrostructures of a text (van Dijk & Kintsch, 1978, 1983; Kintsch & van Dijk, 1975, 1978; van Dijk, 1979). It should be added, however, that although recall of a particular text is indeed based on macrostructure, with only occasional retrieval of lower-level details, local understanding of a news story contributes predominantly to the formation of situation models. Whereas a macrostructure will be sufficient for the activation and top-updating of a model, it certainly is not sufficient to build in the details of a concrete model. These more complete models, even when not directly retrievable as wholes (which was never tested because all experiments ask for textual, semantic recall), are very relevant for the updating of general knowledge. Repetition of details and more complete models should also contribute to better cognitive integration of new information. In other words, more work is needed about other cognitive effects of news story reading, even though it seems rather well established that people in general do not remember more than the main topics of a news article. Other evidence suggests that under special circumstances readers also note salient details. A purely schematic and thematic macrostructure approach cannot explain such special memory for striking details, which was already observed by Bartlett (1932) (see also van Dijk & Kintsch, 1978).

Larsen (1980) did a series of experiments on the comprehension and recall of radio broadcast news, in which he focused on the notion of updating. Larsen also wonders whether we should adopt a special news schema that guides news story comprehension. He does not provide such a schema but suggests that the event–action structures of work on stories might act as a possible framework. Against the background of the text processing model of Kintsch & van Dijk (1978), his experiment with radio news items shows first that in general people do not remember more than about 20% of the propositions of the original items. Katz, Adoni & Parness (1977) found similar percentages of recall. Later items in bulletins are recalled even less. This primacy effect is found in much other work on text and information recall. Larsen also found that there was a significant levels effect: First propositions in the news items (typically lead sentences) are recalled much more often than the later sentences. Apparently, primacy and macrostructure effects combine to produce better recall. At the local level of processing, propositions that must be kept in the STM buffer (the control system)—typically macropropositions or presuppositions that guarantee coherence—are recalled up to 40% of the time. Overall macropropositions appear to be recalled three times as frequently (33%) as micropropositions (11%). The effect of conventional narrative categories in news stories appears to favor the setting category the most and, the complication category least. In other words, best remembered are places and people of news events and much less what actually happened. This setting information was also found to be best known by the subjects. This suggests, according to Larsen, that previous knowledge indeed favors recall from news items: Known information generally is recalled at a rate greater than 30% (where "known" is defined as known to more than 50% of the listeners), whereas less-known information usually does not reach 20% of recall. Similarly, the really important new events in news items were generally recalled less than 20% of the time. Larsen concludes that knowledge updating from the news is quite modest. People tend to recall what they already know; even major new developments or causes of the actual events are frequently forgotten. These results are generally consistent with much earlier work on complex story recall. It should be added, however, that subjects in Larsen's experiments had to listen to and recall four different stories. Single-story recall might be expected to be somewhat better.

The generally poor recall of news items was also found in Katz, Adoni & Parness's (1977) study of radio and TV news items. Up to 34% of radio listeners of a seven-item bulletin could not recall a single item (21% for TV news stories). Higher education appeared to enhance recall in both cases. Pictures do not seem to contribute much to recall: TV news was only slightly better recalled. It should be emphasized that listeners and viewers were doing other things when they heard or saw the news. Hence, these results should be interpreted as data for casual understanding, which is undoubtedly the usual way of news processing in everyday life. Katz et al. also found that domestic items are recalled better than foreign news items, but adding pictures enhances memory for foreign news. News values such as negativity, surprise, and meaningfulness (Galtung & Ruge, 1965) predict better recall, which suggests that such values are shared by journalists and readers. Katz et al. also find a primacy effect: First items tend to be better recalled (which may be partly explained by the factors that condition first position, such as importance, seriousness, or high newsworthiness). Also, longer items are better recalled, which would be at variance with some of the results previously mentioned, where macrostructures are more important than details for recall (but again, longer news items are usually about more important events). In a simple understanding test for key notions from the news, 50% of the uneducated and 35% of the educated subjects did not understand basic news concepts, whether or not they had heard or seen the news. Questions about the causes and conditions of news events appeared to be too difficult to answer for most people. Finally, there was some marginal evidence for the unexplained assumption that viewers tend to agree more with political opinions about the news events than listeners. These various findings also lead to the general conclusion that only fragments of the news are recalled and understood by media users, and that only a few factors may facilitate processing (education, item primacy, news values, and topic category). Differences between radio and TV news are not dramatic, and film barely contributes to recall.

Russell Neuman (1976) asked people in San Francisco what they recalled from the dinner hour TV broadcast news. Of an average of 19.8 stories. viewers recalled only 1.2 stories without help (retrieval cues), whereas half of the respondents did not remember any story at all. When recall was cued by news topic, approximately 20% of the people did recall the item, and about the same number of respondents could recall further details. Having a college education only slightly influenced recall. The same was true for motivation: Those who watch the news to keep informed hardly performed better. People who are most motivated did not appear to have better recall for the more abstract political stories but did appear to do better on human interest items. The weather report and human interest stories have best overall recall (aided and unaided), but Vietnam stories were best recalled when no help was given by the interviewer. Retrieval cues on that topic did not produce more recall than retrieval cues for the other stories. Again, we find that for TV news, overall recall is very low (4%) although recognition scores are usually higher, though seldom more than 40%. According to cognitive theorizing, recognition is different from spontaneous recall: In recognition, a given topic acts as a powerful retrieval cue for macrostructures and models of news event stories.

That different experimental designs may lead to rather different outcomes is shown in the experiments of Gunter (1983), who found that people recalled up to 70% of items in sequences of four groups of three items. Yet, he also found the primacy effect we have encountered: Recall of later items drops to between 40% to 50%.

A more indirect, correlative study was undertaken by Schulz (1982) into the interdependence of media use and knowledge about news events. Frequency of media use, especially viewing political TV programs, reading more than one quality newspaper, and listening to the radio correlate significantly ($>.40$) with recognition and recall (both by mentioning and identifying events). Similarly, there are significant positive correlations among various news structures or presentation forms and the awareness about news events. Frequency of coverage about an event is the best predictor of awareness, followed by maximum and mean length of TV stories in news programs. The same holds for the role of interest for and participation in political affairs. Schulz also found that the news values that define newsworthiness tend to correlate positively with such prominence features of the news. Thus, elite persons and relevance (consequence) correlate highly with position and length of news items. The same is true for valence factors such as controversy and success, and predictable and stereotypical dimensions of news events, as well as proximity, emotional content, uncertainty, and unexpectedness. Similar correlations were found between news values and people's awareness of news events. Only controversies, which are emphasized in the news, are less prominent for media users, whereas the converse is true for proximity. In other words, most news values that underlie the news predict people's awareness of news events. This confirms the conclusion of Katz, Adoni & Parness (1977) that news values are shared by journalists and media users. An important exception to this observation is that journalists tend to pay more attention to distant events and controversies than the news media public.

Much of the work on news comprehension has been done in Sweden by Findahl and Höijer mainly on TV news. Their recent doctoral dissertations (in Swedish) are the only book-length treatments of news understanding and comprehension (Höijer & Findahl, 1984; Findahl & Höijer, 1984; but now also see Robinson & Levy, 1986). Their theoretical framework is similar to the one sketched earlier in this chapter. Their experimental work focuses on variations in presentation of the news and its effects on comprehension and recall. Thus, in an early experiment with radio news, they investigated whether additional verbal information would affect understanding (Findahl & Höijer, 1975). This is important for our discussion because experimental work reviewed previously suggests that, in general, additional details are forgotten: People tend to recall only the major topics. The authors found that whereas recall of the basic message was 25%, adding information about location, participants, causes, or effects boosted recall to values between 30% and 40%. Specification of causes and consequences not only improve recall for these aspects of the news items but also appears to enhance overall recall of the item. In other words, there is a structural effect on news comprehension if coherence is further detailed (typically with information that helps to build models of the situation). Listeners do not have different evaluations of such extended versions: At most, the longer items were found to be somewhat more thorough and less simplistic, as might be expected. There were no differences in ease of understanding. Findahl & Höijer later (1981a, 1981b) explained in more detail the event structures underlying news items, and found that in general some dramatic highlights and major actors may be mentioned in the beginning of an item, but precise conditions and consequences (e.g., in industrial disputes) are not made clear due to the complex arrangement of facts.

The general relationship found later by Schulz (1982) between overall political knowledge and recall of the news was also established by Findahl & Höijer. Simply, those who do not know where Peru is do not remember a news item about Peru. Individual differences in both knowledge and news retention separate middle-aged men with college education from women without college education. That relevance is a major criterion for comprehension and recall may be concluded, however, from the finding that this group of women better recalled news items about the kind of everyday life issues they are confronted with (rising prices, maternity benefits, etc.).

Unlike Katz, Adoni & Parness (1977), Findahl & Höijer (1976) found evidence for the role of pictures in the comprehension of TV news items. Especially when the important structural relationships of cause and consequence are illustrated with special pictures or additional information, recall generally improved. The picture of the situation, that is, what we call a model, seems to be better structured in this way. Recall of consequences, for instance, may go up from 10% to 43% in such cases. News locations are found to be recalled best in general, but a map of a country may improve recall from 45% to 61%. It should be added, however, that later content analyses of news recall (mentioned briefly in Findahl & Höijer, 1981b) show

that people have serious difficulty understanding major relationships because TV news focuses on spectacular events and neglects important
backgrounds.

Turning from conditional factors of comprehension to effects of news
comprehension, the two Swedish authors also found that news items tend to
be confused. Disturbance after a demonstration in Paris may be inserted
into a news item about an environmental bicycle demonstration in Sweden
(Findahl & Höijer, 1973). Against the background of the current notion of
script, this reconstructive recall can be explained easily by the role of models
and scripts of demonstrations, in which civil disturbances are often associated with demonstrations in the press (Halloran, et al., 1970; van Dijk,
1987b). The authors conclude that, in general, news is especially relevant
for the initiated. Contents, presentation, and news values favor those media
users who already know much about the events presented in the news.
Complex relationships within news events tend to be mixed up, if recalled at
all, and generally confuse viewers. This promotes selective attention for the
more dramatic headlines of the news.

Finally, a recent study by Graber (1984) on news processing provides
results of a vast project in which panel media users from the Chicago area
were asked what they remembered of newspaper and network news. Only a
summary of a few major findings of the study, which was partly similar to
ours in its theoretical orientation, can be presented here. The panelists were
categorized into combinations of high- or low-access and high- or low-
interest groups and subsequently interviewed at length about previous news
items. Graber used the massive data from an earlier project, in which some
19,000 stories of the *Chicago Tribune* and about 4,000 stories of each
national network were content analyzed. In the *Tribune* most of these
stories (47%) are about government or politics (mostly about national politics), followed by 28% about various social issues, 14% about economics,
and 10% about human interest; the national networks gave somewhat more
emphasis to national politics and less to social affairs.

Although the panelists generally said they depended most on TV for their
news, information from their diaries revealed that, in fact, 48% of the stories
were derived from the press, 27% from TV, 9% from radio, 8% from
conversation, and 6% from news magazines. These data further support our
initial assumption about the continued importance of the press for news
information. On average, the panelists read one third of all press stories
(especially from the first five pages of the paper), of which more than half
were read completely. Generally, panelists indicated that personal, social, or
job relevance, as well as interest and emotional appeal, were major reasons
for reading a story.

Up to one month, nearly all of the panelists remembered a specific story,
and concrete questions could still be answered for 23% of the stories. Of the

topics recalled and mentioned in diaries, individual crime, the judiciary, and disasters together make up about 40% of all topics (similar percentages were found for the press and TV). Topics such as education, the Middle East, or business crimes each usually score below 5%. In other words, people remember best the kind of emotional stories that also underlie everyday stories and fiction and much less often the more abstract or distant topics. On the other hand, most panelists were relatively well aware of the political issues, such as the stands of candidates from the presidential elections of 1976. Generally, the high-interest and high-access groups remembered several facts from each topic. People who already know much about the news also learn most from it. Forgetting rates, especially for the low-interest or low-access groups, are highest for information about Congress, state politics, the police, corruption, education, and business. Negative stories (crime, terrorism) and relevant stories (energy) are usually best recalled.

Conclusions

From the limited amount of psychological work on news comprehension and recall, a few general conclusions may be drawn:

1. Recall of radio and TV news is generally low. Unaided recall for news in natural situations may be less than 5% of items in a broadcast, whereas recognition may be at most about 40%. In more controlled conditions, recall may be higher (from 20% to 40%).

2. Generally, previous knowledge, either by education or special interest for issues or topics, improves comprehension and recall. Frequent occurrence in the news of given issues tends to contribute most to people's awareness of political events. This also means, however, that people especially tend to recall the information they already knew. Other factors that influence comprehension, attention for specific topics, and hence subjective recall besides knowledge, especially are interest and perspective.

3. Presentation and textual factors that enhance recall are primacy, the verbal or pictorial emphasis of structural factors like cause and consequence, coincidence with general news values, and a number of content characteristics that express such news values (proximity, relevance, unexpectedness, etc.). Important, too, is the existence of a news schema or similar (e.g., narrative) schemata that organize the understanding of news events.

4. In general, macrostructural topics tend to be best recalled. Details are usually poorly understood and are, hence, forgotten. Condensed versions of news articles are understood better than more detailed versions. Yet, under certain circumstances, adding details about

important structural dimensions of news content (e.g.. causes and especially consequences) may help understanding and recall.

5. Generally, people remember best the kind of negative or spectacular stories that also define everyday and fictional storytelling, and/or that have most emotional appeal or everyday relevance: individual, street crime; accidents; disasters; etc. Although national politics is remembered fairly well (e.g., election coverage), more abstract and distant political topics tend to be forgotten.

Most of these findings can be integrated easily into our theoretical model and in fact confirm most of its predictions. Although most results pertain to TV news, we have reason to believe that they are also true for newspaper news. Macrostructures, schemata, detailed models, general world knowledge (scripts), attitudes, perspectives, and news values are the major determinants that account for variance in news comprehension and recall. Those features of presentation and structure that help organize these representations (titles, headlines, primacy, pictures, etc.) favor retention. Social context factors, both structural ones such as education, and ad hoc ones such as amount of attention, can be translated easily into these overall cognitive dimensions. To specify these findings for news retention in the press, let us finally examine some data collected in our own studies of news recall.

AN EXPERIMENT ON NATURAL NEWS COMPREHENSION

To test some of the theoretical notions and their empirical predictions outlined in the previous sections and chapters, a field experiment was carried out in Amsterdam. Two well-known morning newspapers, *De Telegraaf* and *De Volkskrant*, were chosen as sources for collecting data about reader's memory for news. The experiment consisted of three main parts: (1) a free recall interview; (2) a delayed recall interview after two weeks; and (3) a control experiment in the laboratory, using the same materials. The overall aim of the experiments was to obtain data from natural news comprehension and recall because much work on news comprehension is performed in the laboratory or within strictly controlled field experiments. We wanted to be sure that recall post hoc was based on casual, everyday newspaper reading. To establish possible similarities and differences with controlled reading and recall, an additional laboratory test was performed.

Materials

Four articles about the same topics were selected from both *De Telegraaf* and *De Volkskrant* of Monday, March 12, 1984. A Monday was chosen so as to avoid interference with stories in the evening papers of the previous day.

The four articles were about different topics, both on domestic and on foreign news, so that different interests and knowledge of readers would be addressed. The four topics were:

1. Debate among political parties about admitting a third TV channel (the TV-III text).
2. Results of a poll about the preferences of people for a successor of the present social-democratic opposition leader den Uyl (the Poll text).
3. A report about South Africa's willingness to participate in a peace conference on Namibia (the Namibia text).
4. A sport item about soccer fans' criticism of the trainer of a Dutch soccer team, which was defeated 1-7 by another soccer team (the Soccer text).

The first three items appeared on the front page and on the domestic news pages and were all rather prominent. The two newspapers were chosen because of their different style and political–ideological stance: *De Telegraaf* is a conservative, popular newspaper, with the largest number of subscribers/readers in the Netherlands (about 750,000). *De Volkskrant* is a moderately liberal newspaper, widely read among the members of the (social–democratic) center–left and has about 280,000 subscribers. Together, these newspapers serve about 40% of the readers of the national press.

Subjects

Subjects of the field study were divided into two groups. The first group consisted of a heterogeneous set of average readers, selected at random by house calls of interviewers in different parts of Amsterdam. The second group were administrative staff members of the University of Amsterdam and, therefore, more homogeneous regarding education, interests, and perhaps reading behavior. Since *De Telegraaf* readers, who are generally more conservative, are more difficult to find among the University staff, we found fewer readers of that newspaper ($N=21$), than for *De Volkskrant* ($N=33$). Twenty-three readers were women, and 31 were men.

Procedure

Readers of both newspapers were approached during and after lunchtime of the same day by interviewers, who were students taking part in a course on news comprehension. Each student interviewed an average of five readers. Readers were asked whether they were willing to "help the student with a little research project, carried out at the University of Amsterdam." If the answer was positive, they were asked which newspaper they read, and if *De Volkskrant* or *De Telegraaf* was mentioned, a brief standard interview was conducted to collect some demographic data and information about their media behavior. Next, interviewees were asked if they had read the newspaper that morning and if they had, which articles they remembered. Finally, a tape-recorded, free interview was conducted that asked readers to tell in their own words all they could remember of the four stories previously mentioned. Each story, whether spontaneously recalled in the listing question or not, was identified by a brief reference to its major topic. The interview was tape-recorded to analyze all information from the readers in detail, including hesitations, errors, and especially expressed retrieval strategies. It was hoped that this would allow us to examine underlying processes of representation, retrieval strategies, and recall, as well as details of the style of reproduction. Reproduction style is important to learn how readers retell news stories, that is, how stories may be used and reproduced in natural contexts.

General Demographic and Media Use Data

Age. *De Volkskrant* readers were generally younger than *De Telegraaf* readers: Only 6 of 33 readers were older than 40, with ages ranging between 19 and 52, whereas for *De Telegraaf,* 12 readers out of 21 were older than 41, with ages ranging between 23 and 74.

Education. The general education level of *De Volkskrant* readers appeared to be higher. Of 33 *De Volkskrant* readers, 18 had higher education (University or similar), and all others, except one, had a high school diploma. Only 5 out of 21 *De Telegraaf* readers had higher education, whereas most others had middle education diplomas.

Occupation. Of the *De Volkskrant* readers, 10 were administrative staff, and the other occupations were usually distributed across the professions (including teachers, computer programmers, therapists, social workers, etc.). Three readers were students, and three were jobless. *De Telegraaf* readers were more heterogeneous and included all occupations, from housewife, to musician, administrative assistant, secretary, technician, and shopkeeper. There were no students among these readers, and only one was jobless. The overall occupational level was only slightly higher for *De Volkskrant* readers, and especially included various types of civil servants in administration, social work, or education.

Location. The interviews of *De Volkskrant* readers were mostly carried out on the job at the University of Amsterdam or at the homes of the readers.

Some were held in public places like cafés, waiting rooms, or offices. *De Telegraaf* readers were mostly interviewed at home, at work, or in public places.

Media Use. Most (12) *De Volkskrant* readers also regularly read another newspaper, namely, the quality evening newspaper *NRC-Handelsblad;* whereas *De Telegraaf* readers read *De Volkskrant* (9x) as a second paper. Of the 33 *De Volkskrant* readers, 11 read the newspaper practically every day for between 10 and 30 minutes, and 14 spend between 30 to 60 minutes reading the paper. *De Telegraaf* readers take on average some more time for the paper (between 45 and 60 minutes). *De Volkskrant* readers more often watch TV news regularly (19 vs. 14 respectively) which is similar for Telegraaf readers (12 vs. 9 readers). Only a few readers (about three or four) from both groups also regularly watch other news programs (which provide longer background items about recent news issues). The proportion of radio news listeners is higher for *De Telegraaf* readers (9 of 21) than for *De Volkskrant* readers (6 of 33). Conversely, more *De Volkskrant* readers (11) than *De Telegraaf* readers (4) also regularly read a weekly news magazine, which in the Netherlands is the major source of background articles. Surprisingly, readers of both newspapers preferred to read the more liberal weeklies.

Newspaper Reading. Apart from a few special items, such as columns and comics characteristic of each paper, 19 *De Volkskrant* readers indicated that they usually read about various topics, the front page, and domestic news; 12 have special interest for the arts pages; and only 8 for foreign news, 5 for economic affairs, and 4 for the sports pages. Similar proportions were found for *De Telegraaf* readers, except for sports, which interests 10 out of 21 readers, as well as several human interest and crime story categories, which are typical for that newspaper.

Women and Men. There are few overall differences between men and women for these various data. For *De Volkskrant,* men tend to read more often another serious than another popular newspaper, take longer to read the paper, watch less TV news, hear less radio news, and read more weekly news magazines. For *De Telegraaf* there are no marked differences in media behavior between men and women. As for the various news categories, male *De Volkskrant* readers read more foreign and domestic news, more economic affairs, and more sport news. For *De Telegraaf* readers there are fewer differences, except that more women read domestic news, and no women read economic news.

Today's Newspaper

Reading Time. *De Volkskrant* readers of this Monday took much less time reading the newspaper than they indicated as their average reading time: 25 of 33 Volkskrant readers say they read the newspaper within 30 minutes, and the same is true for *De Telegraaf* (14 of 21). Most readers read the newspaper first a little bit in the morning at breakfast and continued reading at or after lunchtime. Few readers still read the morning paper during the evening.

Reading Location. The newspapers were mostly read at home or at work and in various public places (train) in about equal distribution for *De Volkskrant* readers. *De Telegraaf* readers do this mostly at home and much less at work or in public places.

Reading Style. Most *De Volkskrant* readers said they read the paper uninterrupted whereas *De Telegraaf* readers read in installments. About half of the readers of both newspapers reported that their reading that day was superficial, whereas only one third of the readers read attentively. Only a few readers of each paper talked about the news with others.

Categories. What was read that morning was in agreement with the categories usually read: front page, domestic news, and foreign news in that order. Almost all *De Telegraaf* readers had read the sports pages that morning, whereas only four *De Volkskrant* readers had done so. The latter read less art news than they usually do (the Monday newspapers have little art news and much sports news, mostly as a separate sports section). *De Telegraaf* readers also pay more attention to the advertising section, which is most extensive in the Dutch press.

Newspaper reading of that Monday was not markedly different from general newspaper reading habits. The only difference was that male *De Volkskrant* readers read less economic news than usual.

Overall Recall

Table 4.1 indicates the number of readers who remembered the four articles in each of the two newspapers. The data for this analysis were obtained for more readers than for the demographic figures given previously (data collected and analyzed by de Bie, 1984b, and Hermans, 1984).

From this table, we may first conclude that except for the soccer item, the percentage of readers who recall the respective items is about the same.

TABLE 4.1.

Recall of Four News Items by Two Groups of Newspaper Readers

Newspaper	Category of Recall	Articles			
		TV III	Poll	Namibia	Soccer
Volkskrant	a. Recalled by	25 (66%)	21 (55%)	7 (18%)	5 (13%)
(N=38)	b. Total facts	310	225	61	27
	c. Facts/reader	12.4	10.7	8.7	5.4
Telegraaf	a. Recalled by	16 (64%)	14 (56%)	5 (25%)	18 (72%)
(N=25)	b. Total facts	149	136	26	105
	c. Facts/reader	9.3	9.7	5.2	5.8

As expected, there are more *De Telegraaf* readers who recall the soccer item but also a few more who recall the Namibia item. Yet, when we calculate the average length of the protocols, that is the amount of information recalled by the readers, we see that overall, *De Volkskrant* readers tend to recall more. Even for the soccer item, this amount of recall is not much lower than that of the *De Telegraaf* readers. The TV III item is recalled best and by the largest number of readers. The difference between the two domestic items and the foreign news item is remarkable, for both groups: Only 25% of *De Volkskrant* readers and 18% of *De Telegraaf* readers recalled any information from this item; in addition less information is recalled of this item (*De Volkskrant* readers remember somewhat more). It is also interesting that although the sports item is recalled by many *De Telegraaf* readers, the amount of information reproduced from that item is still rather low. In general, a substantial proportion of the recalled information comes from the macrostructural lead: One half to one third of the domestic political items is lead information; if little is retained (as is the case for the soccer item for *De Volkskrant* readers or for the Namibia item for *De Telegraaf* readers), nearly all information recalled comes from the lead. In other words, *if* something is recalled at all, it tends to come from the top, macro, and superstructure of the item. This is a further confirmation of our theoretical predictions.

Variation between the readers is impressive. Some do not recall a single proposition and many only a few, whereas others reproduce dozens of propositions. This variation is such that most differences between the readers of the two newspapers are not significant. There is, however, an overall tendency of *De Volkskrant* readers to reproduce more information once they have read an article. Apparently, more education and more political information from reading other news media (mainly weeklies) is positively correlated to the amount of news information recalled, probably through the specific role of more extensive political knowledge and understanding. In general, male readers have more recall for foreign news and the sports item. Only a few women recall the Namibia text. Besides local and ideological proximity and political knowledge, we see that the factors of relevance and interest play a role in the attention of news items and the amount of recall. In other words, the usual factors that determine news attention and news reading also determine respresentation and recall in natural contexts of reading and memory.

Recall of Content and Structure

An analysis was made of the four experimental news articles in terms of complex propositions, denoting different facts. For each fact, it was determined whether it was recalled by the readers and how often if was recalled. Next, to test recall for various categories of facts, the general notions of cause, main event, and consequences were used, much like in the experiments of Findahl & Höijer reported previously. Similarly, facts about persons vs. institutions and facts about place and time were recorded (data analyzed by De Bie, 1984b).

In both newspapers, most attention is paid to the main event of all articles and least to the consequences. This appears most clearly in the actual news about the poll. Only for the sports item is more attention given to causes than to the major event, which can be explained by the special role of the defeat that caused the criticism against the soccer team trainer.

Institutions are recalled more, and more often than, persons; whereas place and time are much less recalled (contrary to Findahl & Höijer's findings). Total proportion of recalled main events is 42% (scored 212 times), causes 34%, and consequences 26% (percentages rounded). Total recall also emphasizes the main event, whereas only a few readers remember causes, and even fewer recall consequences of events. There are no differences between readers of the two newspapers in this respect. Note that no reader recalled any of the 12 consequent facts in the Namibia article. Generally, the sports item was also poorly recalled. Fifteen of the 20 main-event facts of the TV-III item were recalled, a much higher proportion than for the other items. Note also that whereas more than 40% of all readers recalled any item, the average reader recalled only two or three main events. Analysis of the data also shows that most main events, as well as cause and consequence information, come from the beginning of the articles. As was found by others for TV news, there is a clear primacy effect in newspaper news recall (an effect we have explained in terms of the position of macrostructures in news discourse). Information from the main event category that tends not to be reproduced are evaluative remarks, sources, background information, and all information in later position. What is remembered from the rest of the articles are general knowledge presuppositions, reasons, and consequences.

When we examine the recall percentages of the various structural categories of the news schema, we first find that Lead and Headline are reproduced by most people—which confirms the primary role of the macrostructure of a news article in recall—followed by Main Events, Context, Previous Events, and general Background. History, Consequences, Verbal Reactions, and Comments are recalled less often. These results are in agreement with the lower relevance and later position of these news categories in the news items. *De Volkskrant* readers do somewhat better in recalling general backgrounds, but for the other categories there are no marked differences.

A more detailed analysis was made of the contents and structures of one of the items (the poll item in *De Volkskrant*), which examined what and how readers' protocols (N=21) are related to this input structure (data collected by Diddens, 1984). Of the 83 propositions in the original text, 48 (58%) also occur in the recall protocols. That is, nearly half of the information does not even appear in a single protocol. Only 5 of 83 propositions (6%) is recalled by half or more of the readers. These propositions describe the major participants of the major event of the poll text, namely, the three candidates for the succession to the social-democratic leader (den Uyl), and the candidate who was favorite. The other two main events, namely the information about the current vote percentages the major parties would receive, as well as information on the opinions regarding the siting of cruise missiles in the Netherlands, were recalled only by a few (at most four or five) readers. Most other propositions were recalled only by a few readers (one, two or three). The information best remembered was mentioned first and in the headline and lead of the text. In other words, both macrostructure and relevance structure are best indicators of recall, as predicted by the theories of text recall.

Information least often remembered was of the following types: (1) setting information about the source and media presentation of the poll (in a radio program on the previous Saturday); (2) redundant information, implied by other information mentioned and/or recalled; (3) information about the detailed questions of the poll; and (4) practically all precise numbers (percentages, except for numbers of seats in Parliament, which are remembered by about three subjects). Apart from the macrostructural and superstructural organization of the information best recalled, previous knowledge about the political situation especially seems to influence recall—the three candidates are well-known politicians. Retrieving their names, as well as the limited personal or social models associated with such identities is not difficult for most readers of this social democratic newspaper; for most readers, these three men are members of their own party. The only crucial information to be remembered, then, is (1) that there was a poll, and (2) who came out best. All details that construct this information (the exact questions, setting, and consequences of the poll) may then be forgotten. The same applies to the second and third main topics of the item (party votes and cruise missiles), although these are recalled by only one third of the readers. Then, a few salient details receive some more attention and hence are recalled somewhat better, namely, the fact that the favorite candidate is also the favorite of female and younger voters; and that the second candidate, who is the present chairman of the federation of unions, is not even mentioned most by his own union members. In other words, information with a personal touch, or information that is contrary to expectations, also has higher chances of being recalled.

Overall, it may be concluded that natural news discourse recall is rather poor: Although most of the readers recall an important front page item of domestic news, they only recall the very top of the macrostructure and superstructure, if that is also based on their model of the political situation and if the information has a personal dimension. Most details are not retrieved. Moreover, as is also apparent from the protocol analyses, this information was also predictable. One reader simply says, "I don't know, but I think it is X." In other words, best recall is correlated with plausible expectations (although sometimes unexpectedness may also operate as a representation and retrieval strategy).

Similarly, another analysis was made of the soccer text in *Telegraaf* and of the recall of content and structure (data collected and analyzed by Louwes-Steubing. 1984). The 247 micropropositions of the text were organized into 13 main episodes, which in turn were further analyzed into complex macropropositions (macrofacts), complex propositions (facts), and micropropositions. Twelve of 18 protocols were used for further analysis. Of the episodes recalled, those expressed in headline and lead were best remembered (11 of 12 readers recalled the three macrofacts of the first episode). Of the 49 recalled propositions, 29 occur in the first two episodes. The difference between macroinformation and microinformation is obvious in recall: 16 of 23 macrofacts are recalled, 25 of 51 microfacts are recalled, and only 7 of 72 details are recalled.

Structural organization of the news schema leads to best recall of the information that also has a macrostructural role, namely, of the Headline and Lead (recalled 22 times). Yet, the Evaluation and the Antecedents are also fairly well remembered—the Evaluation because this category dealt with the heavily attitude-dependent information about the harassment of the (losing) soccer team trainer by the supporters, and the Antecedents (the disastrous defeat of the team) because they were the direct cause of the fate of the trainer. A separate narrative analysis of news text and protocol data (see also Thorndyke. 1979), revealed that the major episode and the Setting of the story were remembered best (and these also coincide with the best recalled information of the news schema). There is a tendency to organize main events in a narrative schema during retrieval (and, therefore, during representation) and those readers who organize main events in this way generally show better recall. Finally, it was found that more reading time correlated highly with more information in the protocols. Most readers (>75%) had read the paper that day for 30 minutes or less. The two readers who had read the paper for at least an hour recalled most.

Delayed Recall

Essential in a study of memory for news is what people recall of a news item information after a few weeks. During the same day, subjects may still have access to textual representations in memory, including many other episodic traces, such as layout, location, photographs, or personal associations. After a few weeks, news information, if retained at all, should have been integrated largely into more permanent forms of knowledge. We, therefore, went back into the field after a month to ask other people whether they remembered specific items of information from their newspapers. In this second field experiment, 44 subjects were interviewed: 12 readers of *De Telegraaf,* and 32 readers of *De Volkskrant.* Again, the level of education of *De Volkskrant* readers is higher than that of *De Telegraaf* readers. Media use of these readers was expectedly similar to that of the subjects in the immediate recall experiment. Of the four texts used in the first experiment, three were used in this experiment: the NAMIBIA, POLL, and SOCCER texts. Instead of free recall, which we assumed to be virtually impossible for most subjects, concrete knowledge questions were asked that could be answered on the basis of earlier newspaper items (although some answers can be answered partly on the basis of more general world knowledge). Scoring was based on correct, incorrect or don't know, and half-correct criteria. Data were analyzed by Claver (1984).

Results

The question that was answered best by both *De Volkskrant* and *De Telegraaf* readers was about the favorite successor of the present Labor leader (from the poll text). Two thirds of the readers could answer that question. Note, though, that general political knowledge about the potential candidates is a powerful knowledge base or retrieval cue in this case. Only one third of *De Telegraaf* readers recalled the results of the poll about the actual percentages the major parties would get, whereas this proportion was much higher (59%) for *De Volkskrant* readers. But again, this knowledge can also be partly inferred from other political knowledge about the actual popularity of the major parties. Indeed, the third question about the poll text— the percentage of people who favor cruise missile siting in the Netherlands could not be answered by a single *De Telegraaf* reader and was only answered by one *De Volkskrant* reader. The Namibia and soccer items were much less recalled. Only one fifth of the readers in the two groups knew what specific proposal was made by the South African minister of foreign affairs in the Namibia question and practically no one recalled where the proposed conference should be held. That one third of the readers still remembered which parties should participate in the conference can also partly be explained by general knowledge about the Namibia issue. The soccer item, though initially well recalled, especially by *De Telegraaf* readers, was also difficult to retrieve. One third of the readers in each group still recalled that there were troubles around the trainer of the soccer team, but nobody remembered the occasion or the causes of his fate, let alone the detail about the precise score of the match in which the team was defeated. On all questions *De Volkskrant* readers scored 25% correct on average, and *De Telegraaf* readers 20%, but the range is vast (between 72% and 0%). Yet, only a few people in the two groups said that they had not read the items. There is no direct link between having read and recall of an item: Only 3% of Volkskrant readers indicated that they had not read the Namibia item (17% of *De Telegraaf* readers), yet their recall for this item is only slightly better, and the same holds for the soccer item in the case of *De Telegraaf* readers. The major media use difference between the two groups (38% of *De Volkskrant* readers and only 8% of *De Telegraaf* readers always or regularly read weeklies, which are the main source for political background information in the Netherlands) might account for the slightly better recall of *De Volkskrant* readers, especially of the item about the current popularity of the major political parties. The same may hold for the different in the education level between the two groups. Yet, the overall differences in recall for the three news items are not dramatic.

Discussion and Conclusion

From these results, we may conclude that after a month people say they still recall whether or not they have read an item but that only about one third of the respondents can still answer the major questions about such an item. If main issues are still known, these are often derivable from general political knowledge. Concrete details are nearly always forgotten. There are no dramatic differences between groups in this respect, although the better educated and politically better informed group tended to do slightly better. These conclusions confirm what we know about text comprehension and recall in the laboratory. After several weeks, readers tend to recall at most the highest levels of macrostructure, especially if these are retrievable or reconstructable on the basis of general knowledge. Microlevel information is no longer accessible. This is interesting since, as we have seen in Chapter 2, newspaper news tends to pay much attention to details like numbers and names. On the other hand, what is signaled to be most important in news discourse, the information in headlines and lead, tends to be best recalled both in immediate and delayed recall. Some items that are fairly well remembered in immediate recall (such as the percentage of people who favor siting of cruise missiles) but which had low relevance in the news item, are no longer accessible in later recall. This confirms the well-known laboratory finding that the overall macrostructural and superstructural (relevance) organization of news discourse in memory tends to have an effect on long-term recall of information. This may be explained by better access to the representation of the news item itself, by integration information from such an item in our situation models, or by both factors. Whatever the precise processes at work, it may safely be concluded that the overall organization of news discourse correlates highly with recall of news information: What is signaled to be relevant in the news discourse is also best recalled by the readers. This may be the result of structural organization of this information (macro and/or super) or by shared values and criteria of relevance between readers and journalists or both. Finally, we have seen that recall of news is intricately interwoven with the representation, uses, and updating of more general social and political knowledge. For the average reader, such knowledge does not seem to be highly developed and complex, but rather of the headline type. Only one third to one fourth of the readers can answer concrete questions that in principle could also be derived from updated political knowledge, as was the case in the Namibia item. How exactly social and political knowledge and beliefs influence reading, decoding, interpretation, representation, knowledge integration, retrieval, and other uses or applications of news information is a question that can only be answered through further experimental work.

The Influence of Other Media

Although Monday newspapers were used in our field experiment, some of the items were about issues that were at least also covered by other media during the weekend, especially on radio and TV. This means that at least part of the readers might have known about some of the information conveyed by the press, and this of course would influence their recall of such information (usually positively, but sometimes also negatively). Data about other media sources were compiled and analyzed by Hermans (1984).

During the interviews, therefore, most readers were asked whether they had seen or heard about this news from other media during the weekend (15 were not asked, but two of these spontaneously mentioned other media). This appeared to be the case for all four items, although the Namibia item was hardly recalled from other media information (1 *De Volkskrant* and 2 *De Telegraaf* readers). Most information came from TV (seven subjects had listened to the radio, and two to both radio and TV). In each group, seven readers had heard about the TV III news, six *De Volkskrant* and three *De Telegraaf* readers had heard about the poll, and in each group four had heard about the soccer news. Overall, about half of those readers asked about other media had seen at least one of the items on TV or heard about it on the radio.

Next examined was whether subjects that had access to other media information had better recalled the respective newspaper items. Of the 63 respondents, 26 named other media and knew 533 of a total of 1,039 propositions (51%). Yet, only 288 of these 533 propositions come from the items they have seen or heard about before. Overall, therefore, respondents with other media knowledge knew 16% fewer propositions (53% more, and 69% less) than nonmedia users. However, it is striking that 41% of other media users mention 51% of the propositions. From these figures, we may provisionally conclude that subjects do not exhibit superior recall of items they have heard about before via other media. On the contrary, their overall performance is even poorer. Perhaps interference with the earlier information prevented them from knowing which information occurred in the newspaper item and which information came from the other media. Or else, people who watched TV or listened to the radio have generally lower scores on recall, which again may be conditioned by lower education or less political knowledge.

A Laboratory Experiment

To compare the results of the field experiment with recall results from a better controlled context, a simple recall experiment was conducted in the laboratory. The subjects were 42 psychology students at the University of Amsterdam, who participated to obtain course credits. Two groups were created, the first receiving a few xeroxed pages from *De Telegraaf,* the second a few pages from *De Volkskrant.* They were instructed to read the pages carefully, which took about twenty minutes on average. After a 15-minute break, to prevent immediate literal recall and which would interpolate other (conversation) information, the students were asked to recall as much as they could about the TV III item which was also used in the field experiment. To simulate, as much as possible, the natural reading situation, subjects did not know in advance which article they would be asked to recall. In fact, they did not know the nature of the task at all. Data were collected and analyzed by Greep (1984).

The recall protocols were analyzed into atomic propositions, and for each proposition of both texts it was calculated how many subjects recalled that proposition. It was found, first, that for both articles, the lead and the first sentences were well remembered, which is in accordance with the macrostructural role of the lead or first sentence. Besides this macroinforma-tion, details were recalled about the financial consequences of introducing a third TV channel. The same is true of the information in which a well-known politician (parliamentary fraction leader of a government party) gives his personal opinion about the new TV channel. Generally, information lower in the article is less recalled, especially when the information (as in *De Telegraaf*) was part of the continuation on a next page. Again, we find the relevance and primacy effects, with an additional effect of front-page or inner-page (continuation) location.

Next, recall for this item in the laboratory was compared with that in the field situation. As expected readers in the more controlled laboratory situa-tion recalled the respective propositions much better than the readers in the natural situation, who for the most part had read the newspaper several hours earlier and probably more casually. For both readers of *De Telegraaf* and *De Volkskrant* nearly one third on average recalled the 20 sentences of these two texts, whereas in the natural situation the average score for the *De Telegraaf* article was 19% and that for the *De Volkskrant* was 14%. In other words, recall in the laboratory was about twice as high. Part of this dif-ference may be explained by the fact that laboratory subjects may have read about the event earlier (the laboratory experiment took place two months after the publication of the item). It is interesting to observe that proposi-tions recalled well in the laboratory were also recalled best in the field. Despite this clear tendency, however, there is also substantial variation. In the case of *De Telegraaf*, a few sentences were even better recalled in the field situation. This is the case for instance when a party politician is quoted who made a statement for the radio. In the field experiment situation, readers may actually recall that radio statement. Another difference be-tween the laboratory and field condition is that the recall of sentences is distributed more evenly across the items in the laboratory condition: Final sentences that tend to be forgotten during natural newspaper reading are better recalled in the laboratory. This may be a recency effect, due to a shorter delay between reading and recall in the laboratory, but it may also be the result of partial newsreading in natural situations, where readers often read only the first part of an article. Further, it appeared that recall was relatively good for information about the respective statements and opinions of important politicians involved in the media debate.

Discussion and Conclusions

The two experiments we conducted confirm a number of earlier findings and also suggest some new insights into the nature of news comprehension and recall. Overall, memory for news is quite low, especially in natural reading situations. Whereas in the laboratory, an average of one third of the subjects recall the sentences or propositions of a carefully read news item, at most only one fifth of the subjects recall this information in the natural situation. The fact, however, that information recalled well in the laboratory is also recalled well in the field suggests that there are context independent factors in the representation and recall of news.

In general, it was found again that macrostructure and superstructure organized information in such a way that it leads to better recall for news information high in the hierarchy: Major topics, and information that was signaled to be relevant, was generally recalled best, both in the laboratory and in the field. Previous information from other media did not appear to lead to better recall; on the contrary, there is some evidence that the reverse may be true, maybe because of interference. After a delay of a month, even less information is recalled. Nearly all details have become irretrievable after such a delay. The information best recalled after a month may be derived from or cued by more general political information. More education and, especially, more political information from other media such as weeklies have a tendency to positively influence recall for political items, but the overall differences between groups of popular and quality newspaper readers are not dramatic. From the point of view of knowledge acquisition, it may finally be remarked that the updating of situation models on the basis of news in the press is not impressive. Generally, people only seem to integrate a few macropropositions of each news item and only for those issues directly relevant for their daily understanding of political and social life in their own regional or national context. They know about the debate that might or might not bring them an additional TV channel (and what it will cost them), and they know about the main political parties and leaders and who is favorite among the electorate. Yet, causes, consequences, context, and history of many issues, especially foreign ones (such as in the Namibia case), as well as most details about places and numbers, tend to be forgotten. In other words, only repeated and concurrent information about certain issues may lead to a modest change or construction of current situation models. Usually, only one or two major macropropositions of a news story will be stored such that it can be integrated into more general knowledge representations (models). Conversely, the issues we know most about also lead to better comprehension and recall of such items.

In other words, of the vast amount of information in our daily newspapers (which is still only a tiny fragment of the information available to the media), only a very small amount is actually recalled and integrated into the knowledge system of the readers. Obviously, then, newspaper reading does not primarily serve the permanent updating of our world knowledge, but rather more direct functions such as the satisfaction of curiosity about actual developments, daily conversation about events, and so on. In this sense, newspaper reading is not a very effective way of social information processing and learning: Of the many thousands of propositions, only a handful will actually be integrated into our models each day. Of course, active recall may be lower than recognition: We may need much more previous information to be able to understand actual news information, and we only need to passively recognize the presuppositions of this actual information. Perhaps all that is needed is the processing of vast amounts of structuring, repeated, and coherent information to serve as a basis for minimal extensions or other changes of our world models. Further work on the details of actual news reading, interpretation, representation, and retrieval is necessary to fill in the many details that have not been discussed in the theoretical and experimental work reviewed and reported in this chapter. We still know almost nothing about what media users actually do with the information they get from the news. Thus, many earlier studies of the effects of mass communication appeared to be inconclusive, if not premature. The central component of understanding and memorization is still largely unknown.

5

CONCLUSIONS

NEWS AS DISCOURSE

Throughout this book we have dealt with news in the press as a specific type of discourse. It was argued that mass communication research has paid only marginal attention to its central object of research—the media messages themselves. When they were studied it was usually along the rather superficial categories of traditional content analysis and usually in a quantitative rather than a qualitative perspective. The research carried out on news in the past decade, briefly reviewed in Chapter 1, appeared to provide interesting insights into the microsociology and macrosociology of newsmaking and news institutions but focused on news texts only in a more ad hoc or intuitive way. Thus, we know about the everyday organization of newsmaking, the journalistic routines of newsgathering, and the social and economic constraints of news production rather than how news events or the many source texts that describe or constitute them are actually processed into the news we read in the paper or see on TV. Nor do we know exactly how media users select, read, understand, memorize, or reproduce information from news texts. In recent years, however, especially in Europe, there has been an increasing interest for the linguistic, semiotic, cultural, or ideological analysis of news texts. A discourse analytical approach embodies and further integrates and extends these developments.

Developments in this new cross-discipline of discourse analysis now allow us to study media text and talk in a more explicit, systematic, and interesting way. Within a wider socioeconomic and cultural framework, such an analysis considers media discourse, and hence also news, as a particular form of social, institutional practice. This discursive practice of news production or reception may be analyzed theoretically into two major components: a textual and a contextual component. The textual component systematically analyzes the various structures of news discourse at different levels. The contextual component analyzes the cognitive and social factors, conditions, constraints, or consequences of such textual structures and, indirectly, their economic, cultural, and historical embedding.

Since most recent studies have focused on the socioeconomic context of news, this book studies the sociocognitive interface between text and these socioeconomic contexts, namely, the ways newsmakers and readers actually represent news events, write or read news texts, process various source texts, or participate in communicative events. Without a detailed account of both textual structures and cognitive processing, we are unable to explain how news is actually made, why it has its characteristic structures, or what readers do with the information they get from the newspaper. If we only study journalists as social actors who deal with other social actors or with institutions, we only get a picture of the social macrostructures or microstructures of newsmaking but ignore the other side of these social practices: how newsmakers actually *understand* what is going on, and how these understandings finally shape the news texts they produce. Also, important concepts of the theory of news, such as that of news values, receive a more satisfactory reformulation in terms of the social cognitions of newsmakers and news users. The ideological analysis of news crucially depends on advances in both these textual and contextual dimensions of news and communication processes: They need textual structures for their expression and communication and cognitive representations and strategies for their role in social practices, the interpretation of news events, newswriting, and news understanding by media users.

TEXTUAL STRUCTURES OF NEWS

News reports in the press are a member of a family of media text types that need their own structural analysis. That is, the general properties of discourse they display and the more specific or characteristic structures that distinguish them from other media texts or similar nonmedia texts, such as stories, must be made clear.

Such a structural analysis operates at several levels and dimensions. Obviously, as a form of language use, media texts also display linguistic or grammatical structures of words, word groups, clauses, or sentences. The usual phonological (or rarely, graphematic), morphological, syntactic, and semantic descriptions may be relevant for these structures. Variations and genre-specific structures at these levels also define the style of news discourse. Thus, the use of neologisms, the heavy recourse to nominalizations (instead of verbs), sentence complexity, or word or clause order (such as postpositioned declaratives: ". . . ., the president declared") are examples of these specifics of grammatical style of news discourse. Similarly, syntactic structures may also express underlying ideological positions, for instance by using passive constructions and deleting agents from typical subject positions to dissimulate the negative actions of elite or powerful groups. Finally, lexical choice is an eminent aspect of news discourse in which hidden opinions or ideologies may surface. The traditional example of using "terrorists" instead of "guerrillas" or "freedom fighters" is only one example. The same is true for the use of "riots" instead of "disturbances" or instead of "resistance" or the use of "hooligans" instead of, for example "demonstrators". A large part of the hidden point of view, tacit opinions, or the usually denied ideologies of the press may be inferred from these lexical descriptions and identifications of social groups and their members.

Thus far, discourse analysis runs parallel with linguistics. However, news texts are not simply characterized at the level of individual words or sentences in isolation. They also have structures at higher, more complex, or more extended levels and dimensions. Semantically, for instance, sentence meanings (propositions) are mutually dependent and connected and form coherent sequences. Besides the meanings of words and sentences, world knowledge in the form of models, frames, and scripts represented in memory, is brought to bear by the reader to understand a piece of news discourse as a coherent whole. Conditions, causes, or reasons may be involved in these links between sentences, and obviously these presuppose knowledge or beliefs about how events or situations in the world are organized. Thus, a simple *because* may betray a large set of assumptions about the social or political world the news describes. No wonder that journalists often use the more neutral *while* instead of *because* to avoid ideological identification with their sources or with the events they describe.

Whereas this semantic account still takes place at the more local level, we also analyze the overall, global meanings of news discourse. The notion of semantic macrostructure has been used to make explicit the familiar notion of topic or theme a news report covers. Macrostructures and the cognitive processes on which they are based are crucial for news reports and their production and comprehension: They define the gist, upshot, or most important information of the news report. More than in any other type of text, macrostructures are explicitly expressed in the news report, as headlines and leads. Since they also depend on world knowledge, opinions and attitudes (after all, what is important is ideologically bound), macrostructures and their expressions—e.g., in the headlines—may be subjective and biased. An explicit analysis of the thematic organization of news reports, in terms of macrostructure rules of inference or reduction, allows us to assess such biases, for instance when low level topics are upgraded to main topics and even expressed in the headlines, or conversely. In other words, the definition of the situation as it is provided by the thematic macrostructure of a news report may be vastly different from alternative definitions. Macrostructures, thus, are systematically related to the constraints and conditions of news production: Summaries of news events figure everywhere in newsmaking, as we shall see shortly.

Global meanings or content (topics) also require a conventional or canonical form (like sentence meaning needs syntax for its organization). For different types of text or talk, therefore, each culture has its own global categories and rules to organize discourse or communicative events. The best known examples are the conventional structure of stories (setting, complication, resolution, etc.), or that of arguments (premises, conclusion). Texts that occur frequently and/or are processed routinely within institutions, such as news discourse, often have such a canonical pattern. Therefore, we introduced the notion of a news schema, featuring the usual categories that provide the different functions of information in news reports: Summary (Headline and Lead), Main Events, Backgrounds (Context and History), Consequences (Consequent events or actions and Verbal Reactions), and Comments (Evaluation and Prediction). Some of these categories are obligatory (Summary and Main Event), whereas others are optional. Apart from organizing the global content (themes, macrostructure) of news reports, they have cognitive and social functions in news production and in news understanding and memorization. For instance, journalists may explicitly search for background to a main news event and explicitly ask for, or select from, a wire, the Verbal Reactions of a major news actor.

Characteristic of both macrostructures and superstructures of news is their discontinuous, installment structure: Topics and their schematic categories are realized step by step throughout the news text. The general principle is that of relevance: The most relevant information (from top to bottom) comes first, followed by lower levels, and finally, details of each respective schematic category (from summary, via main events, through backgrounds to comments). Hence, an important verbal reaction may appear before a less important detail of the main event. This relevance structure is intricately linked with news production strategies, the structure of models journalists have of news events, as well as with properties of reading news such as skimming.

Finally, news structures of various levels may feature a rhetorical dimension. Special structures or organizational principles (identity, permutation, deletion, or addition) may operate on sounds, word order, or meanings in order to make them more noticeable, hence more memorable and effective. Although news discourse was found to be nonpersuasive in principle or intention, it may well have a persuasive dimension in a more indirect sense: Even if it does not argue for a position or opinion, it certainly presupposes them, by definition of its social and therefore ideological embedding. But even professionally speaking, a news report will have to signal its credibility and therefore exhibit its truth claims. The major rhetorical aspect of news, therefore, is the characteristic usage of the number game. By signaling precision or exactness. such numbers in the news report rhetorically enhance its effectiveness—like the statistics in a scholarly publication.

This summary of a few structural principles of news discourse suggests that we are not simply interested in news structures per se, even if these also need attention. Rather, we analyze such structures in relation to their context of production and understanding: We want to know their specific functions, for instance, in the expression of underlying knowledge, beliefs, attitudes or ideologies, or as results of specific constraints of newsmaking. Similarly, once we have made explicit such structures, we also know more about the strategies and the representations that play a role in the interpretation, memorization, and reproduction of news information by the readers.

PRODUCTION

Newsmaking is an institutional practice primarily defined in terms of the activities or interactions of journalists in the setting or situations of newsrooms, meetings, beats, and many newsgathering contexts. Whereas such routines and their constraints, as well as the macrostructural goals or institutional embeddings of these activities, have received much attention, a few crucial elements of news production have been largely ignored. From our discourse analytical perspective, this means, first of all, that most stages of news production involve the processing of text and talk. It was argued that journalists seldom witness events as such. Rather, they get coded versions of such events through agency wires, eyewitness reports, other media messages, documentation, interviews. press releases and press conferences, reports, statements, meetings, sessions, and many other forms of discourse. Part of these, such as the declarations of high officials, may constitute news events in their own right.

It follows that the reconstruction and reproduction of news events in the process of newswriting involves both highly complex forms of text processing, as well as the cognitive strategies and representations that underlie these processes. In a field study, therefore, we monitored in detail how journalists use these multiple types of text in newsgathering and newswriting, which information of these texts is addressed, and how such information is transformed into the structures and contents of the final news report.

This account is formulated in terms of current theories in the psychology of text and information processing, which are also used to explain processes of comprehension. For production processes, it is important to analyze how large amounts of source text and talk can be managed and transformed into a relatively small news report. The notion of macrostructure is important in these processes, because it allows us to define the important role of summaries in all stages of newsmaking, from taking notes and asking interview questions, to the formulation of the lead of the final report.

Besides a mental representation of the various source texts, journalists also build a so-called model of the situation, that is, an episodic (subjective) knowledge structure of what these source texts are about. The construction of such models is also fed by more general knowledge scripts, as well as by general attitudes and ideologies. In other words, the model is the crucial cognitive representation communicators (journalists as well as readers) use to understand news events and situations. It is also this model that the journalist wants to convey to the readers through the news report. And the structures of this news report are organized so that the intended model is effectively communicated: What is high in the hierarchy of the model will also feature high the the structural hierarchy of the news text, in headlines or lead.

The combined discursive and cognitive approach to newsmaking also allows us to spell out in detail the structures and strategies of news values and the role of professional and social ideologies in general. How such ideologies, values, or norms actually monitor the interpretation of news events, or rather of source texts, and how they guide the actual production of the news report by the journalist can now be made explicit in such an interdisciplinary approach.

UNDERSTANDING

Similar remarks hold for the process of understanding news reports by readers. Again, we did not focus on the traditional question of mass communication research, that of effects of the news, but examined in more detail its crucial condition, interpretation and representation. The transformation of knowledge, beliefs, and attitudes is much more complex and requires a cognitive analysis that is vastly more intricate than traditionally suggested by effect research.

A review of current work on news understanding revealed that people actually remember very little of news in the press or on TV, especially after longer delays. This also appeared from a field experiment we did on news retention. Generally, readers remember what we called the macrostructures of the news, and after some time, even these merge into more general knowledge structures. In fact, as we suggested above, what readers do is not so much remember news reports at all but rather construct new and update old models of the situation a news report describes. Recall, thus, is based on the partial retrieval of such models. And more general knowledge or attitude changes can be accounted for in terms of the generalization and decontextualization of such models, which feature both the personal and the group-based beliefs and opinions of the reader(s). News that fits the canonical schematic structure of these models, as well as the general knowledge scripts or attitude schemata of the reader, will tend to be remembered best. Indeed, experimental results confirm that people remember best what they already know, that is, the information that retrieves old models, or that simply can be fitted into such models. Also, remarkable emotional events, such as crimes, disasters, or conflicts tend to be well remembered, especially if they fit existing (stereotypical, prejudiced) belief or attitude schemata (such as the assumed participation of Blacks in crime).

Although we focused on understanding and representation of news, these cognitive processes also allow plausible assumptions about the processes of knowledge, belief and opinion transformation, and, hence, about the major component of the effects of media news. If we know what information people notice, represent best and most effectively, and are able to retrieve after longer delays, we also know what information is used in the formation of more general knowledge and attitude patterns.

Final Remarks

This book sketches the outline of a theory of news from a new, interdisciplinary perspective, focusing on the discourse structures of news and the social cognition of production and interpretation. In this respect, it provides an extension of, and a further contribution to, a more general theory of news, which of course also has macrosocial, cultural, historical, and economic subtheories. Our approach, however, is not simply an addition to the current approaches. It also is intended to bridge the gap between the microlevels and macrolevels of news analysis and between media texts and contexts. It has been shown how the complex structures of news reports can be linked systematically to both the cognitive processes of newsmaking and those of understanding by the readers. At the same time, and through this cognitive interface, these structures could be linked to the social practices of newsmakers, their group ideologies, and the institutional constraints of the news media. This means, conversely, that we have outlined how the macrodimensions of social structure, history, or culture are enacted or translated at this microlevel of news discourse and its processing.

Our approach shows how ideologies are related to the cognitive representations that underlie news production and understanding. This allows us to account at the same time for the important reproduction function of the news media. Partly autonomous in their form of cultural reproduction, partly dependent and monitored by more embracing societal structures and ideologies, the news media embody such structures and ideologies in the very routines of newsmaking (e.g., by selection of and focusing on elite actors and sources or understandable and ideologically consonant events) and the conventional structures of their reports. As the central purveyors of public discourse, the news media provide more than the agenda of public topics and discussions. We have seen that understanding news does not imply the adoption of identical models by readers. The influence of the media, therefore, is more indirect and more structural. News reports do not necessarily prescribe the concrete opinions of readers. Rather, they are the main form of public discourse that provides the general outline of social, political, cultural, and economic models of societal events, as well as the pervasively dominant knowledge and attitude structures that make such models intelligible. The structures of news reports at many levels condition the readers to develop such interpretation frameworks rather than alternative ones, in which other goals, norms, values, and ideologies are used to provide counterinterpretations of news events.

Since this study only gives outlines, hence a macrostructure of a theory, its microstructural details still need much research, both theoretical and empirical. We still know little, for instance, about the style and rhetoric of news reports. We have few insights, as yet, in the actual writing processes of news reports and do not know exactly how people read their newspaper. The general framework that embodies our own theory also needs more attention, so that we are able to spell out in detail how macrodimensions such as societal structure (class, gender, ethnicity, power, elite groups, institutions, etc.) are linked to the social practices of newsmaking, to the social cognitions of news participants (journalists, readers), and finally to the discourse structures of news texts themselves. Although much of the microstructure is yet to be identified, and although part of the macrostructures of the theory must be linked with those of other theories, we hope that this study has provided an explicit plan for further research about news and media discourse.

REFERENCES

Abel, E. (Ed.). (1981). *What's news: The media in American society.* San Francisco: Institute for Contemporary Studies.

Abelson, R. P. (1976). Script processing in attitude formation and decision making. In J. S. Carroll & J. W. Payne (Eds.), *Cognition and social behavior* (pp. 13–46). Hillsdale, NJ: Lawrence Erlbaum Associates.

Allport, G. W., & Postman, L. (1947). *The psychology of rumor.* New York: Holt, Rinehart & Winston.

Altheide, D. L. (1974). *Creating reality. How TV news distorts reality.* Beverly Hills, CA: Sage.

Anderson, A. R., Belnap, N. D., Jr. (1975). *Entailment. The logic of relevance and necessity.* Princeton, NJ: Princeton University Press.

Anderson, R. C., & Pichert, J. W. (1978). Recall of previously unrecallable information following a shift in perspective. *Journal of Verbal Learning and Verbal Behavior, 17,* 1–12.

Atkinson, J. M., & Heritage, J. C. (Eds.). (1984). Structures of social action. Cambridge: Cambridge University Press.

Atwood, L. E. (1970). How newsmen and readers perceive each others' story preferences. *Journalism Quarterly, 47,* 296–302.

Atwood, L. E., & Grotta, G. L. (1973). Socialization of news values in beginning reporters. *Journalism Quarterly, 50,* 759–761.

Auclair, G. (1970). *Le mana quotidien. Structures et fonctions de la chronique des faits divers.* Paris: Anthropos.

Bagdikian, B. H. (1971). *The information machines.* New York: Harper & Row.

Bagdikian, B. H. (1983). *The media monopoly.* Boston: Beacon Press.

Baker, B. (1981). *Newsthinking. The secret of great newswriting.* Cincinnati: Writer's Digest Books.

183

Barrett, M. (1978). *Rich news, poor news.* New York: Crowell.

Barthes, R. (1957). *Mythologies.* Paris: Seuil.

Barthes, R. (1966). Introduction à l'analyse structurale des récits. *Communications, 8,* 1–27.

Barthes, R. (1970). L'ancienne rhétorique: aide-mémoire. *Communications, 16,* 172–229.

Bartlett, F. C. (1932). *Remembering.* London: Cambridge University Press.

Bauman, R., & Sherzer, J. (Eds.). (1974). *Explorations in the ethnography of speaking.* London: Cambridge University Press.

Bechmann, R., Bischoff, J., Maldaner, K., & Loop, L. (1979). *BILD. Ideologie als Ware.* Hamburg: VSA Verlag.

Bentele, G. (Ed.). (1981). *Semiotik und Massenmedien.* Munich: Oelschläger.

Black, J. B., & Wilensky, R. (1979). An evaluation of story grammars. *Cognitive Science, 3,* 213–229.

Bower, G. H. (1974). Selective facilitation and interference in retention of prose. Journal of Educational Psychology, 66, 1–8.

Bower, G. H. (1980). Mood and memory. *American Psychologist, 36,* 129–148.

Bower, C. H., Black, J. B., & Turner, T. J. (1979). Scripts in memory for text. *Cognitive Psychology, 11,* 177–220.

Breed, W. (1955). Social control in the newsroom. Social Forces, 33, 326–335.

Breed, W. (1956). Analyzing news: Some questions for research. *Journalism Quarterly, 33,* 467–477.

Brewer, W. F. (1982). Stories are to entertain. A structural-affect theory of stories. *Journal of Pragmatics, 6,* 473–486.

Carbonell, Jr., J. (1979). Subjective understanding. Unpublished doctoral dissertation. Yale University: Department of Computer Science.

Chabrol, C. (1973). *La logique du récit.* Paris: Seuil.

Charniak, E. (1972). Toward a model of children's story comprehension. Unpublished doctoral dissertation. MIT.

Chatman, S. (Ed.). (1971). *Literary style: A symposium.* London: Oxford University Press.

Chibnall, S. (1977). *Law-and-order news. An analysis of crime reporting in the British press.* London: Tavistock.

Chomsky, N. (1981). *Radical priorities.* Edited by C. P. Otero. Montreal: Black Rose Books.

Cicourel, A. V. (1973). *Cognitive sociology.* Harmondsworth: Penguin Books.

Cirino, R. (1971). *Don't blame the people.* New York: Random House. Vintage Books.

Clark, H., & Clark, E. (1977). *The psychology of language.* New York: Holt, Rinehart & Winston.

Claver, H. (1984). Verslag delayed recall onderzoekje (Report on delayed recall research). Unpublished manuscript. University of Amsterdam, Section of Discourse Studies.

Coerts, J. A., & Vermeulen, A. (1984). Strukturen van nieuwsteksten. Een vergelijking tussen kranteberichten en telexberichten (Structures of news texts. A comparison of newspaper reports and wire reports). Unpublished manuscript. University of Amsterdam, Section of Discourse Studies.

Cohen, S. (1980). *Folk devils and moral panics* (2nd ed.). Oxford: Robertson.

Cohen, S., & Young, J. (Eds.). (1981). *The manufacture of news. Deviance, social problems and the mass media* (2nd rev. ed.). London: Constable/Sage.

Communications 4. (1964). *Recherches sémiologiques.* Paris: Seuil.

Communications 8. (1966). *Analyse structurale du récit.* Paris: Seuil.

Connell, I. (1980). Television news and the social contract. In: S. Hall, D. Lowe, & P. Willis, et al., (Eds.) *Culture, media, language* (pp. 139–156). London: Hutchinson.

Corbett, E. P. J. (1971). *Classical rhetoric for the modern student.* New York: Oxford University Press.

Coulthard, M. (1977). *Introduction to discourse analysis.* London: Longman.

Cronkhite, G., & Liska, J. R. (1980). The judgment of communicant acceptability. In: M. E. Roloff & G. R. Miller (Eds.), *Persuasion* (pp. 101–140). Beverly Hills, CA: Sage.

Crystal, D., & Davy, D. (1969). *Investigating English style.* London: Longman.

Culler, J. (1975). *Structuralist poetics.* London: Routledge & Kegan Paul.

Culler, J. (1983). *On deconstruction.* Ithaca, NY: Cornell University Press.

Danet, B. (1980). Language in the legal process. *Law and Society Review, 14,* 445–565.

Danet, B. (Ed.). (1984). Legal discourse. Text 4, nrs. 1/3. Special issue.

Davis, H., & Walton, P. (Eds.). (1983). *Language, image, media.* Oxford: Blackwell.

de Beaugrande, R. (1980). *Text, discourse and process.* Norwood, NJ: Ablex.

de Beaugrande, R. (1984). *Text production.* Hillsdale, NJ: Lawrence Erlbaum Associates.

de Beaugrande, R., & Dressler, W. U. (1981). *Introduction to text linguistics.* London: Longman.

De Bie, S. (1984a). Samenvatten als onderdeel van het produktieproces van nieuws (Summarizing as a component of the news production process). Unpublished manuscript. University of Amsterdam, Section of Discourse Studies.

De Bie, S. (1984b). Weinig nieuws. Een analyse van wat mensen onthouden van krantenniews (Little news. An analysis of what people remember of newspaper news). Unpublished manuscript. University of Amsterdam, Section of Discourse Studies. Student paper.

Dennis, E., & Ismach, A. (1981). *Reporting processes and practices: newswriting for today's readers.* Belmont, CA: Wadsworth.

Diamond, E. (1978). *Good news, bad news.* Cambridge, Mass.: MIT Press.

Diddens, B. (1984). Het onthouden van nieuws (Remembering the news). Unpublished manuscript. University of Amsterdam, Section of Discourse Studies.

Dik, S. C. (1978). *Functional Grammar.* Amsterdam: North Holland.

Downing, J. (1980). *The media machine.* London: Pluto Press.

Dowty, D. R., Wall, R. E., & Peters, S. (1981). *Introduction to Montague grammars.* Dordrecht: Reidel.

Dressler, W. U. (1972). *Einführung in die Textlinguistik.* Tübingen: Niemeyer.

Enkvist, N.–E. (1973). *Linguistic stylistics.* The Hague: Mouton.

Epstein, E. J. (1973). *News from nowhere.* New York: Random House. Vintage Books.

Epstein, E. J. (1975). *Between fact and fiction: The problem of journalism.* New York: Random House. Vintage Books.

Erlich, V. (1965). *Russian formalism.* The Hague: Mouton.

Fillmore, C. J. (1968). The case for case. In E. Bach & R. T. Harms (Eds.), *Universals in linguistic theory* (pp. 1–88). New York: Holt, Rinehart & Winston.

Findahl, O., & Höijer, B. (1973). *An analysis of errors in the recollection of a news program.* Stockholm: Sveriges Radio/PUB.

Findahl, O., & Höijer, B. (1975). Effect of additional verbal information on retention of a radio news program. *Journalism Quarterly, 52,* 493–498.

Findahl, O., & Höijer, B. (1976). *Fragments of reality. An experiment with news and TV-visuals.* Stockholm: Sveriges Radio/PUB.

Findahl, O., & Höijer, B. (1981a). Media content and human comprehension. In K. E. Rosengren (Ed.), *Advances in content analysis* (pp. 111–132). Beverly Hills, Ca: Sage.

Findahl, O., & Höijer, B. (1981b). Studies of news from the perspective of human comprehension. In G. C. Wilhoit & H. de Bock (Eds.), *Mass communication review yearbook* (Vol. 2) (pp. 393–403). Beverly Hills, CA: Sage.

Findahl, O., & Höijer, B. (1984). *Begriplighetsanalys.* Stockholm: Studentlitteratur.

Fishman, M. (1980). *Manufacturing the news.* Austin, TX: University of Texas Press.

Fiske, S. & Taylor, S. (1984). *Social cognition.* Reading, MA: Addison-Wesley.

Flammer, A., & Kintsch, W. (Eds.). (1982). *Discourse processing.* Amsterdam: North Holland.

Forgas, J. P. (Ed.). (1981). *Social cognition. Perspectives on everyday understanding.* London: Academic Press.

Fowler, R., Hodge, B., Kress, G., & Trew, T. (1979). *Language and control.* London: Routledge & Kegan Paul.

Freedle, R. O., & Carroll, J. B. (Eds.). (1972). *Language comprehension and the acquisition of knowledge.* New York: Holt, Rinehart & Winston.

Freeman, D. C. (Ed.). (1981). *Essays in modern stylistics.* London: Methuen.

Galtung, J. & Ruge, M. H. (1965). The structure of foreign news. *Journal of Peace Research, 2,* 64–91.

Gans, H. (1979). *Deciding what's news.* New York: Pantheon Books.

Garfinkel, H. (1967). *Studies in ethnomethodology.* Englewood Cliffs, NJ: Prentice-Hall.

Garst, R. E., & Bernstein, T. M. (1982). *Headlines and deadlines* (4th ed.). New York: Columbia University Press.

Givón, T. (Ed.). (1979). *Discourse and syntax* (Vol. 12) Syntax and semantics. New York: Academic Press.

Glasgow University Media Group. (1976). *Bad news.* London: Routledge & Kegan Paul.

Glasgow University Media Group. (1980). *More bad news.* London: Routledge & Kegan Paul.

Glasgow University Media Group. (1982). *Really bad news.* London: Writers and Readers.

Golding, P., & Elliott, P. (1979). *Making the news.* London: Longman.

Gormley, W. J., Jr. (1975). Newspaper agendas and political elites. *Journalism Quarterly, 52,* 304–308.

Graber, D. A. (1984). *Processing the news. How people tame the information tide.* New York: Longman.

Graesser, A. C. (1981). *Prose comprehension beyond the word.* New York: Springer-Verlag.

Green, G. M. (1979). *Organization, goals, and comprehensibility in narratives: Newswriting, a case study* (Technical Report No. 132). University of Illinois: Center for the study of reading.

Greep, K. (1984). Een experiment met betrekking tot krantelezen (An experiment on newspaper reading). Unpublished manuscript. University of Amsterdam, Section of Discourse Studies.

Greimas, A. (1966). *Sémantique structurale.* Paris: Larousse.

Grice, H. P. (1975). Logic and conversation. In P. Cole & J. L. Morgan (Eds.), *Syntax and semantics 3: Speech acts.* New York: Academic Press.

Gritti, J. (1966). Un récit de presse: les derniers jours d'un grand homme. *Communications, 8,* 94–101.

Guback, T. H. (1968). Reporting or distorting. In: H. J. Skornia & J. W. Kitson (Eds.), *Problems and controversies in television and radio.* Palo Alto, CA: Pacific Books.

Gumperz, J. D., & Hymes, D. (Eds.). (1972). *Directions in sociolinguistics. The ethnography of communication.* New York: Holt, Rinehart & Winston.

Gunter, B. (1983). Forgetting the news. In: E. Wartella, D. C. Whitney, & S. Windahl (Eds.), *Mass communication review yearbook* (Vol. 4) (pp. 165–172). Beverly Hills, CA: Sage.

Gurevitch, M., Bennett, T., Curran, J., & Woollacott, J. (Eds.). (1982). *Culture, society and the media.* London: Methuen.

Hall, S. (1980). Introduction to media studies at the Centre. In S. Hall, D. Hobson, A. Lowe, & P. Willis (Eds.), *Culture, media, language* (pp. 117–121). London: Hutchinson.

Hall, S., Critcher, C., Jefferson, T., Clarke, J., & Roberts, B. (1978). *Policing the crisis. Mugging, the state and law and order.* London: Methuen.

Hall, S., Hobson, D., Lowe, A., & Willis, P. (Eds.). (1980). *Culture, media, language.* London: Hutchinson.

Halliday, M. A. K., & Hasan, R. (1976). *Cohesion in English.* London: Longman.

Halloran, J. D., Elliott, P., & Murdock, G. (1970). *Demonstrations and communication. A case study.* Harmondsworth: Penguin Books.

Hamilton, D. (Ed.). (1981). *Cognitive processes in stereotyping and intergroup behavior.* Hillsdale, NJ: Lawrence Erlbaum Associates.

Harari, J. V. (Ed.). (1979). *Textual strategies. Perspectives in post-structuralist criticism.* London: Methuen.

Hardt, H. (1979). *Social theories of the press: Early German and American perspectives.* Beverly Hills, CA: Sage.

Harris, Z. (1952). Discourse analysis. *Language, 28,* 1–30.

Hartley, J. (1981). *Understanding news.* London: Methuen.

Hartmann, P., & Husband, C. (1974). *Racism and mass media.* London: Davis-Poynter.

Hendricks, W. O. (1976). *Grammars of style and styles of grammar.* Amsterdam: North Holland.

Heritage, J. (1985). Analyzing news interviews: Aspects of the production of talk for an overhearing audience. In T. A. van Dijk (Ed.), *Handbook of discourse analysis* (Vol. 3). London: Academic Press.

Hermans, J. (1984). Onderzoek naar de invloed van andere media op het onthouden van krantenberichten (Research on the influence of other media on recall of newspaper reports). Unpublished manuscript. University of Amsterdam, Section of Discourse Studies.

Higgins, E. T., Herman, C. P., & Zanna, M. P. (Eds.). (1981). *Social cognition. The Ontario symposium* (Vol. 1). Hillsdale, NJ: Lawrence Erlbaum Associates.

Hirsch, P. M. (1977). Occupational, organisational and institutional modes in mass communication. In P. M. Hirsch, P. V. Miller, & F. G. Kline (Eds.), *Strategies for communication research* (pp. 13–43). Beverly Hills, CA: Sage.

Hofstetter, C. R. (1976). *Bias in the news.* Columbus, OH: Ohio State University Press.

Höijer, B., & Findahl, O. (1984). *Nyheter, förståelse, och minne.* Stockholm: Studentlitteratur.

Hovland, C. I., Janis, I. L., & Kelley, H. H. (1953). Communication and persuasion. New Haven, Conn: Yale University Press.

Howard, J. & Rothbart, M. (1980). Social categorization and memory for in group and out group behavior. *Journal of Personality and Social Psychology, 38,* 301–310.

Hulteng, J. L., & Nelson, P. R. (1971). *The Fourth Estate: An informal appraisal of the news and opinion media.* New York: Harper & Row.

Hymes, D. (Ed.). (1964). *Language in culture and society.* New York: Harper & Row.

Johnson-Laird, P. N. (1983). *Mental models.* London: Cambridge University Press.

Johnstone, J. W., Slawski, E. J., & Bowman, W. W. (1976). *The news people: A sociological portrait of American journalists and their work.* Urbana, IL: University of Illinois Press.

Jones, L. K. (1977). *Theme in English expository discourse.* Lake Bluff, IL: Jupiter Press.

Just, M. A., & Carpenter, P. A. (Eds.). (1977). *Cognitive processes in comprehension.* Hillsdale, NJ: Lawrence Erlbaum Associates.

Kahane, H. (1971). *Logic and contemporary rhetoric.* Belmont, CA: Wadsworth.

Kahneman, D. & Tversky, A. (1973). On the psychology of prediction. *Psychological Review, 80,* 237–251.

Katz, E., Adoni, H., & Parness, P. (1977). Remembering the news: What the picture adds to recall. *Journalism Quarterly, 54,* 231–239.

Keenan, E. L. (Ed.). (1975). *Formal semantics of natural language.* London: Cambridge University Press.

Kempson, R. (1975). *Presupposition and the delimitation of semantics.* London: Cambridge University Press.

Kintsch, W. (1974). *The representation of meaning in memory.* Hillsdale, NJ: Lawrence Erlbaum Associates.

Kintsch, W. & Greene, E. (1978). The role of culture-specific schemata in the comprehension and recall of stories. *Discoures Processes,* 1, 1–13.

Kintsch, W., & van Dijk, T. A. (1975). Comment on se rappelle et on résume des histoires. *Langages,* 40, 98–116.

Kintsch, W., & van Dijk, T. A. (1978). Toward a model of text comprehension and production. *Psychological Review,* 85, 363–394.

Kniffka, H. (1980). *Soziolinguistik und empirische Textanalyse. Schlagzeilen- und Leadformulierung in Amerikanische Tageszeitungen.* Tübingen: Niemeyer.

Laberge, D., & Samuels, S. J. (Eds.). (1977). *Basic processes in reading.* Hillsdale, NJ: Lawrence Erlbaum Associates.

Labov, W. (1972a). *Language in the inner city.* Philadelphia: University of Pennsylvania Press.

Labov, W. (1972b). *Sociolinguistic patterns.* Philadelphia: University of Pennsylvania Press.

Labov, W. (1972c). The transformation of experience in narrative syntax. In W. Labov, *Language in the inner city* (pp. 354–396). Phildelphia: University of Pennsylvania Press.

Labov, W. (1982). Speech actions and reactions in personal narrative. In D. Tannen (Ed.), *Analyzing discourse: Text and talk* (pp. 219–247). Washington, DC: Georgetown University Press.

Labov, W., & Waletzky, J. (1967). Narrative analysis. Oral versions of personal experience. In J. Helm (Ed.), *Essays on the verbal and visual arts* (pp. 12–44). Seattle: University of Washington Press.

Lang, K., & Engel-Lang, G. (1982). *The battle for public opinion: The President, the press and the polls during Watergate.* New York: Columbia University Press.

Lange, K. (1980). *Abbildung oder Konstruktion der Wirklichkeit? Politik in der Nachrichtenmedien.* Stuttgart: Klett.

Larsen, S. F. (1980). Memory for radio news. Discourse structure and knowledge updating. Unpublished manuscript. University of Aarhus, Department of Psychology.

Lausberg, H. (1960). *Handbuch der literarischen rhetorik.* Munich: Hueber.

Lendvai, P. (1981). *The bureaucracy of truth.* London: Burnett.

Le Ny, J.-F., & Kintsch, W., (Eds.). (1982). *Language and comprehension.* Amsterdam: North Holland.

Lester, M. (1980). Generating newsworthiness: The interpretive construction of public events. *American Sociological Review,* 45, 984–994.

Levelt, W. J. M. (1982). Linearization in describing spatial networks. In S. Peters & E. Saarinen (Eds.), *Processes, beliefs and questions.* Dordrecht: Reidel.

Lindegren-Lerman, C. (1983). Dominant discourse: The institutional voice and the control of topic. In H. Davis & P. Walton (Eds.), *Lannguage, image, media* (pp. 75–103). Oxford: Blackwell.

Loftus, E. (1979). *Eyewitness testimony.* Cambridge: Mass.: Harvard University Press.

Longacre, R. (Ed.). (1977). *Discourse grammar* (Vols. 1–3). Dallas, TX: Summer Institute of Linguistics.

Louwes-Steubing, M. (1984). Een onderzoek naar de werkzaamheid van kognitieve schema's bij het begrijpen en onthouden van kranteberichten (An investigation into the role of cognitive schemata in the understanding and recall of newspaper reports). Unpublished manuscript. University of Amsterdam, Section of Discourse Studies.

Lüger, H.-H. (1983). *Pressesprache.* Tübingen: Niemeyer.

Lyons, J. (1981). *Language, meaning and context.* London: Fontana.

Maddux, J. E., & Rogers, R. W. (1980). Effects of source expertness, psysical attractivenes, and supporting arguments on persuasion. A case of brains over beauty. *Journal of Personality and Social Psychology,* 39, 235–244.

Mandl, H., Stein, N. L., & Trabasso, T. (Eds.). (1984). *Learning and comprehension of text.* Hillsdale, NJ: Lawrence Erlbaum Associates.

Mandler, J. M. (1978). A code in the node: The use of story schema in retrieval. *Discourse Processes, 1,* 14–35.

Mandler, J. M., & Johnson, N. S. (1977). Remembrance of things parsed: Story structure and recall. *Cognitive Psychology, 9,* 11–151.

Markus, H. (1977). Self-schemata and processing information about the self. *Journal of Personality and Social Psychology, 35,* 63–78.

Martin, L. J., & Chaudhary, A. G. (1983). *Comparative mass media systems.* New York: Longman.

McLaughlin, M. L. (1984). *Conversation. How talk is organized.* Beverly Hills, CA: Sage.

McQuail, D. (1983). *Mass communication theory. An introduction.* Beverly Hills, CA: Sage.

Mehan, H. (1979). *Learning lessons.* Cambridge, MASS: Harvard University Press.

Merrill, J. C. (1983). *Global journalism. A survey of the world's mass media.* New York: Longman.

Metz, W. (1979). *Newswriting: From lead to "30".* Englewood Cliffs, NJ: Prentice-Hall.

Molotch, H., & Lester, M. (1974). News as purposive behavior: On the strategic use of routine events. Accidents and scandals. *American Sociological Review, 39,* 101–112.

Morin, V. (1966). *L'écriture de presse.* The Hague: Mouton.

Neuman, R. W. (1976). Patterns of recall among television news viewers. *Public Opinion Quarterly, 40,* 115–123.

Norman, D. A., & Rumelhart, D. E. (Eds.). (1975). *Explorations in cognition.* San Francisco: Freeman.

Otto, W., & White, S. (Eds.). (1982). *Reading expository material.* New York: Academic Press.

Park, R. E. (1940). News as form of knowledge. *American Journal of Sociology, 45,* 669–686.

Pêcheux, M. (1969). *Analyse automatique du discours.* Paris: Dunod.

Petöfi, J. S. (1971). *Transformationsgrammatiken und eine ko-textuelle texttheorie.* Frankfurt: Athenaeum.

Petöfi, J. S., & Franck, D. M. L. (Eds.). (1973). *Presuppositions in linguistics and philosophy.* Frankfurt: Athenaeum.

Petöfi, J. S., & Rieser, H. (Eds.). (1973). *Studies in text grammar.* Dordrecht: Reidel.

Pols, H. (1984). Citeren in nieuwsberichten (Quotations in news reports). Unpublished manuscript. University of Amsterdam, Section of Discourse Studies.

Powers, R. (1978). *The news casters.* New York: St. Martins Press.

Propp, V. (1958). *Morphology of the folktale.* Bloomington, IN: Indiana University Press. (Original Russian work published 1928).

Reder, L. M. (1982). Elaborations: When do they help and when do they hurt? *Text, 2,* 211–224.

Reder, L. M., & Anderson, J. R. (1980). A comparison of texts and their summaries: Memorial consequences. *Journal of Verbal Learning and Verbal Behavior, 19,* 121–134.

Robinson, J. P. & Levy, M. R. (1986). *The main source. Learning from television news.* Beverly Hills, CA: Sage.

Roeh, I. (1982). *The rhetoric of news.* Bochum: Studienverlag.

Roeh, I., & Feldman, S. (1984). The rhetoric of numbers in frontpage journalism. *Text, 4,* 347–368.

Roloff, M., & Miller, G. R. (Eds.). (1980). *Persuasion.* Beverly Hills, CA: Sage.

Rood, T. (1984). Een dag Oost-Europa berichtgeving in NRC-Handelsblad (One day of reporting about Eastern-Europe in NRC-Handelsblad). Unpublished manuscript. University of Amsterdam, Section of Discourse Studies.

Rosenblum, M. (1981). *Coups and earthquakes. Reporting the world to America.* New York: Harper & Row.

Roshco, B. (1975). *Newsmaking.* Chicago: University of Chicago Press.

Rothbart, M., Evans, M., & Fulero, S. (1979). Recall for confirming events. Memory processing and the maintenance of social stereotypes. *Journal of Experimental Social Psychology,* *15,* 343–355.

Rumelhart, D. (1975). Notes on a schema for stories. In D. G. Bobrow & A. Collins (Eds.), *Representation and understanding* (pp. 211–236). New York: Academic Press.

Sacks, H., Schegloff, E., & Jefferson, G. (1974). A simplest systematics for the organization of turntaking for conversation. *Language, 50,* 696–735.

Sanches, M., & Blount, B. G. (Eds.). (1975). *Sociocultural dimensions of language use.* New York: Academic Press.

Sandell, R. (1977). *Linguistic style and persuasion.* London: Academic Press.

Sanford, A. J., & Garrod, S. C. (1981). *Understanding written language.* New York: Wiley.

Saussure, F. (1917). *Cours de linguistique générale.* Paris: Payot.

Saville-Troike, M. (1982). *The ethnography of communication.* Oxford: Blackwell.

Schank, R. (1979). Interestingness. Controlling inferences. *Artificial Intelligence, 12,* 273–297.

Schank, R. C. (1982). *Dynamic memory.* London: Cambridge: University Press.

Schank, R. C., & Abelson, R. P. (1977). *Scripts, plans, goals and understanding.* Hillsdale, NJ: Lawrence Erlbaum Associates.

Schegloff, E., & Sacks, H. (1973). Opening up closings. *Semiotica, 8,* 289–327.

Schenkein, J. (Ed.). (1978). *Studies in conversational interaction.* New York: Academic Press.

Scherer, K. R., & Giles, H. (Eds.). (1979). *Social markers in speech.* London: Cambridge University Press.

Schmidt, M.-A. (1977). *Tagesberichterstattung in Zeitung und Fernsehen.* Berlin: Verlag Volker Spiess.

Schoenbach, K. (1977). *Trennung von Nachricht und Meinung.* Freiburg: Karl Alber.

Schulz, W. (1976). *Die Konstruktion von Realität in den Nachrichtenmedien.* Freiburg: Karl Alber.

Schwartz, H., & Jacobs, J. (1979). *Qualitative sociology.* New York: Free Press.

Schwitalla, J. (1981). Dialogsteuerungsversuche interviewter Politiker. In: G. Bentele (Ed.), *Semiotik und Massenmedien* (pp. 108–127). Munich: Oelschläger.

Searle, J. (1969). *Speech acts.* Cambridge: Cambridge University Press.

Sebeok, T. (Ed.). (1960). *Style in language.* Cambridge, MA: MIT Press.

Siebert, F. S., Peterson, T., & Schramm, W. (1957). *Four theories of the press.* Urbana, IL: University of Illinois Press.

Sigelman, L. (1973). Reporting the news: An organizational analysis. *American Journal of Sociology, 79,* 132–151.

Sinclair, J. M. & Brazil, D. (1982). *Teachers talk.* London: Oxford University Press.

Sinclair, J. M., & Coulthard, M. (1975). *Towards an analysis of discourse.* London: Oxford University Press.

Spiegl, F. (1983). *Keep taking the tabloids!* London: Pan Books.

Spiro, R. J., Bruce, B. C., & Brewer, W. F. (Eds.). (1980). *Theoretical issues in reading comprehension.* Hillsdale, NJ: Lawrence Erlbaum Associates.

Strassner, E. (Ed.). (1975). *Nachrichten.* Munich: Fink.

Strassner, E. (1982). *Fernsehnachrichten.* Tübingen: Niemeyer.

Sudnow, D. (Ed.). (1972). *Studies in social interaction.* New York: Free Press.

Tannen, D. (Ed.). (1982). *Analyzing discourse: Text and talk.* Washington, DC: Georgetown University Press.

Taylor, S. E. (1981). The categorization approach to stereotyping. In D. Hamilton (Ed.), *Cognitive processing in stereotyping and intergroup behavior* (pp. 83–114). Hillsdale, NJ: Lawrence Erlbaum Associates.

Thorndyke, P. W. (1977). Cognitive structures in comprehension and memory of narrative discourse. *Cognitive Psychology, 9,* 77–110.

Thorndyke, P. W. (1979). Knowledge acquisition from newspaper stories. Discourse Processes, 2, 95–112.

Todorov, T. (Ed.). (1966). Textes des formalistes russes. Paris: Seuil.

Todorov, T. (1969). Grammaire du Décaméron. The Hague: Mouton.

Tuchman, G. (1972). Objectivity as strategic ritual: An examination of newsmen's notions of objectivity. American Journal of Sociology, 77, 660–670.

Tuchman, G. (1974). Making news by doing work: Routinizing the unexpected. American Journal of Sociology, 79, 110–131.

Tuchman, G. (1978a). Making news. New York: Free Press.

Tuchman, G. (1978b). Professionalism as an agent of legitimation. Journal of Communication, 28, 106–113.

Tuchman, G., Kaplan Daniels, A. & Benét, J. (Eds.). (1980). Hearth and home. Images of women in the mass media. New York: Oxford University Press.

Tunstall, J. (1971). Journalists at work. London: Constable.

Turner, R. (Ed.). (1974). Ethnomethodology. Harmondsworth: Penguin Books.

van Dijk, T. A. (1972). Some aspects of text grammars. The Hague: Mouton.

van Dijk, T. A. (1976). Philosophy of action and theory of narrative. Poetics, 5, 287–338.

van Dijk, T. A. (1977). Text and context. London: Longman.

van Dijk, T. A. (1979). Recalling and summarizing complex discourse. In W. Burghardt & K. Hölker (Eds.), Text processing. (Textverarbeitung) (pp. 49–118). Berlin: de Gruyter.

van Dijk, T. A. (1980a). Macrostructures. Hillsdale, NJ: Lawrence Erlbaum Associates.

van Dijk, T. A. (Ed.). (1980b). Story comprehension. Poetics 8, nrs. 1/3 (special issue).

van Dijk, T. A. (1980c). Story comprehension: An introduction. In T. A. van Dijk (Ed.), Story Comprehension. Poetics, 9, nrs 1/3, special issue, 1–21.

van Dijk, T. A. (1981a). Studies in the pragmatics of discourse. Berlin/New York: Mouton.

van Dijk, T. A. (1981b). Pragmatic connectives. In T. A. van Dijk, Studies in the pragmatics of discourse (pp. 163–176). The Hague: Mouton.

van Dijk, T. A. (1982a). Episodes as units of discourse analysis. In D. Tannen (Ed.), Analyzing discourse: Text and talk (pp. 177–195). Washington, DC: Georgetown University Press.

van Dijk, T. A. (1982b). Opinions and attitudes in discourse comprehension. In J. F. Le Ny & W. Kintsch (Eds.), Language and comprehension (pp. 35–51). Amsterdam: North Holland.

van Dijk, T. A. (Ed.). (1982c). New developments in cognitive models of discourse processing. Text, 2, nrs. 1/3, (special issue).

van Dijk, T. A. (1983a). Minderheden in the media (Minorities in the media). Amsterdam: Socialistische Uitgeverij Amsterdam.

van Dijk, T. A. (1983b). Discourse analysis: Its development and application to the structure of news. Journal of Communication, 33, 20–43.

van Dijk, T. A. (1984a). Prejudice in discourse. Amsterdam: Benjamins.

van Dijk, T. A. (1984b). Structures of international news. A case study of the world's press. Report for Unesco. University of Amsterdam. Department of General Literary Studies. Section of Discourse Studies (Available from ERIC, and summarized as a chapter in van Dijk, 1986d).

van Dijk, T. A. (Ed.). (1985a). Handbook of discourse analysis (Vols. 1/4). London: Academic Press.

van Dijk, T. A. (Ed.). (1985b). Discourse and communication. New approaches to the analysis of mass media discourse and communication. Berlin: de Gruyter.

van Dijk, T. A. (1985c). Structures of news in the press. In T. A. van Dijk (Ed.), Discourse and communication (pp. 69–93). Berlin: de Gruyter.

van Dijk, T. A. (1985d). Cognitive situation models in discourse production. The expression of ethnic situations in prejudiced discourse. In J. P. Forgas (Ed.), Language and social situations (pp. 61–80). New York: Springer-Verlag.

van Dijk, T. A. (1986). News schemata. In C. Cooper & S. Greenbaum (Eds.), *Studying writing: Linguistic approaches* (pp. 155–186). Beverly Hills, CA: Sage.

van Dijk, T. A. (1987a). *Communicating racism. Ethnic prejudice in thought and talk.* Newbury Park, CA: Sage.

van Dijk, T. A. (1987b). *News analysis. Case studies in international and national news.* Hillsdale, NJ: Lawrence Erlbaum Associates.

van Dijk, T. A. (1987c). Episodic models in discourse processing. In R. Horowitz & S. J. Samuels (Eds.), *Comprehending oral and written language.* New York: Academic Press.

van Dijk, T. A. (1987d). Mediating racism. The role of the media in the reproduction of racism. In R. Wodak (Ed.), *Language, power and ideology.* Amsterdam: Benjamins.

van Dijk, T. A. (1987e). Elite discourse and racism. In I. Zavala, T. A. van Dijk, & M. Diaz-Diocaretz (Eds.), *Approaches to discourse, poetics and psychiatry.* Amsterdam, Benjamins.

van Dijk, T. A., & Kintsch, W. (1978). Cognitive psychology and discourse. Recalling and summarizing stories. In W. U. Dressler (Ed.), *Current trends in textlinguistics.* Berlin: de Gruyter.

van Dijk, T. A., & Kintsch, W. (1983). *Strategies of discourse comprehension.* New York: Academic Press.

Véron, E. (1981). *Construire l'événement. Les médias et l'accident de Three Mile Island.* Paris: Minuit.

Wicker, T. (1978). *On press.* New York: The Viking Press.

Wilensky, R. (1978). *Understanding goal-based Stories.* New Haven, CN: Yale University, Department of Computer Science. Research report #140.

Wilensky, R. (1983). Story grammars versus story points. *The Behavioral and Brain Science, 6,* 579–623.

Williams, A. (1975). Unbiased study of television news bias. *Journal of Communication, 25,* 190–199.

Wilson, D. (1975). *Presuppositions and non-truth conditional semantics.* New York: Academic Press.

Woodall, W. G., Davis, D. K., & Sahin, H. (1983). From the boob tube to the black box. In E. Wartella, D. C. Whitney, & S. Windahl (Eds.), *Mass communication review yearbook* (Vol. 4) (pp. 173–194). Beverly Hills, Ca: Sage.

Wyer, R. S., Jr., & Carlston, D. E. (1979). *Social cognition, inference and attribution.* Hillsdale, NJ: Lawrence Erlbaum Associates.

AUTHOR INDEX

SUBJECT INDEX

197